# *BEING* BRITISH MUSLIMS

*Beyond Ethnocentric Religion and Identity Politics*

## DR MAMNUN KHAN

*AuthorHouse™ UK*
*1663 Liberty Drive*
*Bloomington, IN 47403 USA*
*www.authorhouse.co.uk*
*Phone: 0800 047 8203 (UK landline)*
*+44 1908 723714 (International)*

*Published by AuthorHouse 05/29/2019*

*ISBN: 978-1-7283-8264-7 (sc)*
*ISBN: 978-1-7283-8265-4 (hc)*
*ISBN: 978-1-7283-8266-1 (e)*

*Print information available on the last page.*

*This book is printed on acid-free paper.*

*Because of the dynamic nature of the Internet, any web addresses or links contained in this book may have changed since publication and may no longer be valid. The views expressed in this work are solely those of the author and do not necessarily reflect the views of the publisher, and the publisher hereby disclaims any responsibility for them.*

# Contents

Dedicated to my late father, Haji Faizur Rahman Khan (1944-2019) *rahimahullah* (may God's Mercy be upon him), who by the grace of God nurtured me and taught morals.

The Prophet of God said: "The ones who are merciful, the Most Merciful will have mercy with them. Have mercy with those on the earth, and He who is in the heaven will have mercy upon you"
*al-Tirmidhi.*

God said regarding the universality of justice throughout time and cultures:
"O you who believe! Stand firmly for justice, as witnesses to God, even though it may be against your interests, or your parents, or your kin, be they rich or poor, God is a better protector to both. So, follow not your desires, lest you may avoid justice, and if you distort your witness or refuse to give it, verily, God is Ever Well-Acquainted with whatever you do"
*Qur'an,* 4:135.

"Good and evil are not equal. Repel (evil) with what is best, and you will see that the one you had mutual enmity with him will turn as if he were a close friend"
*Qur'an,* 41:34.

# Foreword by Shaykh Mohammed Nizami

The believers of every age and generation are endowed with a responsibility towards the divine message, to make sense of it and to uphold it by fittingly applying the principles God sets forth within it. Today, British Muslims find themselves at various crossroads, and the one that concerns this anthology of essays presents the challenge of advancing from the racialisation of religious commitment rooted in an immigrant experience, to the inexorable acculturalisation of succeeding generations. Unfortunately, this has meant that communal conversations on the role and status of religion in Britain descends into polarising debates, impelled either by immigrant anxieties and a resistance to perceived western cultural hegemony, or the presumed need to overcompensate or conform. On the former, the reaction has been a heady thrall to a version of the Muslim past whilst struggling to meet the challenges of the present. Indeed, any study of history is useful in determining how we might conceive of a productive future, yet for the modern Muslim narrative history becomes a tragedy episodically lamented.

Yet not all British Muslims relate to this condition. Increasingly, there are voices with the proclivity and aptitude to present intelligent and confident ideas that consider the acculturalisation of immigrant communities through a lens primarily preoccupied with the question: "What does God want of us today?" It is increasingly coming to be understood that our task is not to stand a mournful watch over rhetoric enshrined in historic documents and views of elderly moralists, nor that godly values are simply to be memorialised in the commemoration of old intellectual battles and ancestral deeds, but to recreate those values to deliver new vitality to a godly discourse whilst renewing commitments meaningfully. These impulses are not motivated merely by pragmatic, worldly urges, but by a religious sensitivity that seeks solutions to manage a godly outlook and lifestyle in a context dominated by the secular.

In the ongoing quest to make faith relevant, a lack of creativity is not the only impediment that is being challenged. The nurturing of values that maintains our moral tone and our embrace of revelation as an action-guiding force that looks to faith in accordance with the surrounding realities of modern life means that we must look to faith as something that is going on in the habitual routines of everyday life. Values are constantly in a process of becoming whereby people make and remake connections between what God intended and the human experience, between what God has said and what they believe, and between what God wants and the choices they make. Faith is not simply a sombre exercise in ancestral piety found in the serene corner of a mosque, but goes on in the clamour of the classroom, the din of the marketplace, around an animated dinner table, in terse posts on social media, and in homes up and down the country; true faith ought to communicate itself more vividly through what people do than abstract debates and intellectual musings.

The task of coming generations will be to pioneer creative ideas and a fresh outlook that speaks to the masses in a way that is relevant and inspiring. It requires those unsullied by past failures and anxieties, so that they have the promise of being able to create a positive narrative. If the revival of Abrahamic monotheism is to be our deliverance in an age that witnesses the collapse of reason and tolerance, the rise of vacuous self-indulgence and the persistence of cognitive dissonance that results from an implicit tension between body, mind and spirit that modern "religion" seems to generate, addressing internal dilemmas is of utmost importance and urgency. The contemporary turn away from a holistic conception of faith rooted both in first-principles and the revealed word has produced both an impoverished and highly politicised condition that seem susceptible to the same secularising tendencies that have afflicted the adherents of major European faiths.

This collection of thoughts, observations and meditations provides a welcome perspective to the ongoing crystallisation of religiously-inspired thinking in Britain, and whilst addressing issues at an appropriate level of generality, attention to the specificity of those ideals in application will prove invaluable to the reader. This is not to say everything in this anthology will evade disagreement, but contention inducing viewpoints ought to be welcomed; it is in the spirit of communal deliberation and intellectual enquiry that this anthology constructively demonstrates how we might proceed.

---

Shaykh Mohammed Nizami is a British scholar and has graduated from LSE, Warwick and Al-Azhar universities in political science and international relations, political and legal theory and Islamic law. He has also studied traditional Islamic studies in Makkah. At the grassroots level, he advocates a return to a God-centred approach to religion and Western life, with a focus on using *Qur'anic* narratives to inform us how to live meaningfully, specifically as Western Muslims. For more, visit www.nizami.co.uk.

# Introduction

In the name of God, the most Compassionate, the most Kind

In early 2015 I was encouraged by members of Luton's Muslim community to play a more active role in the community. This coincided with the rise of social media platforms like WhatsApp which were used by community and other interest groups to share information, co-ordinate projects or simply to discuss current affairs, geopolitics, and football and so on. For many, such forums satisfied the need to be connected to a community, with a sense of being engaged and productive. For others, it carried a sense of hope that despite being a free-for-all platform, individuals would step up to benefit others, and in turn they would be supported to drive much-needed projects tackling the challenges within Muslim communities.

However, the reality was rather different. Most of these forums lacked appropriate rules and were essentially online communal hang out places where people spent hours on end expressing divergent views and engaging in bluster with each other. It became clear that despite much keyboard speak as it were, there was still a debilitating unwillingness and lack of capacity in the community to deal with their frustrations. It certainly wasn't the case that British Muslims weren't increasingly socially mobile and therefore couldn't organise to improve conditions that were within their gift to improve for themselves. Nevertheless, these forums were in the main disorganised meeting places for disparate individuals who weren't meaningfully invested in each other, nor did they necessarily share a common vision for social development. In ensuing debates on matters that didn't concern them, and in which they lacked expertise in, those who took part wasted a great deal of energy in pointless attempts to impress others.

In spite of these drawbacks, being present in these forums was on balance still worthwhile. It was a means through which I could connect with others whom I may not have otherwise come across. Equally important perhaps, is it gave me first-hand insight into goings-on within the different strands of Britain's Muslim communities both online and offline.

In particular, I made the following brief observations. (1) Muslims nominally place a high value in Islam as the ultimate source of meaning but have poor knowledge of Islam limited broadly to ritualism. (2) Third generation Muslims are still negotiating trans-national belongings and prefer to retain some aspects of their ethnic identity (e.g. language, cuisines, cultural dress) while accepting the eventual loss of ethnic expressions over time. (3) Muslims generally perceive that the diverse ethnic rooting is increasingly being substituted by an Islamic rooting and consciousness. However, the look and feel of it isn't clear and consistent to them due to the lack of consensus between the diverse communities, religious factionalism and questions about modernity which remain unsatisfactorily answered. (4) There are many growing socio-demographic and generational disparities among Muslims, for example those with higher social mobility tend to be more socially liberal compared to those with lower social mobility who are perhaps more conservative in their public engagement.

Overall, the evidence for me pointed to a largely ethnic commitment to religion, entanglement with identity politics and a kind of ethnic identity that arguably didn't have much substance to begin with, conforming to the "old ways," routines and expressions found in rural Pakistan or Bangladesh. I was convinced that these factors played an important role in the way Muslims "do Islam" in Britain today. The multifarious conflations and imaginings have many consequences which have remained unexplored.

There's no doubt that the Islamic faith has productively informed aspects of South Asian culture historically and continues to do so. However, to implant those expressions into the space and context of the UK one would have to assume that South Asian expressions aren't subject to contextual changes and therefore fit and proper for British Muslims living in the UK. Limiting the *Qur'an*, Prophetic *Sunnah*[1] and Islamic

---

[1] The *Sunnah* is the established way of the Prophet, usually found in reliably transmitted *hadith* texts (statements and actions of the Prophet) and in the continuous practices (*'amal*) of the early generations who came after the Prophet, the Companions (*Sahabiyyah*) and their followers (*Tabi'een*) etc.

scholarship in this way has rarely happened in Muslim civilisation, and simply risks perpetuating the same restrictions, errors and ways of "doing Islam" in South Asia. This isn't in the slightest to disparage ethnic culture. As someone with a Bangladeshi heritage and an awareness of Bengal's rich literature and history, I realise that being comfortable in the right way with one's own skin as it were and owning differences (be it Bengali, Indian, Pakistani, Arab, Somalian, Nigerian etc.) will do much to alleviate modern identity crisis for many. My contention isn't with ethnic culture *per se* but rather the way Muslims "do Islam" in the UK today through an ethnic commitment to religion and identity politics.

I was also acutely aware that such discussions weren't specific to Luton, but generic concerns and points of contention to British Muslims across the country. It's not surprising why. The making of today's world is synonymous with globalised information flows which meet and interpenetrate almost everything giving a free market of ideas. But it's not just ideas. Disparate people who don't necessarily share similar viewpoints and worldviews come into contact with each other. The authority of any message appears negotiable and subject to different standards and life politics. While these facets of modern life aren't completely new, the intensity with which they occur and the lack of common frameworks of ideas, restraints and ethics to handle polarities has perhaps never been as impactful before. With that comes a great deal of turmoil, impacting people generally.

In this tumult, the unnuanced or non-syncretic voices often gain strength. People feel victimised and threatened, whether it's Muslims as minorities who feel that they're under attack from Islamophobia, black people whose race is seen as being sidelined for far too long or white working-classes who feel that their jobs and school places are being taken by immigrants. In all of this, there is a feeling that it's not them who need to change and conform to society's values but the surrounding society which needs to change to accommodate them. People feel that society doesn't value who they are or what they're doing any more, which gets translated into the feeling that others are stealing their culture, inner identity and ultimately their destiny. These and other general observations pointed to a number of broad problem areas.

(1) There is a growing perception of a universalising Islam despite the reality that it isn't mainstream Islamic thought. This perception works both for extreme right-wing nationalists and those who aren't sufficiently aware who see Western Muslims as a threat to Western identity, and for many Muslims it works to confirm an idealisation of a global *ummah*.

(2) The politics of identity and recognition has grown at the expense of accommodation and exploring new intercultural approaches to diversity and difference. Responding to this and in attempts by British Muslims to engage identity politics: (a) the substance of what God has revealed has struggled to be discovered and brought to the fore; and (b) it has distracted from the need to be constructively self-critical to move conditions and polities in new and improved directions in pursuance of being subservient to God.

(3) For British Muslim communities the stock of Islamic knowledge has struggled to be contextualised to the UK, making it rather difficult to draw upon revelatory guidance in a manner that relates to people's intuitions and experiences of living in the UK. Islam from the very beginning impelled Muslims towards an open civilisation, open to learning from other peoples while still preserving the Islamic tradition, thought and ethics, yet today's British Muslim communities generally remain quite parochial and insular.

(4) While things are changing, third generation Muslims still largely conform to ethnically-committed religion, which makes for conflating "culturally Asian" with being Muslim. This is not to discount the contribution of ethnic communities to the social, political and economic life of the UK, which is broadly recognised. My point here is that if people who earlier self-identified as "British Pakistanis," "British Bangladeshis," "British Somalis" etc. and have remained predominantly rooted in their ethnic mores, and now demand public recognition as "British Muslims," then it necessitates looking at things through the lenses of "what does it mean to be God-centred?" Whether Muslims follow God's guidance or the extent to which they do or don't do so is of course a function of "being Muslim," it still doesn't absolve them from

the responsibility to strive to be "Muslim to God." Thus, while the rhetoric of identity has progressed, the way British Muslims "do Islam" has struggled to be contextualised to the UK.

Trends like these required examining in order to articulate how we might critically understand and reconcile dilemmas and challenges in an intellectually credible and emotionally intelligent way. To be a Muslim requires not simply conformity to community expectations but the involvement of all one's being, including intelligence and judgement. Faced with the pressures of modern life, and perhaps living in a majority non-Muslim country, many British Muslims have let their faith be diminished into something simpler and less relevant to their actual lives than should be the case. Yet, God impels Muslims to be steeped in the virtue of high aspiration (*'uluwwul himmah*) built on knowledge (*'ilm*) and desire (*irada*) to achieve excellence (*ihsan*).

My overarching call in the book is for British Muslims to respond to their current situation as an opportunity to concentrate on the essentials of being Muslim and Godliness and to apply these to best effect. By doing so, British Muslims stand a better chance of contributing to wider society and outwardly be seen as living examples of the value of being Muslim. In fact, I would argue that the very notion of British Muslim rests on a new impetus to explore and discover what this means and what we should aspire to. While bringing about change is never easy, as Muslims of the UK into our third and fourth generations it's incumbent on us to forge new horizons and strategic directions.

Indeed, my involvement in these community forums initially led me to write for Islamicate, a small niche blogsite founded in 2014 by Dr Sameer Mallick, which had already established a reputation as a non-sectarian, independent and critical-minded blog. Prominent scholars like Shaykh Mohammed Nizami and Shaykh Surkheel Sharif were already regular contributors. Hence, upon a request by Sameer asking for new writers to come forward, I was convinced that it was the right platform.

I present here an edited anthology of the articles I wrote for Islamicate from 2015 to 2018. Looking back at the topics I covered, it is clear that they were pertinent and would remain not just relevant but equally educational. Hence, I decided to compile them in the form of a book. Books have obvious advantages over blogs in that they don't rely on the shelf life of a website. Current affairs blogs in particular are usually written in-the-now and with each new post they progressively become less noticed even though the content could remain as relevant as ever. Aside from this, it isn't unusual for short articles and essays to be collected together to form a longer book, such as Charles Dickens' *The Pickwick Papers* or the collections of letters published in book form in the *maktubat* genre in Islamic literature.

In compiling this book, I have adopted a thematic approach with three broad sections. Whilst the articles don't touch every aspect of what is a very diverse British Muslim experience (from 2015-2018) which would of course be a daunting task, I have focussed on specific topics that are directly relevant and, I would argue, among the most important to a theocentric British Muslim outlook. Section one explores aspects of faith, reason and progress, taking a look at such things like the virtue of learning though questioning, a theocentric mandate for problem-solving, what it means to be a scholar (*'alim*), our use of language and labels, intra-religious identity dynamics of British Muslims etc. The latter is a completely new section addressing Sunni factionalism in the UK. Section two focuses on religion in society and takes a broad look at various social phenomena such as the nature of serving others (*khidma*), *zakat* in the UK, fake news, the future of our mosques etc. Section three is about integration and the politics of cultural recognition, including political and other impactful events that took place from 2015 to 2018 which generated much discussion among British Muslims, often mirroring the wider British society. In the final chapter, I provide some brief concluding remarks summarising the meta-trends and challenges covered in the book. I also offer some broad counsel in the form of a seven-point charter for British Muslims, which I hope can help show how we might pursue a contextualised theocentric British Muslim experience.

In addition to minor corrections to the original articles, where necessary I've expanded the body of the text and added basic footnotes to provide background and context to the discussion. Where I've referred to the *Qur'an,* I've provided the citation in brackets following chapter-verse numbering, and kept *hadith*[2] references in the footnotes.

I would like to extend my deepest thanks to Sameer for giving me the opportunity to write for Islamicate. I am also grateful to Shaykh Mohammed Nizami for not only writing the foreword, but also for his very useful feedback on many of the articles. Thanks also to acclaimed literary critics and authors, Mike Sherborne and Muhammad Mojlum Khan, for their invaluable feedback, for which I am very grateful. I am also forever indebted to my wife, Fatihah, for her immense patience, sacrifice and suggestions for improvements, without which finding the time to write simply wouldn't have been possible. Lastly, I thank my mother, Mariam Begum, for all her prayers and wishes over the years which have no doubt rendered their invaluable blessings on me. All views, errors and omissions in the book are mine alone and do not necessarily reflect the opinions of anyone else. I pray that God accepts this work, counts it among the good deeds of my father, Haji Faizur Rahman Khan *rahimahullah* (may God's Mercy be upon him), who taught me morals, and makes it a source of benefit for those who read it.

23 March 2019.

---

[2] A *hadith* (plural *ahadith*) is a written report about what the Prophet said, did, approved, and disapproved of, explicitly or implicitly. It is one of the main sources used to define Prophetic tradition (*Sunnah*).

# – 1 –

# Faith, reason and progress

## 1.1 The virtues of learning through questioning

"If you don't ask, you don't get" is as much applicable to learning about religion as it is about anything else in life. Yet, too often, whether it's in relation to tradition, traditionalism,[3] ethno-cultural idioms or other parochial discourses, there is a general lack of a questioning ethic. For one reason or another if we're not already conforming to it, we succumb to unquestioningly accept what we're told, not necessarily because it's self-evident but because we assume that the person speaking knows it, or that it is how things have always been or ought to be. Unfortunately, this engenders a perception of familiarity, whose very lenses often veil our senses from the wondrous nature of any phenomena through which God's attributes reveal. Yet, the *Qur'an* encourages us to cast aside the veil of familiarity to see the mundane or ordinary things anew, as signs of God.

There is also a presumed fear that if we ask too many questions, we risk opening up a Pandora's Box containing all the evils of the world as it were. One question leading to another, and before we know it a juggernaut is unleashed seeking to unpick hitherto well-established assumptions of

---

[3] See: Mohammed Nizami, *Choosing tradition over traditionalism,* 26 July 2017. "Traditionalism" is the trend whereby religious rhetoric is premised on staying true to the past and a commitment to the past, and not necessarily on embracing the revealed texts and Islamic scholarship to make revelation relevant and applicable to today's context. Whereas, Islamic scholars have always understood "Tradition" as always "in the making," and subject to contextualising to people's lived circumstances, time and place.

profound meaning from which we can't seem to recover easily nor prepared to deal with its theological and intellectual complications. Understandably, a reactionary defence develops in the name of protecting us from asking such questions. But in doing so we unwittingly lock ourselves into a culture of learning that doesn't require us to test the integrity of what we've learnt.

Yet, everything we know about the *Qur'an* would suggest that it teaches us "how" to think and "what" questions to ask. Asking questions is arguably a necessary path to being guided and being able to distinguish truth from falsehood, virtue from corruption, justice from injustice, ethics from hypocrisy and so on. A profound example of this is that God opened even the angels to question Him as to why He should place Adam on earth knowing that his progeny would spread mischief and bloodshed (2:30). It was to make God's intention known to us.

We must of course keep in mind when reading the *Qur'an* that it is God Who is Divine, and is talking to us on a level that we can understand. Hence, God uses words like *hal* ("is/has there…") and *afala* ("do they not…") to make us think and reflect. As human beings we have a profound psychology when it comes to questions. Questions engage and compel us to seek answers. In God conversing with the reader, the reader is also building rapport with Him. Above all, through questions in the *Qur'an*, God invites us to self-discover, and helps us to examine or manage preconceived filters through which we see the world or process information.

This of course doesn't mean that the *Qur'an* signifies only those meanings that we're already familiar with, or we read from *Qur'an* exegetes (*mufassirun*) in which there can be quite diverse opinions in any case. A good example is our understanding of the word *dukhaan* (41:11) which is typically translated as "smoke," something which the early Muslims would have been able to relate to. But unlike them, today we associate it to scientific theories about the explosion that set the universe up, a conceptualisation which wasn't possible in earlier times. Evidently, we can only appreciate this if we ask the right questions.

However, being able to ask the right questions is only part of the story. In order to benefit, we usually need the help of someone capable of discerning well-reasoned arguments or positions. In this regard, as many scholars have said, we shouldn't uncritically take religion from anyone who we simply come across. The age we're in is, after all, one that celebrates the "*da'wah* man," "televangelists" and highly adept social media activists and influencers, with thousands of followers, keen to publicise their opinions on just about everything. Unsurprising, the average Muslim is much prone, and unable to resist their populism as a definitive marker of credibility. All of which can be a recipe for confusion and chaos.

One scholar advised that we shouldn't learn religion from anyone whose intelligence we haven't tested. Another advised that we should seek out the knowledgeable with authority to teach or impart guidance. Or, it could be that there are multiple perspectives which in their own way go somewhere towards answering the question, but tend to leave the questioner seeking to reconcile for themselves. An enquiring mind will no doubt attempt to reconcile. Most, however, will settle for the easiest answer, where the bar of acceptability is often set very low, thus compounding the issue further.

Indeed, the Prophets also questioned. Abraham, for example, asked: "My Lord! Show me how You give life to the dead?" to which God replied, "Do you not then believe?" to which Abraham replied, "Yes, but [I ask] in order that my heart may be at ease" (2:260). This is an engaging discussion that God intends for us to learn from. The Companions of the Prophet also asked the Prophet probing questions to clarify matters. And the Prophet, in turn, often answered by asking the Companions a question to encourage them to think at a deeper level. One example which I find incredibly meaningful is the incident when seeing the Prophet pray at night until his feet swelled up, A'isha, his wife, asked the Prophet, "Why do you do this…", [especially], "…when God has forgiven your past and future sins?" The Prophet replied with the question: "Should I not be a grateful believer?"[4] recognising, perhaps, both the genuine nature of the question and the need to open up A'isha's mind so that she could self-discover the link between gratitude (*shukr*) and prayer (*salat*).

Such an approach is discernable as we go through school and as we move into our professional lives. In high school, in order to prove Pythagoras' theorem ($a^2+b^2=h^2$) we cut out squares and counted their area. We were encouraged not to simply take our Math teachers' word for granted, but to empirically test it for ourselves. Similarly, in our professional lives we don't just accept new proposals, especially without critically evaluating them in light of evidence, standards and alignment to strategy. This isn't scepticism

---

[4] *Hadith* narrated by A'isha in *Sahih al-Bukhari*.

for its own sake. As we gleam from *Qur'anic* lessons it's about asking the right questions to make sense of things. Asking questions allows us to create greater order in how we approach things and to prioritise effectively. In fact, in itself, it does great service to filter out weak and untested ideas.

However, some argue against asking tricky questions on the basis that God mentions, "O you who have believed, ask not about things which, if they are shown to you, may cause you trouble" (5:101). Yet, this verse of the *Qur'an* is referring to the futility of unnecessary questioning, which serves the purpose of prying into things, to split hairs or to make things needlessly particular and restrictive. The background to this revelation (*asbab al-nuzul*) makes it clear that the Prophet didn't wish to obligate Hajj every year and that it was sufficient to leave it as the Prophet had explained. Unfortunately, hair-splitting, minutest questions in the fields of *'aqidah* (creed) and *fiqh* (Islamic law) has become widespread today - something which many scholars even in classical periods frequently spoke out against. In the grand scheme of things not only do they have little significance, the reality is that we'll never be able prove them one way or the other, nor remove them of their intrinsic neuro-linguistic variation.

It seems, as the world around us changes, our engagement with religion has become so simplistic that we've become disconnected to the reality of our wider lived experiences. I am wondering how much of this is because we don't ask the right questions? Have we created a culture where we shut down or ignore people who ask questions, conveniently pushing them aside as "wayward," "deconstructive," "modernist" or "unorthodox" perhaps? Isn't the pursuit of truth, enquiry and meaning integral to scholarship leading to holistic and nuanced understanding of reality? And why is it that we prefer to tread on paths that are least taxing to our minds? Does it really have to be like this? Is this really the legacy of Islamic thought and scholarship?

# 1.2 Faith demands lean problem-solving

Spending some time studying communities and institutions, one of the first things one notices is the need for more problem-solving skills. Seemingly good initiatives that set out to address problems of society often turn out to be far too unfocussed or fringe attempts. Usually, it's our inability to transcend existing cognitive filters, or our lack of emotional intelligence to mutually co-operate with others that trip us up. Worst still, despite evidence to the contrary, we often escalate commitment towards sub-optimal, indeed in their most egregious, false paths that harden into dogma. Before you know it, an industry or movement is born whose entire *raison d'être* relies on such sub-optimal or false paths. It then turns out like a self-fulfilling prophecy, as if, as Abraham Maslow famously said, "…it is tempting, if the only tool you have is a hammer, to treat everything as if it were a nail."[5] Of course, there are politics involved in all of this; people have underlying positions or philosophies that they're committed to, for good or bad reasons. Whilst these are challenges one generally encounters in the art of problem-solving, the prudent thing to do as a starting point is to at least equip oneself with the necessary skills and training on how to problem solve.

After all, the problems of communities and institutions generally don't have easy fixes, as with many things in life. As a Muslim I would even argue that embracing problem-solving is an integral feature of being Muslim to God. All Prophets were after all problem-solvers in one way or another. What God reveals in the stories of the Prophets (*qasas al-ambiya*) are a myriad of ways and insights into "what" and "how" to solve seemingly inevitable problems of human behaviour and institutions. Hence, it's not surprising that among nobility and scholars of Islam there is a unifying attitude and cognitive focus on real life problem-solving. The meta-narrative *Sunnah* is to take ownership of one's own problems, not to blame others, and doing what one can to get the best outcomes, appropriate to one's space, context, situation, abilities and sphere of influence.

So where do we start? The first thing is to define a problem properly. A well-written problem statement, concisely and specifically, clarifies a situation by identifying a problem and its severity, impacts and when it

---

[5] Abraham H. Maslow, *Toward a Psychology of Being*, 1962.

happens etc. In other words, it's easily grasped by others and serves as a point of communication about what one is trying to achieve. As a Muslim, a few relevant guiding principles become relevant here.

Firstly, as individuals we're not responsible for everything that merely comes to our attention. The scope of our responsibility is entirely determined by our own competencies and the roles we play (duties and rights - *huquq*), say, within an organisation, in our families, communities, in civic life etc. "Every soul," God reminds us, "is not burdened by more than what they can bear" (2:286). In the Prophet's life, too, you can see examples of how he solved problems differently depending on whether he was asked to arbitrate as a judge (where the nature of the dispute and the wider implications of the decision were also relevant variables), in his role as a husband or a friend, or as a leader etc. The second thing to note is the need to focus on things that concerns one,[6] and generally not trying to fix some other problem "out there" as it were. The point is "to keep things real."

Analysing a problem to better characterise it becomes the next step. Most problems of human behaviour or institutions have multiple root causes. Causes can be disconnected or connected to each other, stacking horizontally on top of each other or vertically, and together make up the holistic experience of the problem. Putting in the detailed work upfront to identify and understand underlying causes and their relative contribution to a problem is crucial. Whilst it would be ideal to quantify the contribution of factors using robust data (quantitative or qualitative), in the event that this isn't possible, inductive reasoning[7] is still a useful tool.

A good way to start analysing is by laying out what we know and what we don't know. We can then build on this by gathering information to fill in gaps and identifying "what goes wrong" in a fuller, more structured way. The rule of thumb here, as C. S Lewis famously said, is that "… only by going back till you find the error and working it afresh from

---

[6] *Hadith* reported by Abu Huraira in *Sunan al-Tirmidhi*: "Part of one's perfection of Islam is leaving that which does not concern one."

[7] Inductive reasoning is to make broad generalisations from specific observations that may be true most of the time but may not hold true all of the time or for specific cases. It is often used when making predictions and forecasting, e.g. "most of the time when there is a storm trees are damaged."

that point, never by simply going on"[8] can you characterise the fuller dimensions of a problem. There are many techniques for this, the macro-pattern of which can be applied to any problem, whether in the home, at work, in the community or in institutes. For example, asking the question "why" repeatedly (known as the "5 Whys") can help one trace back to the source of a problem. Moreover, clustering relevant factors appropriately, for example into "push" and "pull" or into "structural," "internal" and "external" categories etc. can also help draw out insightful, common themes and interconnections.

Robust analysis should lead to greater focus on the specifics of a problem and prioritising the most important and doable things to resolve it. Not least because we'll always be restricted by the range of options available to us, and constraints of resources, buy-in by stakeholders, expertise and time. A problem may have multiple root causes, some of which may be easily fixable, others may not be, or they may need different treatments, short- and long-term etc.

Prioritisation also applies to the next step, which is to identify options for fixing the cause(s). Here, seeking advice from others with experience or expertise is good practice, not least to reasonably check if at least all the known angles have been covered and evaluated. Evaluating options is in essence arguing and scoring the pros and cons of each option. Another way is to look at the impacts of each option and the effort needed to put them into practice. It should be a habit of the believer to continually evaluate and optimise for continuous improvement even after actions have been put in place (*muhasabah*).

In problem-solving there are always falsities and red herrings that can be quite easily distracting and prevent us from effectuating lasting change. Delivering change in any domain of life can be quite tricky at times, and to succeed a great deal of commitment and motivation is required, which means that we can easily lose focus. At the other end, we overinflate our own abilities and pursue options that seek to solve complex problems of human behaviour and institutions in grandiose steps, "boiling the ocean" as it were. Often, these intentions, while made in good faith, are reflexes of sorts to a seemingly "runaway world," confusions in modernity, or self-complexes and not necessarily focused on the specifics of a well-understood

---

[8] C. S. Lewis, *The Great Divorce*, 1946.

problem. It can also be a lack of holistic understanding of the co-operative and competitive contexts, when the two get mixed up because we try to address both internal Muslim issues as well as perceived and real external threats to Muslim identity, but do it in a high-handed or one-dimensional way. In this scenario, the "us and them" exclusivism gains favour, whilst internally it takes the veneer of "speaking up for truth." Another frequent failure point is our poor use of language. Inaccurate, overly-emotive, pessimistic or cynical language can be enough to demotivate people or become yet another barrier to creating the right positive "can do" attitude and mindset necessary to embrace problem-solving properly.

Admittedly, whilst these skills are lacking in far too many Muslim activists, scholars, institutes and initiatives, one thing is for sure, faith demands lean problem-solving

# 1.3 The constriction of *'alim* and *'ilm*?

The word *'alim/'alima* is typically used to describe someone who's completed an *'alimiyyah* degree at a specialised institution of learning,[9] or someone who's earned authorisation (*ijazah*) to teach to a requisite level by his/her teacher(s). Similarly, the word *'ilm* takes the meaning of "knowledge of Islam." However, after a long line of discussions on this, including with a Professor of Physics,[10] I'm led to believe that we've constricted their definitions far too much. To the extent that, today, it's become a sorry reflection of a "crisis of intellect" in how Muslims do religion.

In the well-known example of an *'alimiyyah* course, the *Dars-i-nizami*, students are put through studies in the traditional Islamic sciences (*Arabic*, *qira'a, Qur'an, tafsir, fiqh, sirah, hadith, usul al-fiqh, 'aqidah* and so on). Syllabuses have in some places evolved to include subjects like critical thinking and history, and vary between institutions in their teaching methods and texts studied. On the face of it, it's not too dissimilar to a Classics or Theology course at university; common to both is the study of, in essence, literary texts, law and theology. Though of course, the content and emphasis in their application to the modern world differs greatly. As well, one presumes, the Godly-intention and learning the "stuff" of growing close to God, and helping ordinary Muslims fulfil their basic obligations. In the UK, the *'alimiyyah* course is taught alongside the national curriculum too.

At the end of their studies, if they pass their exams, students gain the *'alimiyyah* certification, attaining the title *Mowlana* or *Shaykh* to distinguish them as "learned in the religion" or *'alim*. Fortunately, we have many institutions that offer the *'alimiyyah*, supplying communities up and down the country with a steady stream of men and women acquainted with some level of Islamic knowledge.

That said, the traditional *'alimiyyah* has its fair share of critics. Some argue that most *'alimiyyah* courses have become overly institutionalised into the ethno-cultural, sectarian and school-based process by which God's words are filtered. The texts, too, are not critically studied it is argued, and hence fail to be integrated and contextualised to the modern world.

---

[9] For example, a college, *madrasah* or *Darul 'Ulum* etc.

[10] Shamsher Ali, Professor Emeritus, Southeast University, Dhaka, Bangladesh.

There are also those who argue that the so-called "Islamic universities" are "not really Islamic universities because they teach the *Shari'ah*, Arabic and Islamic History but other subjects are not integrated."[11]

Keeping these discussions aside, there is an even more basic question of who we can call *'alim* which I would argue goes to the crux of the problem. I say this because it seems a little odd that in the English language we don't constrain the word "scholar" to someone who's only completed the *'alimiyyah* course. Instead, we use "scholar" in a broader sense, to describe anyone who's spent some time studying any field and reaching a level of technical and practical knowledge. If we want to be specific, we use the term "Islamic scholar" in English to mean an "Islamic *'alim.*" You would think that it's entirely reasonable, then, to interchangeably use *'alim* for "scholar" to call someone a "Physics *'alim*" or a "Geography *'alim*." After all, *'alim* in Arabic, linguistically, is someone who has knowledge about a particular matter which need not be confined to *'alimiyyah* courses. But this linguistic definition usually remains unexplored.

In earlier Muslim societies "the learned" were people who didn't just learn the religious sciences, they were also well-acquainted with a broad range of subjects, like mathematics, astronomy, medicine, geography, philosophy, chemistry etc. What existed among the elite centres of learning was a much more dynamic and, arguably, superior knowledge culture or ethic, which grew out of *Qur'an* texts commanding Muslims to contemplate creation, and to place a culture of inquiry and learning at the heart of faith and civilisation.

For example, references to Crescent Moons (*ahilla*) in the *Qur'an* as "signs to mark fixed periods of time for mankind and for the pilgrimage" (2:189) had strong implications for Muslims to understand the knowledge of Moon phases. Similarly, "Read in the name of the Lord … Who taught man through the use of the pen what he did not know" (96:1-5) accorded, says Umer Chapra, "a high place to reading and writing in order to learn what one did not know."[12] These indications (and there are many others), and the opportunities that they opened up, led early Muslims to establish multidisciplinary research academies like the "House of Wisdom" (*Bayt*

---

[11]  Statement of Professor Seyyid Hossein Nasr.

[12]  M. Umer Chapra, *Musllim Civilization - The Causes of Decline and the Need for Reform*, The Islamic Foundation, 2008.

*al-Hikma*) by Harun al-Rashid (763-809), for research and education in fields such as agriculture, astronomy, chemistry, mathematics, medicine etc. Over time, knowledge in these fields led to scientific and technical development, for instance in building hospitals, public baths, guest houses, roads, water supply systems, bridges, navigation tools, mosques with multi-dome complexes and so on. The purpose, says Charles Le Gai Eaton (1921-2010), was "concerned on the one hand with discerning the 'signs of Allah' in natural phenomena, and on the other with observing the forces and laws of nature … [to better] co-operate with them, so that the human family might be more comfortably fitted into its God given environment."[13]

Incidentally, despite this explosion of discoveries and thinking, earlier Muslims didn't seek to Islamicise subjects, as many attempt today using labels such as "Islamic astronomy," "Islamic chemistry" etc. There is a subtle and humbling lesson in this for us. That, whilst Islamic texts might have in some way pointed Muslims, or triggered their interest, in a specific direction of curiosity, it was still up to human ingenuity to discover and to seek out truth. And this ingenuity is a quality inherent to human beings themselves. The role of Islamic texts is simply to remind Muslims of that.

There were clear reasons for this, which relates to how earlier societies understood the term *'ilm*, which, arguably, much like the term *'alim* we've narrowed far too much. Mining the *Qur'an*, it becomes apparent that the various terms used to describe "those who know" or "those who use their intellect" (2:164) doesn't limit it to the study of Islamic texts *per se*. Instead, it focuses on contemplating and investigating creation as a path to glorifying God.

Earlier Muslims had a broader understanding of *'ilm* (knowledge). It was immensely powerful, furnishing a positivistic, integrated and interdisciplinary outlook that did much to maintain an intimate contact between people's material needs, the unseen world and the spiritual culture of Islam. Their understandings were simple yet sophisticated and varied, starting off with two broad categories of *'ilm*: beneficial and non-beneficial. Non-beneficial knowledge, which comes under the category forbidden (*haram*) or disliked (*makruh*), is knowledge that when applied results in unethical, immoral or corrupt outcomes or means. Beneficial knowledge

---

[13] Charles Le Gai Eaton, *Islam and the Destiny of Man*, Islamic Texts Society, reprinted 1994.

on the other hand brings well-being and ease to life, and which can be further classified into: that which is obligatory for each individual (*fardh al-'ayn*) or collectively obligatory (*fardh al-kifayah*); desirable (*mustahab*); and permissible (*mubah*)). Each individual is obligated to learn the basic knowledge of worship (*fara'ida*) and good character (*adab*). And knowledge of collective obligations ensures that every locality has learned people in both the obligatory religious knowledge, such as the Islamic sciences, the *'alimiyyah* type, as well as knowledge necessary for human well-being such as medicine, science, mathematics, geography, economics, sociology and so on.

These categories of knowledge sit in pitiful contrast to the popular categories of "secular subjects" and "*deeni*/religious subjects" which Muslims habitually use today. It's incredibly dubious that the study of the natural world, languages and people could be passed off as "secular subjects" when God speaks of them in the *Qur'an* in a positive light. Such views are premised by the fear that so-called "secular subjects" might teach values contrary to Islam. However, I would argue that this is a smokescreen for the lack of intellectual grounding in people's own faith assumptions in the "crisis of the intellect." You only have to ask yourself why would have earlier scholars gone to such great effort to categorise the different types of knowledge, and especially if *'ilm* only ever meant religious knowledge? The deep wisdoms in this are worth pondering over.

Unfortunately, today's tendency to reduce terms like *'alim* and *'ilm* is unhelpful. It does sometimes feel that far too many of us seek to minimise possibilities of meanings to produce tight-fisted, no-nonsense answers, as if this is what's needed for ordinary people to understand and as a necessary response to the perceived wishy-washy relativism of modernity. But in doing so, we also score many own goals. We reinforce the idea of the "religious man" as distinct to the "thinking man," and our most learned in religion appear not as people who think, ponder and ask questions, but exactly the opposite.

These are not new problems. But the big difference in our times is that we don't have figures like al-Ghazali (1058-1111), Ibn Rushd (1126-1198), Qutub al-Din al-Shirazi (1236-1311), al-Biruni (973-1050), Shibli Nu'mani (1857-1914) etc. to help us. What we do have at the very least though is the choice to gain a more nuanced understanding of these basic terms.

# 1.4 Knowing when "Islamic" isn't "Islamic"

Perhaps like me you've often asked yourself when do we call something "Islamic" as opposed to "Muslim"? And what, if any, differences and limits do these two terms have? Whilst they're interchangeably used by scholars and laity alike, in ensuing discussions we're often left in all kinds of knots and confusions. I know we can easily get caught up in semantics. However, it's worth exploring words and their usage to understand things better, not least because language actually matters. With every word there is context, implication of its use, and frameworks by which we understand it. The *Qur'an*, for example, was revealed and recorded in the specific dialect of the Quraysh. Language offers immense opportunity to both mystify and clarify things. It's possible for those who master a particular language to control and influence the rest of society, for good or bad. And we know how difficult it can be to put thoughts and experiences into words. In this sense, in celebration of languages on International Mother Languages Day (21st February) it's worth recognising that language can be a slender resource with inherent traps, but we can't do without it. Thus, we can only face up to the challenges of using it expediently and honestly if we're to be truthful, as commanded by God.

When it comes to the use of the word "Islamic" a number of areas are worth considering. The first, and perhaps the most common, is to recognise the cultural, technological and intellectual contributions of Muslims of the past, most notably during the so-called "Golden Age of Islam,"[14] or post-classical periods, in the form of "Islamic astronomy," "Islamic chemistry," "Islamic trigonometry," "Islamic pharmacology," "Islamic art" etc. "Islamic" here is intended to differentiate from the "non-Islamic" other, and thus to highlight history or features that might otherwise be

---

[14] The so-called "Golden Age of Islam" covers the period in the history of Islam from roughly the 8th century to the 14th or 15th century, during which Muslim societies produced the peak of economic, cultural and scientific outputs. However, it should be noted that from a God-centred perspective this is somewhat of a contradiction since the period doesn't cover the era of the Prophet and the Companions, which Muslims would nominally hold as the most blessed or golden period. Interestingly, the term was likely first coined within Orientalist literature, for example by Josias Leslie Porter in *A Handbook for Travelers in Syria and Palestine*, 1868, p. xlix: "Damascus is rich in such buildings - relics of the golden age of Islam, long since passed."

overlooked or dismissed as having Islamic roots, particularly as a tactic in today's identity politics. But this shorthand way of looking at Muslim history obscures the other basic fact: that earlier contributions weren't explicitly expressions of religion, in or of themselves, but merely the outputs of human beings, who happened to be Muslims, who sought to enquire into the miraculous nature of God's given world.

Yes, one can argue as the likes of al-Shirazi (1236-1311) have, that there are explicit and implicit indications (*ishara*) in the *Qur'an* that we can interpret as "signs" (*ayat*) which inspired a knowledge culture which in turn led to discoveries. Hence, in this sense, using "Islamic" it could be argued is meaningful. However, I think this refers only to the inspiring factor or value rather than the output because otherwise we can apply the same generalisation to everything to the extent that anything and everything can become a marker of "Islamic," which thankfully we don't.

For example, we hardly ever hear anyone say "Islamic camera" on the basis that the pinhole camera was invented by the Muslim polymath Ibn al-Haytham (965-1039). Or "Islamic refinery" on the basis that Ibn Hayyan (721-815) advanced the knowledge of distillation. This could perhaps also explain why "Islamic" wasn't added to words used during the so-called "Golden Age of Islam" such as *al-kimiya* (for alchemy which chemistry is derived from) or *'ilm al-falak* (for astronomy). Applying this to "Islamic art" we can see that it's not Islam in or of itself, but inspired by concepts like *husn* (beauty) and *ihsan* (achieving excellence) in Islam.

The second type are subject areas that are intrinsically Islamic such as "Islamic learning" referring to learning about the *Qur'an*, *fiqh*, *hadith* etc. There are also other times when it's necessary to use "Islamic," such as "Islamic prayer" in the context of religious worship or in comparative studies of religion. The same perhaps applies to "Islamic education" particularly if we're looking to differentiate from other fields of study today.

The third is the use of "Islamic" for current involvement of the *Shari'* dictates in specific fields like "Islamic Inheritance." Here, the law being referred to is intrinsically Islamic, and it can be reasonably argued that prefixing "Islamic" in these cases is necessary in order to differentiate from other legal systems. However, it's important to realise that sometimes what is labelled as "Islamic finance" or "Islamic investment" is debatable, and the opinions of some scholars may be somewhat of a stretch and not necessarily amount to what might please God as the Ever Watchful, Knower of what is hidden within us. This also raises an important point of "technical norm implementation."[15] Whereby, the label "Islamic" rather simplistically purports to "Islamicise" things, as automatically approved in the religion, in both spirit and form, when the reality is that upon examination they dismally struggle to go beyond the rhetoric, "techniques in law" or populism.

The fourth area, which is perhaps most egregious, is the use of "Islamic" for human organisations and institutions such as "Islamic political party," "Islamic state" or "Islamic government." You might be forgiven for thinking that if Islam means to be subservient to God, then a political party or government that sets out to implement Islamic law, the *Shari'ah*, in a rightful way could be truthfully called "Islamic." However, this is highly problematic in a number of ways.

Political parties and governments are human institutions and ways in which people organise to get things done; they're not intrinsically in and of themselves Islamic like for example the five daily prayers. Whilst their moral philosophy can be informed by Islamic values and law, they're still human systems in and of themselves, where power, policy choices and money matter. If we apply the same logic at an individual level, we certainly don't call ourselves "Islamic people" much as we intend to follow Islam 100%. What if a party or government only implements the *Shari'ah* 10% or 90%, do we risk faking religion for the non-compliant portion? In this sense, doesn't it fall on ordinary people, opposition parties or the judiciary to keep so-called "Islamic political party/government" or any government for that matter in check? However, it would be rather strange to restrain something we call "Islamic" if it's meant to be subservience to God. It seems, like the perversion of "Islamic camera," references like "The Islamic State/Government of the Umayya/Abbasiyya/Uthmaniyya" etc. were unsurprisingly quite unheard of at the time. Worst of all, some Muslim groups, most recently in the form of ISIS, but as well many so-called "Islamic political parties" across the world, have been happily appropriating "Islamic" in statecraft to suit their own political or narrow ends for well over a century.

---

[15] Tariq Ramadan, *Radical Reform, Islamic Ethics and Liberation*, OUP USA, 2009, p. 251.

The good news in all of this is that there is a term that we can use, in God's own description of believers, in the term "Muslim" as a submitter, or one who is subservient, to God. What Muslims achieve, do or don't do, is because of their efforts, priorities and inclinations. Whether Muslims understand or follow God's guidance or not, it's a function of "being Muslim." God gave us the label "Muslim" and called the religion "Islam" to make this distinction clear.

The rush to prefix things "Islamic" today, whilst often just sloppy, has a tendency to idealise or romanticise history and traditions. But, if anything, the signs are quite clear for Muslims. The lack of clarity and muddled understandings of what "faith" is by Christian scholars at the onset of European Enlightenment some three centuries or so ago, is something Christianity hasn't been able to recover from to this day. To the extent that the West is often described as "Christian West" despite increasing fewer Westerners recognising the value of religion,[16] and even fewer who go to Church, and still even fewer who learn or seek to apply the teachings of Jesus.

Thus, we ought to take heed by using the term "Islamic" truthfully, knowing when and how to use it in the right place and time, for the right purpose.[17]

---

[16] According to Theos (a UK based Christian think tank) in a poll conducted by ComRes, "Nearly half of British adults (47%) agreed that the world would be a more peaceful place if no one was religious, and a remarkable 70% agree[d] that 'most of the wars in world history have been caused by religions'." While the report overall presents a confusing picture of the value of religion, the changes in attitude is challenging to all religious people, especially when compared to previous centuries. See: https://www.theosthinktank.co.uk/in-the-news/2018/07/23/half-of-british-adults-say-the-world-would-be-more-peaceful-if-no-one-was-religious, retrieved 30 July 2018.

[17] See: Shahab Ahmad's *What Is Islam? The Importance of Being Islamic*, Princeton University Press, 2015. I think the author has confusing takes between being Muslim in the activities as human beings and Islam as guidance from God. See also Khaled Abou El-Fadl's critique of Shahab Ahmed's *"What is Islam?"* https://www.youtube.com/watch?v=aJooVgiqhQI, Usuli Institute Halaqa, Part 3 Q&A, 25 August 2018.

# 1.5 Why language and labels matter!

There are many reasons why in an age where news and information are readily available that we come across a great deal of high-handed, unkind, inappropriate or antagonising rhetoric. In response, we tend to react in the moment and not necessarily with well-thought-out reflections. That aside, with Trump, Brexit and a growing mandate for the far-right across Europe, politics has taken a definite rightward shift in recent years. In the UK, we've also seen a more organised, energised left, which has shifted further to the left. In societies like ours in the UK that take pride in being "open," much of this plays out in the media, where views, interpretations and ways of doing things are cast against one another. Whatever the wrongs and rights of this, the reality is that we've inherited and continue to build society's checks and balances in this way. As active Muslims engaged in this environment, whether it's related to the public understanding of religion or Muslim identity, or negotiating public self-assertion, there are many added challenges of representation and agency. What isn't so much in focus, however, which I would argue is vital in bringing about beneficial, mutually-assured outcomes, is the language we use to influence and engage in the different realms of public activism.

It's well-known in behavioural and cognitive sciences that our use of words to describe phenomena, inferences or feelings carries meanings which in turn affect our own attitudes and assumptions. If we get this wrong, it can quite easily lead to a yet more narrowing mindset where we completely shut down external viewpoints and perspectives, and lay ourselves open to blind spots that we can't, or refuse to, see. To the extent that we stop listening to others and shut them out from benefitting us. This kind of stubbornness is a basic feature of human psychology. It affects everybody to varying degrees no doubt, whether we're from the political right or left or in academia or business, in religious settings and so on. Thankfully, we can break away from this. Inherent social and metaphysical systems often have their own ways of settling things, sometimes serendipitously even. And of course, as human beings we possess a great capacity to think critically and to achieve levels of self-awareness that help us to at least consider ideas which we may have disagreed with at first, and to change our positions, behaviours and attitudes, whether our own or those of wider society.

To take an example, consider the words "stuck between a rock and hard place," "difficult," "challenging" and "tricky." Whilst they can all be interchangeably used, they have very different and real impacts on us. This isn't about an exercise in linguistic gymnastics, but about the art of negotiating or expressing our own internal states to give ourselves energy to be productive and useful. For Muslims it's also about making it easy for others to understand our viewpoints as a sign of affirming Godliness (*ihsani*) when interacting with others. That is, words signal our intent and approach to outcomes. What we shouldn't do, as Professor Jaques[18] argued, is "use all types of descriptions without thinking about the implications of their use, or frankly, out of a need to say things quickly because audiences do not have the time to read long explanations."

However, it's become far too normal, for instance, to amplify words of damnation or polemics using harsh or inappropriate words in order to hit home, whether from the mosque pulpit, on YouTube or on social media. Thus, in religious circles, we see child-like use of terms like "wobbler" as cognate of "straying" from a perceived normative convention, or dubious headlines like "Sinners Summit" and "Shirkmas." How many times do we hear male preachers overly focus on children, women and wealth in the context of only a narrative of damnation or *fitna* (test)?

Similarly, in the struggle for social justice, many activists are trigger-happy in their use of the term "white power" without distinguishing "hard right" or "white supremacy" from say casual or institutional racism. In such popular discourses, use of such terms isn't usually in context, but rather used in a cursing mode, in angry, predatory, amplified voices, so that they can be heard. Yet, most white people don't have the foggiest idea of what this label actually means nor are they responsible for what they're being accused of historically or today. Being white in a generalised way becomes wrongly cognate of injustice, just like being black was once cognate of being fit for enslavement by Europeans. Oddly, those who use such shorthand labels are often quick to point out that the term "Islamist terrorism" is a contradiction in terms, yet are only too happy to use shorthand labels when venting their own frustrations. Oddly, still, much of the structural socio-economic injustices, class- and caste-based

---

[18] R. Kevin Jaques is Associate Professor of Religious Studies at Indiana University specialising in Islamic legal history.

inequalities, social mobility issues etc. are found right across the world, and so reducing problems of the world to primarily a cause of "white power" would be quite naïve. If anything, it would create an unnecessary wedge with the very people whose potential for virtue needs unlocking.

In an age of information and disinformation, we're constantly bombarded with bad news and problems of our society, and it's very easy to get frustrated. What we shouldn't forget though is that whatever battles we're fighting we have choices, and choosing what's right usually starts with using the right words. By doing so, we stand a far better chance of healing the troubles of our world.

# 1.6 Moral philosophy in the face of neo-liberal and far-right extremism

In the wake of Brexit and the Trump vote, the term "neo-liberalism" has surfaced time and time again, amidst the soul-searching and political recriminations that have since followed. According to Encyclopedia Britannica, "neo-liberalism" is an "ideology and policy model that emphasizes the value of free market economics ... most commonly associated with *laissez-faire* economics ... often characterised in terms of its belief in sustained economic growth as the means to achieve human progress, its confidence in free markets as the most-efficient allocation of resources, its emphasis on minimal state intervention in economic and social affairs, and its commitment to the freedom of trade." However, as Barak Obama pointed to, "It did not start with Donald Trump," "He is a symptom, not the cause. He's just capitalizing on resentments that politicians have been fanning for years, a fear and anger that's rooted in our past, but it's also borne out of the enormous upheavals that have taken place in your brief lifetimes."[19]

Here's part of the challenge. Money whispers seductively because, generally speaking, as human beings we "love wealth with immense love," (89:20) and it's usually the morally depraved among us who cave in. Almost two years before the Credit Crunch, Bill Bonner wrote that everybody likes a credit boom and believes that they have money. "The businessman believes there is more demand for his products than there really is. The consumer believes he has more purchasing power than he really has. The lender believes the borrower is a better risk than he really is. All these mistaken judgements lead," according to Bonner, "to spending, investing and lending - which look for all the world like a *bona fide* boom."[20] And sure enough, the penny sank for some, as Will Hutton remarked, "Now we know the truth. The financial meltdown wasn't a mistake - it was a con."[21]

On the plus side, globalisation, hailed by some as the triumph of

---

[19] Barak Obama's speech at the University of Illinois on 8th September 2018.
[20] Bill Bonner, *Ponzi Economy*, 2006, https://dailyreckoning.com/ponzi-economy/, retrieved 21 November 2016.
[21] Will Hutton, *Now we know the truth. The financial meltdown wasn't a mistake - it was a con*, The Guardian, 19 April 2010.

neo-liberalism, has brought millions across the world out of poverty within a just few decades, and, together with modern technology, it's enabled greater transnational interconnectedness in the exchange of ideas, people and commerce. It is, on the face of it, "a great moral improvement over being driven by fervour, craving and tyrannical propensities," as Amartya Sen pointed out.[22] Yet, at the same time we've also seen the ugly side of "runaway globalisation" with worsening income inequality between the haves and have-nots, flouting people's spiritual needs and historically-proven social structures, as well as damaging the environment irreversibly. It's become okay, if you like, for society to develop paying least attention to local contexts, communities, nature, social history and spiritual needs.

These failures show that free markets work for mutual benefit when the right "institutional structure[s] and behavioural codes"[23] are in place. The intervening actions of regulatory bodies overseeing ethical and consumer standards, as well as preserving things significant to people, their own values, the environment and ethical standards, to name a few.

However, it's worth pointing out, as many economic philosophers have, that the free market mechanism (supply, demand, prices, advertising, competition etc.) isn't outside of moral choices *per se*. When market factors move (to reach "market equilibrium," perhaps) they do so because of choices people make. Buyers, sellers, suppliers, customers, regulators - they're all people partaking in the free market mechanism. Their actions reflect worldviews, identities, information available to them, values, needs and lifestyle choices. Notwithstanding the unintended consequences and the limits of human agency, one can argue that free markets are not devoid of free moral choices, albeit it's not necessarily coordinated; it's not just an abstract system, but the intentions and behaviours of human beings which are at the heart of it. And, of course, as with most things in life, choices and whether or not one succumbs to a particular grievous marketing claim, requires scruples and awareness of one's needs, blind spots and limits. Such qualities are not straightforward, and can themselves often be confused with "desire," where "unhealthy instincts" can appear under the guise of "rational arguments."

The story for far-right extremism is arguably linked to the story of

---

[22] Amartya Sen, *Development as Freedom*, Oxford University Press, 2001.
[23] Amartya Sen, ibid.

neo-liberalism. The 20ᵗʰ century was by far the most devastating in the history of humankind, driven by the belief in the exclusivity of national identity. Iblis's promise to delude human beings (15:30-39) coming to fruition as it were. The same egoistic impulse which prevented Iblis from obeying God's command to prostrate to Adam, which led to the angels consulting God as to whether Adam's progeny would cause carnage on earth as they vie to be superior to one another (2:30), would still be the same character defect for human beings to contend with in the 20ᵗʰ century.

Thankfully, a world ravaged by wars leading up to modernity eventually heralded the formation of supranational institutions like NATO, UN, WTO, the EU and decolonisation. This reversing of what had preceded in the last 500 years was a welcome relief. Human fraternity seemed to have matured at last, geared through mutual collaboration, not only lessening the chance of a despot wreaking terror in the West, but also to become more mutually productive, strengthening the international rules-based order and establishing peaceful societies. Some even claimed that the human race was marching towards greater security where the past no longer mattered.

However, as with most things in life, globalism has its own set of challenges. Increases in cross-border flows of capital, information, people and ideas inevitably lead to new forces of pluralism and decentralisation of local, ethnic and religious definitions, impacting not just the ability of governments to manage their own economies, but also their ability to create values and definition of citizenship.[24] This conjoining has consequences at all levels of life and tests people's ability to manage impacts, tolerance and patience etc. In the absence of clear demonstration of the value of globalisation, there can often be an unfortunate tendency for suspicion of "otherness." And when new immigrant communities develop within "cultural microcosms," a feature natural to diaspora communities almost anywhere in the world, they look far beyond national borders to other parts

---

[24] See: Hassan Hakimian and Ziba Moshver, *The State and Global Change: The Political Economy of Transition in the Middle East and North Africa (Institute of East Asian Studies)*, 1ˢᵗ edition, Routledge, 2000.

of the world because of economic, cultural and religious ties,[25] and the zealot claim of ghettoised no-go zones can easily gain traction. Coupled with the post-industrial breakdown of working-class white communities in Western societies, what we get is a fertile ground for extremism by white supremacist groups, racists and hatemongers.

For people of virtue and morality, the response to these things cannot be like that of Iblis, but like God's rebuke of him in the dialogue with the angels, when God said: "I will make upon the earth a successive authority" (2:30). One might ask themselves, who will work to renew the modern conscience and work to heal the deep wounds of neo-liberal and far-right extremism today? Who will engage the tough questions of our time with moral philosophy, graceful manner and wisdom, and bring into focus renewed ideas and arguments that enlighten the human conscience? The mesmerising part of the *Qur'an*, that "Human beings are in a state of loss except those who have faith, and do righteous deeds, and join together in the mutual teaching of truth, and of patience," (103:1-3) surely, must mean something.

I very much doubt if this is about partaking in the usual unoriginal ideological way that the right and left tussle each other. It's also not about the Huffington Post's and The Guardian's versus the Breitbart's and The Sun newspapers of the world. Neither is it about in-your-face, populist self-righteous "*da'wah*" or identity politics. Today, such unoriginal engagement has led many to join in with the popular abusive tirades against public figures or people whose opinions might offend. And it's not just the likes of Trump, but it seems anyone critical or scathing of Muslims or Islam too. For too many Muslims react to being offended in abrasive, ideologically motivated, vindictive tone. Such undignified reactions are antithesis to God telling the Prophet, "And if you had been rude [in speech] and harsh in heart, they would have disbanded from about you. So pardon them and ask forgiveness for them and consult them in the matter" (3:159). What it shows is just how flawed our grounding on moral philosophy has become.

Erdogan may have had a point when he said that denouncing Donald Trump was "disrespecting democracy." Similarly, the Electoral College system in America has its pros and cons, but Obama was right to remind

---

[25] For extensive discussion see: Amjad Muhammad, *Muslims in Non-Muslim Lands: A Legal Study with Applications*, The Islamic Texts Society, 2013.

people that democracy isn't easy. And who these days seriously studies American culture to see that America is actually built on contradictions? Christopher Bigsby identifies America as a secular country immersed in religion, where, "All expensive hotels will have a Gideon Bible," yet American culture is at the same time, "a puritan culture in love with pornography." It is said that some "11,000 adult films were released in 2000," and "it gave the world Playboy magazine."[26] America, Bigsby goes on, "celebrates the individual," yet its citizens are "always joining clubs, cults, good fellow societies, teams. In its films America is drawn to apocalypse provided it is followed by redemption. It weds violence to sentimentality, invincibility to vulnerability. America celebrates the family while for every two marriages there is one divorce."

It's clear in all of this that unnuanced, unmannered populism has overtaken far too much in society, and it is our most important asset, moral philosophy, which is being eroded.

---

[26] Christopher Bigsby, *The Cambridge Companion to Modern American Culture*, Cambridge University Press, 2006.

# 1.7 Beyond pre-assumed fault lines with the natural sciences

God's command to "Observe what is in the heavens and earth" (10:101), you could argue, has a two-pronged indication (*ishara*). The first being the natural science agenda of working out what makes life and nature work. The second being the Islamic scholarship agenda for deciphering God's law. However, despite much common ground, far too many on both sides lack awareness, verging on misunderstanding, of how science and religion work in relation to one another. On one end science is seen as the "bad guy" driving a wedge against religion, while on the other it is held as a "saviour" and the only source of "knowing" and values. Muslims also have to contend with the culture of proving the scientific content of revelation. Yet the *Qur'an* and Prophetic examples were never meant to be about science, or were they?

When we put these questions and dilemmas in context to wider post-modern scepticism of both science and religion, and subsequent defence, understandably, things become not just a degree more complicated but also unnecessarily divisive. Protagonists on all sides, rather than engage meaningfully and productively with each other, retreat to positions that serve to enhance their starting positions and self-image. Yet, with a little more insight and maturity it's possible to see parallels between Islamic and the natural sciences. Thus, when scholars or activists on both sides bludgeon one another, it is, as I argue here, a betrayal of the very methods that underpin their respective disciplines.

Just like groups of Islamic scholars come together to decipher a religious ruling or viewpoint on an issue (*mas'ala*) in the course of which they see patterns within revelation, from which they deduce principles (*usul* and *qawaid*) to organise religious thought, scientists also collaborate with each other to understand natural phenomena, forming hypotheses and theories. A hypothesis is simply a supposition or proposed explanation made on the basis of limited evidence as a starting point for further investigation. A collection of hypotheses which have been repeatedly tested and shown to be correct often leads to a theory. A theory is a supposition or a system of ideas intended to explain something, especially one based on general principles independent of the thing to be explained.

Just as Islamic jurists (*fuqaha*) use systematic and methodical frameworks to decipher Islamic law, such as principles that dictate the valid use of analogical reasoning (*qiyas*), scientists use the "scientific method" to collect, verify and evaluate evidence about natural phenomena. The philosopher Karl Popper (1902-1994) called this "falsification": the idea that something can't be true if it's contradicted by observation or experiment.

It's also worth pointing out here that just as there are ongoing discussions about how principles of Islamic sciences (*usul, qawaid*)[27] are applied in conjunction with contextual knowledge,[28] there is a fair amount of debate among philosophers of science about the nature of "facts" and "proofs" and how we arrive at conventions that we call scientific "laws" and "theories" from them.

As with any endeavour that involves investigating something whether it's in *'ilm al-hadith* (the sciences of *hadith*) or trying to work out the double helical structure of DNA, research entails evaluating methods and the results that those methods yield. Despite years of painstaking research, we can get conflicting results that, far from being useless, open up yet more questions which lead us to refine a hypothesis or theory. Sometimes we reach an impasse. Sometimes, albeit rarely, we get paradigm shifts. Through such iteration, both natural and Islamic sciences have developed over time and have become more and more concise or sophisticated as the case may be.

In all of this, there is a fair amount of competition too. For scientists, being first to discover something gives them kudos and euphoric moments, published papers, research grants and salaries. If we were to travel back in time to the medieval period, in places like Baghdad, Tunis, Cordoba, Cairo or Isfahan, I would argue we would be able to substitute the polities of scientists today with the polities of Muslim scholars as lawyers, chemists, philosophers, physicians and so on. Much like scientists today, they were

---

[27] For example, the relative preference for the principle of "public benefit" (*maslaha mursala*) versus "juristic discretion" where circumstances dictate a different solution (*istihsan*), in the classical Maliki and Hanafi schools of Islamic law (*madhahib*), respectively.

[28] For example, the knowledge of sociology, economics, medicine, computing etc.

funded by government patronage and endowments. A mix of meritocracy and favour from ruling classes raised their rank and status.

There is yet more common ground when it comes to the outputs of both scientists and Islamic scholars. Both of their works are subjected to peer-review. In science, results are independently assessed by other scientists, who give feedback and ask for clarifications or further experimentation to substantiate their claims before the science is accepted for publication. Independently, other scientists are at liberty to publish contrary findings. Equally, in Islamic scholarship, there is a strong culture of refuting ideas and beliefs, which can be likened to rejecting hypotheses. Historically, the most famous example is perhaps the refutations and adjustments centred on the philosophical musings of Ibn Sina (980-1037), al-Ghazali (1058-1111), Ibn Rushd (1126-1198), Ibn Taymiyyah (1263-1328) and Mulla Sadra (1574-1640), which spanned hundreds of years. I would also argue that a competitive spirit among both scientists and Islamic scholars helps prevent society from being perpetually blinkered. Finally, just like Islam can be misreported, misunderstood or misinterpreted, the same can happen in science.[29]

Yet, despite these similarities between the two disciplines, advocates on both sides often needlessly sour the air. Not because that's how these two arenas of knowledge meet in their truest forms, but because many on both sides aren't prepared to understand and reconcile each other's methods. It happens particularly when the relationship between science and Islam is reduced to a few big contentious questions.

The first of these, "Can science prove God?" is somewhat a misleading question from the offset. Among philosophers of science, there is a fair degree of consensus that things come under the purview of science only if they can be independently tested. God, however, reveals that "there is nothing like Him" (112:4). Hence, the thought of subjecting the

---

[29] For general themes around misreporting and abuse of science, see examples and discussions in these papers: (1) Hans Peter Peters, *Gap between science and media revisited: Scientists as public communicators*, Proc Natl Acad Sci U S A. 2013 Aug 20; 110(Suppl 3): 14102-14109, retrieved 10 August 2018; (2) Damaris Rosado *et. al. The Use and Abuse of Science*, 2007, http://cstep.cs.utep.edu/research/ezine/Ezine-TheUseandAbuseofScience.pdf; (3) *Abuses of Science: Case Studies*, https://www.ucsusa.org/our-work/center-science-and-democracy/promoting-scientific-integrity/abuses-science-case-studies#.W6i_TnXrvIU, retrieved 10 August 2018.

Omnipotent (*Al-Qahir*), Everlasting (*Al-Baqi*), Most Loving (*Al-Wadud*), incomprehensible entity (*dhat*) to some notion of "test" seems absurd. The fact that God can't be subjected to such "scientific testing" of sorts, it could be argued, serves to illustrate His incomprehensibility.

My point here is that stress-testing whether something should come under the purview of science (or religion) is an important first step. By getting this right we stand a better chance of developing a cogent view of how science and religion can productively interact. This is to say that science tries to tell us about the physical world and how it works, whilst religion gives us values, morals and meaning to the world and to our place in it. Moreover, for Muslims there is yet something beyond the phenomenal realm, as God hinted: "How can you be sure that if a sign came [that] they would still not believe[?] … even if We had sent to them the angels, made the dead speak to them, and gathered before them all things before their eyes, they would not have believed" (6:111).

The second contentious area is explaining the origin of life. The theory of evolution tries to explain how the vast similarities and diversity of life came about, and looks for evidence in life forms (in fossils, phylogenetics, physiology, gene sequencing, behavioural adaptations etc.) to propose a mechanistic view of how life may have evolved. It's a theory because, fundamentally, many things remain unexplained. Evolutionary relationships can't themselves be observed *in situ* through a real-life time-lapse video of millions of years for instance, and hence scientists need to make reasonable assumptions to piece together gaps in the evidence. Scientists generally don't deny this, which is partly why there is so much ongoing research activity in this area.

Interestingly, evolution theory doesn't directly test "causality" in itself, and assumes that the evolutionary mechanisms such as natural selection are in themselves spontaneously causative. This notion itself causes all sorts of problems for philosophers of science. Nevertheless, the theory of evolution as a plausible explanation of the diversity and origin of life is the working paradigm today and unifies the entire subject of biology. In some respects, it reflects how the human mind naturally works. We observe and analyse patterns, and seek connections between variables, so that we can explain phenomena better. Though, for Muslims there is also a metaphysical consideration in the belief that everything is dependent on

God and happens by His Power (*Qadar*) and attributes (*sifat*) whether we realise it or not.

The geological migration of the Pangaea supercontinent over millions of years into the dispersed continents today is a good example of how scientists search for and make use of evidence to make connections that enable them to propose mechanistic explanations (theories) of why the earth's land topology is the way it is today. Another good example is the "variations in your languages" (30:22). No one denies that languages which have reached us today evolved through different roots and fusions. In fact, the very subject of Etymology, which is the "study of the origin of words and the way in which their meanings have changed throughout history," enables entire languages to be classified into families based on their similarities.

Indeed, rather than taking a closer look at the philosophy of science and how science works, as Muslims we often base our defence of religion through populist reactions against secular evangelical evolutionists like Richard Dawkins. The meeting point isn't necessarily formed on the body of deep Islamic scholarship and a structured way of approaching ideas and problems through the right perspectives. As my former Professor of Immunology, Denis Alexander,[30] argued, Dawkins isn't as respected by everyone in the scientific community as people from the outside might assume. Nevertheless, in doing so, we forget that the theory of evolution remains partly unexplained and instead succumb to thinking that our faith assumptions are threatened. We then feel compelled, verging on religious obligation, to take to the hammer and uncritically refute evolution theory, come what may.

Moreover, we forget that there's plenty of speculation among Islamic scholars, for example about the "spiritual ascent to God."[31] The point is, there are things in Islamic scholarship which we've taken as *fait accompli* for centuries, yet whilst evidences and arguments have their own merits, they are largely speculative compared to definitive things like the verse "Say, God is One" (112:1) or the phenomenon of gravity. Moreover, speculation

---

[30] For brief biography of Professor Denis Alexander, see: https://www.faraday.st-edmunds.cam.ac.uk/Biography.php?ID=9, retrieved 6 July 2018.
[31] Through processes known as *fana* (annihilation) and *baqa* (subsistence) etc. For details see: Riyad Asvat, *Sufism: the Living Tradition*, Diwan Press, 2017.

of this kind isn't automatically a fruitless exercise. Some Islamic scholars argue that the doctrines around the spiritual ascent to God help believers to deepen their servitude (*ma'arifah*) in God, whereas scientists in the realm of biology could equally argue that the theory of evolution helps them to understand and organise biology.

So, what exactly is the problem and how do we resolve things? It seems the entire problem we have with evolution theory centres around whether the *Qur'anic* account of Adam's creation is incompatible with man having evolved. In answer to this question the claim that God has explicitly or implicitly informed us that it is impossible for one sort of being to come out of another (speciation) is nowhere to be found. In fact, there is arguably evidence in support. God mentions in the *Qur'an* (7:166)[32] the metamorphosis of a disbelieving group of *Bani Isra'il* into apes, which isn't disputed in exegetical (*tafsir*) literature. Similar references to metamorphosis also exist in *hadith* literature.[33]

However, while speciation isn't necessarily negated for other species, the view for man in the *Qur'an* is that God created Adam as the first human being (*bashar*) and placed him in Paradise (*Jannah*) and not on earth as we know it (38:71-76). It also hints that God created in a particular unbeknown way by virtue of "fashioned him" (*sawwaituhu*) "with My hands" (considered figurative speech) and "breathed into him My spirit." Hence, it could be argued, if man wasn't on earth when he was created, how then is it possible that he evolved out of a precursor who was on earth?

Now, one could also argue that there could have been a process of evolution that did happen which produced something similar to man (e.g. Neanderthals, *Homo Erectus* etc.) which became extinct, but it was Adam's progeny (human beings as *Homo sapiens*), having been "put on earth" as it were, who came to disperse as God intended. One could also argue that the use of "fashioned him" applies to being fashioned on earth, particularly given that God says, "I am going to create a human being from clay" - "clay" arguably referring to an earthly material. Though, these are all speculative of course.

Moreover, where God tells us that He has created us in the "best of

---

[32] This is not disputed in exegetical (*tafsir*) literature.
[33] Examples from *hadith* narrated by Ibn Mas'ud in *Sahih Muslim* and others: https://sunnah.com/search/?q=apes, retrieved 6 July 2018.

form" (*ahsani taqweem*) (95:4), it doesn't necessarily negate evolution *per se*. It's merely stating, as a matter-of-fact, that the human form is the "best of form" in its physique, and rational and spiritual qualities. The point is, if God hasn't explicitly revealed such details to us, in their absence, perceiving phenomena and events which came before "all that exists" or life forms as we know them will always be somewhat speculative. A good example of this is the soul (*ruh*): despite being an entity which people at the time of the Prophet accepted, it was God who ended speculation by saying we "have been given very little" (17:85) of the knowledge of some things like the soul.[34]

What are we to do with such matters? Firstly, it's worth noting that the question of whether the *Qur'anic* account of creation is incompatible with man having evolved has only arisen and broadened in modern times, thanks to Darwin and the expansion of biology as a subject. And so, it's up to contemporary scholars to investigate. There's little point looking for explanations from classical scholars and thinkers despite finding references like that of Ibn Jahiz (776-689)[35] because, quite simply, the theory of evolution as a broad field of modern evolutionary biology didn't exist then. Muslim theologians in the past did have a remarkably expedient way of defending the body of sound Islamic beliefs (*'aqidah*) through simple and specific statements. Classical *'aqidah* texts are all in the main made of these statements. It's therefore not unreasonable, and certainly I don't think it would be a betrayal of Islamic scholarship to simply assert: "We believe in what has been related in the *Qur'an* and authentic *hadiths* regarding the creation of Adam and do not necessarily deny what is evident according to

---

[34] See *tafsir* literature to understand the background to this verse.

[35] Primary example, and perhaps the earliest in Muslim scholarship, is Ibn Jahiz (776-868/9), whose *Kitab al-Hayawan* (*Book of Animals*) discusses the phenomenon of competition between species leading to survival of the fittest and natural selection, see: Zirkle C (1941). *Natural Selection before the "Origin of Species"*, Proceedings of the American Philosophical Society, 84 (1): 71-123.

scientific inquiry" and to leave it at that.[36] Beyond this, to make explicitly binding belief statements about evolution (which is subject to revision in any case) may be problematic and unwittingly confuse Muslims to needlessly doubt revelation or science.

That aside, it is understandable that some Muslims feel threatened by evolution theory as a concept, and possibly science more generally. There are many reasons for this. The first is the line of thinking that Godlessness (*fawahisha, jahiliyyah, gaflah* etc.) in today's world comes at a time when science has presided over it. People instinctively see science as enabling the modern world's sophistry, including its troubles. However, this is a narrow analysis and doesn't consider macro factors associated with the Muslim civilisational ("ummatic") experience (e.g. the lack of education, civil strife, silo mentality, crisis of intellect, colonisation etc.).

Admittedly, among many Muslims, rightly or wrongly, as Shaykh Abdul Hakim Murad observes, there is a sense of mounting "attempts to unpick all transhistorical notions of meaning and canonicity." Whilst this might be the case in the abuse and misreporting of science,[37] it is not a reason to blame or be overly-sceptical of science *per se*, because science is fundamentally a values-neutral enterprise. Most scientists, says Denis Alexander, whilst not dogmatically against traditional conventions, accept a "moderate form of constructivism of science, not so much for ideological reasons but because the evidence supported it."[38] This kind of scientific

---

[36] The *'aqidah* text of the 12th century theologian of the Maturidi school Imam Abu Hafs Umar Ibn Ahmad al-Nasafi known as *Al-'Aqidah al-Nasafiyyah*, for example, introduced the statement affirming "reason" (*'aql*) as a source of knowledge in addition to the "sound senses" (*al-hawas al-salima*) and "true narration" (*al-khabar al-sadiq*), which was not present in earlier creedal texts such as its 9th century predecessor *Al-'Aqidah al-Tahawiyyah* of Imam Abu Jafar al-Tahawi. Al-Nasafi states: "With regards to Reason, it is also a source of knowledge. Whatever is established by it by way of intuition (*badiha*), it is of necessity, as the knowledge that everything is bigger than its part." Inclusion of such viewpoints is arguably proof that creedal statements should be developed in context to the times and places in which Muslims live. In this sense, making reference to science as a source of knowledge would simply fit into that schema which has been in play in Islamic scholarship since classical periods.

[37] Not just from what I would argue is an abuse of science but also in other fields like sociology, psychology etc., where the deconstructive tendency can be far more overt.

[38] Denis Alexander and Ronald Numbers, *Biology and Ideology - From Descartes to Dawkins*, Chicago University Press, 2010, p. 6.

constructivism typically expresses itself in the form of "expertism" and correlational studies, inviting individuals to adapt their behaviours. However, it still remains the job of Muslims to evaluate them through the prism of well-reasoned arguments of the *Qur'an* and *Sunnah*.

Moreover, some philosophers of science, the "Positivists," like Paul Fayerabend (1924-1994) take the view that an obsession with science leads to individuals losing their freedom to make up their own minds about lifestyle choices, beliefs and factors that define their identity. Fayerabend's argument was against extremist scientists who sought to legitimise the use of science to prescribe human behaviours and social arrangements because they reckoned that these things are inevitably determined by genes and biology alone. This sentiment is very much alive among many Muslims, most likely as a result of poor understanding.

Whilst there is much more to be discussed, I think many Muslims genuinely fear, as Imam al-Ghazali noted, the continuous search "for the cause of the world" as nature for them becomes "barren" and "dark" as it's not spiritualised through the knowledge of God.[39] However, it's the responsibility of religious institutes to produce thinkers and professionals who can show how one can be in search of the causes of the world while remaining grateful believers immersed in Godliness. Believers ought to accept that science as a rational approach to understanding the physical world is emphatically encouraged in Islam. Being alert to the potential misuse or poor practice of science (eroding values, ethics, faith and Godliness etc.), should be based on robust understanding of both science and revelation and not on speculation of revelation imposed on science or vice versa.

---

[39] Abu Hamid al-Ghazali, *The Niche of Light (Mishkat al-Anwar)*, Brigham Young University Press, 1998, p. 46.

# 1.8 Idealism and realism: rebalancing the Muslim mindset

The unrealistic belief in or pursuit of perfection and ideal state, "idealism," gives human beings motivation and courage. However, without being true to life, "realism," our approach to things can, and so often does, turn into false hope, cynicism and sometimes even a blame culture. It seems, our perceived and real lack of control of modernity's rapid changes has a tendency for idealism at the expense of realism, as at any time in the past. Yet, for the sincere believer, the strain between idealism and realism is a struggle to, on one hand, defend the truth no matter how unpopular it may be, and on the other hand, to embrace the right "attitude or practice of accepting a situation as it is and being prepared to deal with it accordingly." Far from being an emerging so-called apologetic or post-modern reflection, this balancing of idealism by realism has always had a deep intellectual wisdom in Islamic scholarship.

We might expect an idealist to look at things as they ought to be, whereas a realist might look at things as they are actually experienced. While an idealist may not be satisfied until they see reality achieve its optimal state, a realist may be content with the most pragmatic state. Idealists might argue that colonialism, for example, should never have occurred; a realist might argue that it was inevitable since human beings have always vied to dominate one another and God reminds us of it (57:20). An idealist might advocate a classless society, but a realist might opine that human societies, even the Madinan society of the Prophet, have always resisted a kind of sameness between people where meritocracy didn't matter. God in the *Qur'an* repeatedly alludes (e.g. 39:9) to the basic difference between those who know and those who don't know.

The implications of such an outlook are immense. Whether we're conscious of it or not, we might become fixed to seeing the world in all its flaws versus seeing the world through its inherent restlessness made up of good, bad and mundane experiences. It is true that we imagine and represent things in our minds, and in doing so form perceptions of things often in a highly personalised way. The possibility of such intimate realisations, however diverse, can only be a mercy from God. But such perceptions are altogether something else when we seek to project them onto others as "the ideal."

It's hard to find idealism as a mode of normative thinking in Muslim civilisation. Human beings could not be made into a single sort of being, which God actually rebukes (49:13). Muslim societies thus expressed universality as a plurality of cultures, ideas and peoples. The Madinan society of the Prophet, for example, was forged on alliances between people of different religions, tribes, social and economic standing and immigrants.[40]

Yet, the realist in me tells me that the dominant motivity in Muslim discourses today is idealism. In Islamic concepts, like *ummah* ("global Muslim community") for example, we idealise it as a consciously homogeneous community where faith alone is operative, which we then project as authentic today. Premised on this kind of idealism, it is often the case that for anyone differing on a matter of geopolitics or social policy, or theology even, they face being castigated for apparently breaking "unity" or deviating from an apparent "original *Sunnah*." Unity within this *ummah* is often taken up in the imagination of the unreal conformity or uniformity. However, we know that the diversity of races, languages, cultures, grades of knowledge, class and ideas is a well-recognised existential reality in the *Qur'an* and Prophetic example. The Companions, as bearers of Prophetic Sunnah *par excellence*, too, differed on many matters and grappled with the challenges and opportunities of being human.

Another common idealism is that of so-called "political Islam," which is common to violent groups and post-colonial "Islamic political parties." What you often see in them is an idealist view of history, where "political Islam" becomes the hubris of the "zero point," the untouchable memory, one that if you go against, you're seen as a "sell out," "apologist" or "modernist." Many people struggle to see this for what it is, and perpetuate reactions that take little account of vastly different processes underway today than at any point in the past.

Idealism in juristic school-based institutions is also quite prevalent. Fixing historical texts into today's contexts in matters of ambiguity (*thanni*) seems a far cry to the kind of observations made by the 10th century geographer, al-Muqaddasi (946-991). He recalls a level of realism that, at times, led scholars in the 10th century to present "their opinions, advancing

---

[40] See: M. Hamidullah, *The First Written Constitution in the World*, Lahore: Ashraf Press, reprinted 1975.

on one point, then retreating; granting, as it were, then contradicting; allowing, then disallowing; permitting, then forbidding - and people have accepted this, and have been satisfied with it, and no intelligent person has denied them the right to do this."[41]

However, idealism in this area has convinced many Muslims that Divine revelation offers answers to life's ever-changing circumstances without having to make sense of, and strive with, the external environment and our own inner psychological space. Ironically, it's become automatic for many to approach "sacred texts" as remote and "untouchable" due to their very sacredness. And on a macro level, too, today's ethno-factional identity politics is partly a reflection of this kind of inflexibility and "crisis of the intellect."

From what I can see, idealism in the Islamic paradigm is a subjective notion. Not least since acts of subservience to God (*taqwa*) outside of core aspects of worship (*'ibada*) vary from one person to another according to the specifics of their own space, time and contexts. There are many Prophetic examples that bespeak of the Companions learning about the actual nature of the world.[42] To experience and represent things in "ideal" form, or as they might or should be, is quite simply the effort of striving to act out of being in awe of God (*taqwa*), sincerity (*ikhlas*) and applying one's best discretion (*ihsan*). And even so, whilst there may be signs in one's behaviour, one doesn't know for certain if God has accepted one's good deeds. The Islamic paradigm, it could be argued, recognises human beings as continuously wavering around "nonideal" positions, between gratitude and sin.

Idealism can quite easily lead to psychopathic, hard-nosed,

---

[41] Al-Muqaddasi, *The Best Divisions for Knowledge of the Regions: Translation of Ahsan al-Taqasim fi Ma'rifat al-Aqalim*, translated by Basil Anthony Collins, Ithaca Press, 2000, p. 223.

[42] Examples include a *hadith* narrated by 'Abdullah in *Sahih al-Bukhari*: "The Prophet drew a square and then a line in the middle of it and let it extend outside the square and then drew several small lines attached to the central line, and said: 'This is the human being, and this, [the square] in his lease of life, encircles him from all sides, and this [line], which is outside [the square], is his hope, and these small lines are the calamities and troubles [which may befall him], and if one misses him, another will snap [overtake] him, and if the other misses him, a third will snap [overtake] him.'"

over-confident positions, often concealing the real nature and features of our experiences of life. In turn, pushing the line of thinking that circumstances beyond our own spaces and contexts are the real drivers for moving things forward, to improve conditions and so on. But, this is a kind of false lure that we must check using the very existential reality that idealism seeks to obscure.

# 1.9 The trouble with American preacher-scholars in the UK

The frequency with which American preacher-scholars come over to the UK would have you think that British scholars, advocates of the Islamic faith, or community workers were few and far between. There was of course a time when the likes of Shaykh Hamza Yusuf, Imam Siraj Wahaj, and others, came over frequently and quite rightly commanded our awe. You could argue in those days there weren't many British scholars or activists who could articulate faith or reason well in English. However, times have changed, and this is no longer the case. Thus, the proliferation of American preacher-scholars visiting the UK, arguably, risks becoming an unhealthy intrusion into the making of British Muslim identity. There are, as I argue here, compelling reasons for a corrective change in course.

For a start, the American preacher-scholar phenomenon, unlike in the UK, is significantly dependent on social media. With that come all the good and ugly aspects that fragment and homogenise religious learning, as well as, unfortunately, periodic scandalising and self-righteous frenzies. Many preacher-scholars often take time to thank their followers having reached a certain milestone in the number of followers. What they don't publicise so much is the responsibility, need for training and care required of them when communicating about matters of religion to such broad audiences.

As we have seen, the gluttony for numbers usually leads to a self-satisfying drive to supply visually-stimulating content crafted to keep people glued to the screen. Fueling what has now become the ubiquitous modern-day spiritual malady of "infotainment religiosity." Where the teaching of religion is: (1) fixated onto the screen for very broad audiences; (2) there is no checking if audiences have correctly understood and applied the content; (3) the audience's learning and interacting with local teachers, mosques and educational institutes is abandoned in favour of those whom they may never meet nor meaningfully interact with in person; and (4) the focus on deeper study is substituted by what Shaykh Mohammed Nizami described, "tidbits of information and divergent perspectives of an incoherent patchwork of learning."[43]

This isn't at all surprising. In fact, as Neil Postman wrote, the problem

---

[43] Personal communication with Shaykh Mohammed Nizami.

is not that the blue screen presents us "with entertaining subject matter but that all subject matter is presented as entertaining."[44] One commentator retorted how they have actually become "a fly-zapper for exhibitionists - they see that blue glow and they just can't help flying towards it."[45] Societies driven by what goes on television and mobile phone screens arguably seem set to follow the American way, as Postman described, of not talking but entertaining each other, exchanging images instead of ideas, and arguing "with good looks, celebrities and commercials" instead of "with propositions."

My question is, if preacher-scholars feel satiated with such big audiences, are we seeing the kind of faith-based change in the quality of "Islamic being" of British Muslims that warrants celebration? While "guidance and success is from God," we're encouraged to be critical and to ask questions in search of necessary and better means.

This also raises some serious questions about the tendency of British Muslim organisations to fly-in American preacher-scholars for fundraising campaigns. It clearly doesn't help develop the many graduates of our own. Nor does it, qualitatively speaking, help us overcome sectarianism, unresolved ethno-cultural baggage, "groupie mentality" and religious illiteracy closer to home, all of which hinders the formation of a confident British Muslim experience.

When American preacher-scholars talk about issues to do with feminism, racism, liberalism, scientism, capitalism, political engagement or some other issue that happens to take their fancy, it's usually not based on the British experience of those conditions. Indeed, the British experience is often vastly subtler and more nuanced. More than a thousand-year history of interaction and deep fascination between the people of the British Isles with Muslims create a different environment in the UK compared to America in which interactions between people of the Islamic faith and others can take place today. Whether it's King Offa of Mercia (d. 796) minting coins in the name of Abbasid Caliphs of Baghdad, or Queen Elizabeth I (1533-1603) meeting the Saadian ambassador-cum

---

[44] Neil Postman, *Amusing Ourselves to Death: Public Discourse in the Age of Show Business*, Penguin, 2005.

[45] Thomas Sutcliffe, *When fifteen minutes of fame drags by*, The Independent, 9 June 2008.

Shakespeare's *Othello*-like caricature, or the half a million or so Muslims who fought alongside the British army to defeat Nazism, or one of the great 20<sup>th</sup> century Muslim philosopher's, Muhammad Iqbal (1877-1938), studying at Trinity College Cambridge, are just a few examples of the varied and rich shared history of interaction. Given this, my question is: can American preacher-scholars appreciate the lived subtleties of this if they haven't been to our schools, colleges, employers, engaged civic bodies and so on?

In fact, the reality is that few preacher-scholars stay in the UK long enough to have meaningful interactions or to deliver structured courses over a period of time, the kind of time that true cultivation (*tarbiyyah*) requires. The marketing machinery around a flying visit exhibits all the show-business power of American branding culture. While branding might be necessary, the sincere believer's seeking decorum (*tawadu'*) is arguably much more in keeping with the good aspects of British sentiments and where celebrity-style endorsement is much subtler and certainly nowhere near as rampant.

Interestingly, many American preacher-scholars argue against the personality cult, yet seem all too happy to be paraded in promotional videos. And, talk of "how" to do community work by American preacher-scholars can be condescending to UK audiences, particularly given that it is those very preacher-scholars who seek mileage out of Facebook rants about not just Muslims being under siege in America by the KKK, Trump, liberals and so on, but also of personal politics between them. No doubt we have our own expressions of this in the UK too, but its scale is limited in comparison, and has separate historical roots in factionalism, religious illiteracy and ethno-culture.

The making of contextualised Islam in the UK is an ongoing exploration for British Muslims. Both British organisations who invite them and American preacher-scholars who come over to the UK would do well to recognise this. After all, as Professor Christopher Bigsby[46] having studied American culture concluded that it's built on contradictions. It remains to be seen if the American phenomenon of preacher-scholars is any

---

[46] Christopher Bigsby is a Cambridge University Professor at the time of writing, and fellow of the Royal Society of Literature and the Royal Society of Arts.

different. However, given the genuine creativity and intellectual potential of American preacher-scholars, and the reality that British Muslims will likely continue to take an interest in them for leadership at least for some time, it's in our interest that they're able to overcome these challenges.

# 1.10 What do we understand by "Prophet of Mercy"?

Every year with the passing of the month of Rabi' al-Awwal many of us find ourselves pondering over the life of the Prophet Muhammad. Rabi' al-Awwal being the month in which the Prophet was born in the year 570, many Muslims throughout the world do something to remember, honour and celebrate his life. How we do this can and does often differ of course. Some increase sending salutations to the Prophet. Others attend events known as *mawlid* or *sirah* conference to commemorate the birth and life of the Prophet. Yet others read articles, watch educational clips on YouTube about the Prophet etc. Some remain completely oblivious too. In all of this, we might get a glimpse into why the Prophet consistently comes at the top of any surveys of the most influential people to have ever lived.[47] However, just as populist distractions grip many Muslims from attending to priority areas, it seems that the idea that the Prophet was "sent as a mercy" too often becomes just another piece of information that doesn't trigger deeper thoughts or actions.

The Prophet came at the end of a long line of people to whom God revealed guidance. It's a chain which started from Adam and includes, among others, Noah, Abraham, David, Moses and Jesus. They were chosen by God as message-bearers on earth to guide human beings towards their well-being, virtue and righteousness and to enable them to carry out responsibilities laid upon them.

We know that God has given Prophets the ability to perform miracles of various forms to help convey their message. Many of these miracles are well-established not just in the *Qur'an* but also in the Old and New Testaments. For instance, among the many miracles God gave Jesus was the miracle of curing blindness and bringing the dead back to life. Moses turned his rod into a serpent (79:20) and caused the sea to split. The Prophet Muhammad, too, had many miracles. The greatest of which was the *Qur'an* itself, which unlike perhaps the miracles of other Prophets was auditory and preserved in time, consistent if you like with being, as Muslims believe, the Prophet for all times.

Whilst the *Qur'an* is a literary miracle, at the same time, it conveys reality, story and meaning, from which a comprehensive spiritual paradigm,

---

[47] Michael Hart, *The 100: A Ranking Of The Most Influential Persons In History*, 2001.

moral guidance, a place of solace, legal code and social, economic and political cosmos are brought into awareness. It is in this very *Qur'an* that the Prophet Muhammad is described as a "mercy for the universe" (21:107). Yet, he was human and subject to physical conditions outwardly just as any other person. He suffered from fatigue, sickness, hunger, pleasure, and was afflicted with heat and bitter cold. Inwardly, though, he had spiritual-metaphysical qualities such that, as he described a quality bestowed on Prophets, "Our eyes sleep but our hearts do not sleep."[48]

What perhaps distinguished him most was his character (*shamail*) as "the most beautiful example" (33:21), details of which have come down to us in the *Qur'an* as well as through corroborated reports and in the continuous practices of the Companions (*Sunnah*). They bespeak of his: justice; firmness; trustworthiness; sedateness; silence; excellent conduct; abstinence, fear of God and intensity of worship; integrity; modesty; probity in contracts and in maintaining kinship ties; compassion; good manner and good nature; courage and generosity; forbearance; intellect and sense of humour and so on.

The word "*mercy*" in Arabic is "*rahmah*," which is derived from the root *ra ha ma*, which curiously, doesn't mean "mercy" but is the noun for the "womb of a pregnant mother." And so, importantly, "*rahmah*" meaning "mercy" is to be understood as complete protection, nourishment and unconditional care that we received while in our mother's womb.

When we speak of the Prophet as a "mercy for the universe," like many aspects of religion that have today lost their nuance, or become jingoistic or politicised, it is often the case that we say he is a "mercy" without contemplating any deeper and recognising how or why that is. Most of us habitually interchange the word "mercy" with "compassion" or "love," for example, in the sense that the Prophet was patient, kind, envied no one, never boasted, nor was conceited, nor rude, never selfish, never one to take offence and so on. But too often we stop here, and don't look to see how "mercy" has much greater meaning. As a result, we fail to benefit from Prophetic examples and wisdoms in a deeper, more fulfilling way.

For example, among the noble characteristics of the Prophet is his character as *Muhammad al-Amin* ("Muhammad the Trustworthy"), which

---

[48] Qadi Iyad, *Muhammad, Messenger of Allah: Ash-Shifa of Qadi Iyad*, Madinah Press, 1999.

was a title he was widely known by even before receiving the first revelation. This was because what he said and did could be trusted; there was no pretence or disingenuous state or act involved; and despite the prevalence of idolatry he believed in One God and refrained from blameworthy behaviours (backbiting, cheating etc.).

There are deep wisdoms in this. Trustworthiness is actually a primary function of "mercy." It is often not so much "what is being said" that moves the human conscience but "who is saying it" and "how it is said," and so for "mercy" to be established there must be trust to begin with. As human beings, we evaluate people's trustworthiness, to be fair, just and well-intended. We're more receptive to a trusted friend than someone we dislike, has bad character or we perceive to harbour ill-intentions or self-interest. By the same measure, when we evaluate trustworthiness, we need to be fair in order to be trustworthy ourselves.

Trustworthy also entails being straightforward, having integrity, being clear and meeting expectations that we set. And the Prophet emphasised these qualities in his teachings. For example, in being *al-jawami' al-kalim*: succinct in speech, whilst still carrying the fullest meanings. For ambiguity is usually a cue for a lack of trustworthiness.

Much of the troubled world we live in bears the scars of a breakdown in trust between human beings and institutions. Whether it's a breakdown in our families, communities, media, corporates, governments, processes, systems, or peoples, it seems, we cannot get away from the question of trustworthiness. By taking utmost attention to being trustworthy and building trust in processes, systems and interactions with others, we draw upon the sources of mercy that God has made implicit in creation. By doing so, we follow in the very footsteps of that unlettered, orphaned child, who God honoured as "mercy," Muhammad, the Trustworthy one, peace and blessings be upon him, *sallallahu 'alaihi wa sallam*.

# 1.11 The esoterism of Ramadhan

Ramadhan is in many ways a very different time of the year. Not just for its outer expression in *iftar* parties (where Muslims break their fasts), charity appeals, the hustle and bustle of finding parking space at the mosque, or viewing live streaming of *tarawih* (night prayer) from Makkah, but for what happens deep within us. Whether we fully realise it or not, fasting modulates the body's neuro-physiological and perceptual responses triggering seemingly out of the ordinary consciousness and feelings. Visible signs of wilful consumption turn into deprivation and hunger, idle chit-chat turns into silence, libido turns into abstinence, muscularity reduces to gentleness, and individualism is at least partially replaced with communion and so on. These first-hand experiences in turn, to the inward or esoteric sense, go some way in instilling the meaning of faith (*iman*) and demonstrate the will to submit to God (Islam). Though, they're most effective if we pay careful attention to them of course.

It's well-known that by around eight hours into a fast, the body switches to a "fasting state." At this point it starts metabolising fat stored in adipose tissues instead of sugars. As the fasting day progresses our energy levels drop and our perceptions and interactions with the world changes. The gradual build from a slight growl to the feeling of an empty stomach can be hard to ignore too.

Yet we refrain from eating. In some cases, counting down to the last few seconds, or even adding a minute or two to be sure. We go to this trouble because, regardless of how religiously devout we are outside of Ramadhan, we instinctively want to get this right, and thus we're prepared to be patient (*sabr*). At stake is the very mark of our own inner determination to be meticulously subservient to God. Fasting, God says, "is for me,"[49] which is made all the more acute because it only comes around once a year. In the process, we may realise that it is God who provides or we may become more disciplined - all part of the wider merits of fasting. And whilst the quality of this connection may differ from person to person, the core lesson of submitting unquestioningly, "we hear and we obey" (2:285), seems uncomplicated and much more easily realised.

At the same time, our minds shunt into a more relaxed, introspective

---

[49] *Hadith* narrated by Abu Huraira in *Sahih al-Bukhari*.

state of awareness. Hunger signals bring about a consciousness of going without food. In other words, we experience what it's like being unable to eat despite the desire to or feeling hunger in our stomach. As it turns out, these are normalised every day experiences of hundreds of millions who go without meals or have no idea where their next meal will come from. Increased empathy and charitable giving are therefore natural reflexes of fasting. And to top it off, increased mental sharpness that also comes with fasting, perhaps, helps concentrate mere concern or intent into conscious acts of giving (*sadaqa, zakat*).

There is also the disruption to our natural circadian rhythms of the day that comes in the month of Ramadhan. *Tarawih* in the summer can easily take us up well into the early hours of the morning. The length of such prayers is a useful tool, even if in prayer our minds wonder elsewhere. The words of the *Qur'an* echoing from a melodious reciter can be mesmerising. And as scholars have pointed out, standing in complete stillness in prayer for prolong periods can by itself help bring about or sustain a state of humbleness (*khushu'*). As beggars standing before God, even if as late as the last few units of prayer we achieve some mindfulness in the form of a split moment of intimate realisation of God's presence, sending electrifying goosebumps through the body, or a sudden moment where the meanings of the words of God truly hit home or make us weep in awe, it would still be well worth it. These are precious moments when time and space become at once vacuous to our consciousness, and our focus suspends into a state of metaphysical elevation in the Divine presence. And it happens perhaps because, at a basic level, we've understood God's words in a deeper, more meaningful way.

This kind of "*ihsani*" ("illuminationist-like") connection is common to those with deep attachment to Prophetic knowledge and gratefulness to God, which can explain why they get so besotted with prayer throughout the night. The pious, according to Imam al-Ghazali, "considered their prayers to be perfect when they were unaware of the people to their right and left."[50]

As with most things, there are inherent obstacles to overcome and false paths to avoid. Lack of food can quite easily lead to outbursts of mild anger

---

[50] Al-Ghazali, *Inner Dimension of Islamic Worship*, translated by Muhtar Holland, The Islamic Foundation, 2002.

or frustration. It can also lead to binge eating once the fast is over. The test to refrain from overindulgence, eating only portions that satiate a third of the stomach and avoids wastage are important Prophetic remedies to a world that seemingly thrives on consumption and appropriation. That very human desire to enhance dignity in the eyes of others in acts of obedience to God (*riya*) can also completely undo the esoterism of Ramadhan.

But as always, we have to be sincere in our intentions (*niyyah*), hope for God's grace (*tawfiq*), and strive (*mujahada*) to understand the *Qur'an* and be subservient to God to stand a chance of benefiting from the esoteric fruits of Ramadhan.

# 1.12 Making sense of news about instability in our times

It was the sociologist Richard Sennett who said that instability woven into everyday practices in modernity is "meant to be normal."[51] Sure enough, the level of instability and anticipation of looming crises in recent years has been quite breathtaking. We've become accustomed to near daily supply of harrowing stories of atrocities, conflict, indiscriminate killings of innocent bystanders, and anarchy in countries like Syria, Yemen, Iraq, Libya, and elsewhere. Nearer to home, we've seen growing mistrust and inequality between the haves and have-nots in society, racism, Islamophobia, hate speech, social media-driven anxieties and so on. As news of these things reaches us, it adds to the sense of a runaway world in deep trouble. Moreover, voices of reason and virtue are easily drowned out by a virulent lack of realism as people default to cynical and pessimistic impulses and neuroticism when the going gets tough.

In light of this, I would like to pause briefly to reflect on our existential condition. For those who traverse multiple groups both online and offline, chances are they'll have seen just how easily people become high-handed or narrow-minded responding to news of instability of one kind or another. It's like being in a football stadium where we'll hear expletives from otherwise well-spoken people. The need to keep grounded leads us to question the impact of the constant supply of news is having on our consciousness. Can we oscillate between periods of meditation and engagement? Is it our responsibility to fix things that happen completely outside of our influence or competence? What would happen if, say, we didn't come across some news of police brutality or a racist gun attack happening in the USA?

Impulsive sharing of news and analysis isn't always a virtuous act, and certainly not as much as we might believe it to be based on its cathartic effect on us or the feeling that it's a natural reaction to shock and outrage. Mere awareness or knowing something doesn't mean that it's coherent or appropriate, or even helpful in achieving restitution or beneficial outcomes.

---

[51] Richard Sennett, *The Corrosion of Character: The Personal Consequences of Work in the New Capitalism*, W. W. Norton & Company, 1999.

Interestingly, there's plenty of research[52] that shows that people can quite easily become less convinced or move further apart as they're given more information.[53]

As a believer I have to constantly remind myself that sharing unverified news or information that causes people undue anxiety could be sinful (49:6). Thus, engaging the news industry's never-ending battle of ideas, analysis and propaganda, requires a minimum standard of scruples, good faith and good intentions.

That aside, our response to news of instability is often a sign of frustration with our own lack of spiritual, mental, institutional and intellectual preparedness to deal with what life throws at us. Of course, this is an ever-moving target. But there are perspectives we can use to build resilience (some of which I mention below) so that by God's grace (*tawfiq*) perhaps we don't fall into heedlessness (*gaflah*), cynicism, pessimism or a fatalistic mindset.

Firstly, it's worth comparing our own situation to earlier times. We live in homes with thick carpets, unlimited supplies of drinking water, temperature-controlled air, video-on-demand, automated machines and internet connected devices, modern medicine and food from around the world. There's no doubt we live more comfortably today than the kings of earlier times. Is there, then, a disconnection between lamenting the apparent doom hanging over the world, and our actual experience of creature comforts and stability? Are we missing out on opportunities to show gratitude and having a positive outlook? Is it a question of priority for the right time and place for dealing with our troubles too?

Secondly, it's worth appreciating that every generation faces its own challenges. Whatever one's beliefs are, the nature of our life on earth is that it has "tests" and uncertainties in its path. Nothing is, to put it bluntly, final until death. And we can be sure that our desires and egos as well

---

[52] For a good example see discussion by Ezra M. Markowitz & Azim F. Shariff, *Climate Change and Moral Judgement*, Nature Climate Change volume 2, pp. 243-247 (2012).

[53] Sunniat Rahman, *Climate Change: Why we just don't give a….*, https://minimolecule.com/2012/04/12/climate-change-why-we-just-dont-give-a/, 2012. Reasons offered are: abstractness and cognitive complexity; the blamelessness of unintentional action; guilty bias; uncertainty breeds wishful thoughts; moral tribalism; long time horizons and faraway places.

as circumstances beyond our control will drive us to moments of regret, hardship, joy and so on. Tests and calamities will befall us, and if one thing doesn't affect us something else will, as the Prophet explained. The Prophet drew a square and then a line in the middle of it and let it extend outside the square and then drew several small lines attached to the central line, and said: "This is the human being, and this, [the square] in his lease of life, encircles him from all sides, and this [line], which is outside [the square], is his hope, and these small lines are the calamities and troubles [which may befall him], and if one misses him, another will snap [overtake] him, and if the other misses him, a third will snap [overtake] him."[54]

Thirdly, sometimes things remain unresolved and fester in our minds, sending us into a spiral of pessimistic and cynical mood. Such moments require taking time out. Here, it helps to keep the company of our loved ones, "elders,"[55] scholars or "*murabbi*" (guardian) figures and those who radiate warmth and peace, who bring out the good within us, and instil in us a deep sense of desire to do better for ourselves, others and the environment. What they will remind us is that change/idleness, justice/injustice, rises/falls, happiness/sadness, power/weakness, wealth/poverty etc. all exist for a reason. They exist, as scholars say, to differentiate and elevate people who remain, and strive to be, truthful and sincere to God and people, from those who don't. They will also remind us that everything we see happens in "order that the Divine names such as *Ar-Rafi'* 'He Who Raises,' *Al-Khafidh* 'He Who Abases,' *Al-Mu'ti* 'He Who Gives,' *Al-Mani'* 'He Who Withholds,' *Ar-Rahim* 'the Merciful,' *Al-Muntaqim* 'the Avenger,' *Al-Latif* 'the Subtlely Kind,' and so on - may be manifest."[56]

Fourthly, it's worth reflecting on the fact that anxiety is a function of uncertainty and is inherent to time. As such, it need not automatically lead to doomsday scenarios. Granted, the modern "rush culture" tends to exacerbate our anxieties. However, a glance at history perhaps reveals something quite different: moments of experiential meaning such that, as one scholar said, "When there is nothing, there is still God." The Muslim civilisation, much like other civilisations, also experienced its

---

[54] *Hadith* narrated by 'Abdullah in *Sahih al-Bukhari.*

[55] Mohammed Nizami, *Distinguishing elders from the elderly,* 2016.

[56] Nuh Ha Min Keller, *Islam and Evolution - a letter to Suleman Ali*, http://www.masud.co.uk/ISLAM/nuh/evolve.htm, 1996.

highs and lows. Its lows arguably included events like the battle between Companions of the Prophet at Karbala (680), the repeated attacks on the Ka'bah, persecution of the *Mihna* (833-848), the marauding Mongol destruction of Baghdad (1258) and the Eastern regions, the Spanish *Reconquista*, outbreaks of plagues, civil wars, wars between rival Muslim powers, colonisation and so on. The scale of devastation and uncertainty often led scholars who witnessed them to think that the end of times was imminent.

The approach of the year 1000 Hijri[57] was also one such occasion. In response, Imam al-Suyuti (1445-1505 AD or 849-911 Hijri) examined the events of the end of times foretold in *hadith* literature and plotted them on a time line. His findings led him to argue that the end of times would at best be well into the second Hijri millennium.[58] His point was: no one can truly know when the end of times will be, but fearing that it would be specifically the year 1000 Hijri was unwarranted. Whilst relating this story, a contemporary scholar reflected that if you apply Imam al-Suyuti's calculations to today, it would perhaps be yet another 250 years or so before the end of times - only God knows for sure of course.

In the meantime, as I was reminded by a fictional character, whatever instability comes our way, whatever battles we have raging inside or outside of us, we always have choices. It's the choices that make us who we are, and we can always choose to do what's right.[59]

---

[57] *Hijri* is the Islamic calendar which is a lunar calendar consisting of 12 months in a year of 354 or 355 days. It starts from the Gregorian year 622 AD which marked the Prophet's migration from Makkah to Madina/Yathrib and is denoted by AH.

[58] *The Oxford Handbook of Millenialism*, edited by Catherine Wessinger, Oxford University Press, 2001, p. 271.

[59] Quote adapted from the film Spider Man 3.

# 1.13 When revisionism takes hold of history - Aurangzeb goes from *Sufi* to *Salafi*

I felt the urge to write this article having read a blog titled, *Aurangzeb: the Salafi Mughal Emperor*.[60] The blog is a good example of historical revisionism[61] as it claimed that the so-called "*Salafi* way" defined the 6th, and perhaps the most devout, Mughal Emperor, Muhyiuddin Muhammad Aurangzeb Alamgir (1618-1707). Lacking nuance, research and contextualisation, the article seemed well-tuned into the Information Age's endless misinformation and opinions. Initially, it caught my attention triggering the memory of a pamphlet I read in my teenage years which similarly claimed that the Indian scholar Shah Waliyullah al-Dihlawi (1703-1762) was a *Salafi*. *Déjà vu* aside, unlike then, I felt it was necessary to help readers unfamiliar with Mughal history recognise the need for nuance and corroboration to avoid giving legitimacy to crass articles that so often masquerade as authoritative.

"A *Salafi*," according to the article, "is someone who believes in strict monotheism, that nothing can be added to Islam after the Prophet and that the first three generations of Muslims (the *Salaf*) ought to be emulated." Curiously, by this definition, to be *Salafi* one isn't required to have lived at the time of the first three generations, but by merely following those who did. Though, by the same logic few would ever claim to be a *Sahabi* (Companion of the Prophet) by following the *Sahabah* as it were, and rightly so. A *Sahabi* is of course a special designation of a believer who saw the Prophet in person. It's also odd that the term *Salafi* should be appropriated given that Muslims are latter-day Muslims or *Khalafi*. Thus, calling today's Muslims *Khalafi* would be more reflective of our inherent

---

[60] Shoaib, *Aurangzeb: The Salafi Mughal Emperor?*, https://www.muslimworldjournal.com/aurangzeb-the-salafi-mughal-emperor/, retrieved 8 July 2016.

[61] Some may refer to this as "historical negationism" or "denialism," taking the view that "revisionism" is an ongoing process which tweaks and makes history more accurate, whereas "negationism" arguably goes a step further and denies actual historical facts despite the evidence. However, I have used "revisionism" here because the blog I have critiqued here does not deny but rather tries to revise history based on some preconceived notions.

lack of spiritual and intellectual character requiring humility, particularly in the face of universalising modernity.

Nor am I convinced if the term *Salafi* can truthfully differentiate one group of Muslims over another. After all, it's virtually unheard of to find Muslims who don't believe in Islam as a purely monotheistic (*tawhid*) faith or don't consider the first three generations as rightfully to be followed in matters of religion. There is then the equally contentious shorthand label, *Ahl al-hadith*, which the article defines as, a "follower of the Prophet's *Hadeeth* (words or actions)." As it turns out, so the article states, *Ahl al-hadith* (literally "people of *hadith*") is just another term for *Salafi*. Yet, oddly, many Muslims today would happily identify as people who follow *hadith* but would still not call themselves *Ahl al-hadith*. There are good reasons for this.

Terms like *Salafi*, *Ahl al-hadith* and the many other shorthand identity labels are highly contentious, misused and often mean different things to people in different periods and places. Their use requires contextualising both to the times they applied to and the purpose they served. For example, the Kufan school of Islamic law (*fiqh)* in classical Muslim civilisation was known by some as *Ahl al-ra'y* ("the people of opinion") in contradistinction to the label *Ahl al-hadith*. Over time, such dichotomy became muted with the realisation that both juristic reasoning/opinions and *hadith* are more or less relied upon by all reputable scholars, and have always been so. The tendency today, however, is that such terms are abused in the politics of religious authenticity and self-righteousness.

The article doesn't provide a definition for *Sufi* or *Sufism* which seems somewhat careless given that *Salafi* and *Ahl al-hadith*, for which definitions are provided, are framed in antonymic fashion to *Sufism*. For the critical minded, however, the term *Sufi* arguably describes at least four different forms, which shouldn't be crudely grouped together as if they were all one and the same, as implied in the article: (1) charlatan *Sufis*;[62] (2) mainstream *Sufis*; (3) those who identify with *Sufi* scholars but are themselves indifferent to its methods; and 4) those considered pious using the term *Sufi* sometimes as an expression of ridicule or dissatisfaction.

The article rightly describes Aurangzeb as a devout man of faith

---

[62] Charlatan *Sufis* do not adhere to the *Shari'ah* on many aspects of mainstream belief and religious law, and are not considered mainstream *Sufis*.

(*iman*). My own notes have him down as someone who "always prayed in congregation (*jama'at*), strictly adhered to Hanafi *fiqh*, memorised the *Qur'an* after becoming Emperor, authored (*arba'een*) forty collections of *hadith*, wrote the entire copy of the *Qur'an* (*mashaf*) in his own handwriting, observed *i'tikaaf* (staying in a mosque for a set period for the purpose of worship, particularly in the month of Ramadhan), habitually fasted on the days of *ayyam al-bidh* (13-15 of each lunar month), paid *zakat* on his own wealth, didn't wear silk or listen to musical instruments" and so on.[63] Yet, despite being a strict Hanafi and having commissioned the multi-volume text of Hanafi edicts known as the *Fatawa-i-'Alamgiri*,[64] the article claims that Aurangzeb adhered "to the grain of *Salafiyyah*."

Rather than see this for what it was, the article seeks to explain away the real significance of the apparent contradictions. Drawing parallel with Muhammad bin Abdul Wahhab (1703-1792), who the article states was himself Hanbali in *fiqh* yet had unquestionable "*Salafi*" credentials because he, like Aurangzeb, "fought against polytheism (*shirk*) and *bidah* [innovation]." The article implies that because the different schools of *fiqh* weren't available for Aurangzeb to choose from in 17th century India, it's justifiable to identify Aurangzeb as "*Salafi*." Even if we accept this for the sake of argument, it still seems a little odd that someone could be seen as *Ahl al-hadith* yet fails to make much reference to *hadith* in a major codification of their *fiqh*.

The article then goes on to make subtly disparaging remarks about how the spread of Hanafi *fiqh* was due to the appointment of Hanafi scholars as state judges who refused to allow other schools of *fiqh* to grow, which in turn meant that ordinary people couldn't choose an alternative *fiqh*. What seems missing in this line of thinking is that whilst there was competition between legal schools, the early Hanafi *fiqh* had advantages over other schools in its remarkable consistency and inductive power to organise Islamic law. For instance, it made use of hypothetical cases, which enabled Hanafi scholars to test legal principles and procedures, and

---

[63] Personal notes from classes on *Fatawa al-'Alamghiriyyah* with Shaykh Mohammad Akram Nadwi.

[64] Also known as *Fatawa-i-Hindiyyah*, which is a popular reference in the Hanafi School of *fiqh* especially in South Asia.

do so consistently.[65] As a result, it wasn't surprising that the early Hanafi *fiqh* became the adopted *fiqh* of the Abbasid state (as did the Ottomans, Mughals and many other dynasties). After all, it was for state officials to institute laws which they thought were in the best interest of people and territories under their rule.

The article then boldly claims that Shaykh Abdul Qadir Jilani (1078-1166) and a list of other scholars were all *Salafi*. Just how Abdul Qadir Jilani, the very scholar who initiated the central *Sufi* practice of giving allegiance (*bay'ah*) to a spiritual mentor, could be *Salafi* is puzzling to say the least.

In fact, the overwhelming historical evidence pinpoints Aurangzeb as a "*zinda pir*" ("living saint"). [66] He was a disciple of the *Sufi* Khwaja Muhammad Ma'sum, who was a deputy (*khalifah*) of Muhammad Tahir Lahori. Muhammad Tahir Lahori was, in turn, a *Sufi* discile to one of India's greatest *Sufis* and renovator (*mujaddid*) Shaykh Ahmad Sirhindi (1564-1624). In other words, Aurangzeb was initiated into the very famous Naqshabandi *Sufi* order (*tariqah*) whose spiritual lineage in the Indian Subcontinent was popularised by Shaykh Ahmad Sirhindi. In fact, Aurangzeb was in close contact with many renowned Naqshbandi *Sufis*. Khwaja Muhammad Ma'sum, for example, frequently visited Aurangzeb, whose sons were close friends.[67] Aurangzeb is reported to have given them expensive gifts while visiting them in Sirhind. He is also reported to have read Imam al-Ghazali's *Ihya' 'Ulum al-Din* (*The Revival of Religious Knowledge*) to a scholar by the name Sa'id Mulla Jiwan.[68] Moreover, among the leading scholars commissioned to compile the *Fatawa-i-'Alamgiri*, there were many famous *Sufi* scholars, including the likes of Shaykh Abdur Rahim who founded the famous Madrasah-i-Rahimiyyah in Delhi, as well as being the father and Naqshabandi *Sufi* teacher of Shah Waliyullah al-Dihlawi.

---

[65] Mohammad Akram Nadwi, *Abu Hanifah: His Life, Legal Method and Legacy*, Kube Publishing, 2011.

[66] Muhammad Mojlum Khan, *The Muslim 100: The Lives, Thoughts and Achievements of the Most Influential Muslims in History*, Kube Publishing, 2008.

[67] Ibid, pp. 281-291. Also known as Imam Rabbani or Mujaddid Alf-i-Thani - "the renovator of the second millennium" of Islam.

[68] Annemarie Schimmel, *Islam in the Indian Subcontinent*, Brill, 1980.

Hence, the idea that Aurangzeb was against *Sufism per se* is simply not true. To understand Aurangzeb one would need to understand the religious discourse and socio-politics of his time. It might explain why Aurangzeb took a stricter stance on things in line with the legacy of Shaykh Ahmad Sirhindi's efforts to maintain mainstream *Sufism's* conformity to the *Qur'an* and *Sunnah*.

Having considered these points, it's clear that unnuanced, retrograde fitting of significant historical figures into today's popular, contentious labels of *Sufi, Salafi* or *Ahl al-hadith* (or other identity labels[69] - the ones I've used here are just for illustration), is to unwittingly revise history using shorthand terms that are current reflexes in the politics of religious identity and authenticity.

The wider import is the need for nuance, consistency and accurate use of terms like *Sufi, Salafi, Ahl al-hadith* etc., not by presenting filtered definitions that trap us into the politics of face-value identity, but rather, by looking at their real socio-religious contexts and experiences. The intrinsic pluralism and complexity of Godly life within Muslim communities today requires thorough investigation and reconciling conflicting viewpoints by teasing out intelligible nuances. Academic rigour in such matters will no doubt help British Muslim communities develop greater understanding and respect for differences of opinion and to come together in mutual service and benefit to one another.

---

[69] Other prominent groups include *Barelvi, Deobandi, Ikhwani, Shi'a* and *Jamati* etc.

## 1.14 The roots of intra-religious identity politics and ethno-cultural commitment to Islam

History has plenty of examples of movements and groups, and religious movements and groups are no different. One of the first things groups seeking public recognition in pre-modern societies often did was to create a sense of their history, to own and determine that history. Their ideas sometimes found eager audiences and attained favour among the ruling classes and people of influence. Self-expression, ambition and power had as much to do with the appearance of these groups as their underlying ideas and beliefs. In Islamic civilisation such internal oppositions were perhaps as important to its development as the external opposition by members of other religions and powers. As early as the 9th century, Imam al-Tahawi (843-935) listed at least ten of these major factions or sects.[70] Many of them are now extant as formal groups, however their ideas live on in various forms. This article isn't about them.

For British Muslims, the dynamics of their intra-religious groups has been challenged to work out how best to live with differences and disagreements between themselves, particularly with the growing questions about integration and threats from the far-right and racists. British Muslims are a relatively small set of communities, yet despite its overall size, as Shaykh Shams ad-Duha noted, it is "a melting pot of every idea and movement known in Islam." Increasingly under global interconnectedness, this "melting pot" characterises communities throughout the world. Finding ways to live with differences has thus become "extremely important," not least because, "Our future and our community's well-being depend on it."[71]

Sunni Islam in the UK largely mirrors South Asia with four major factions, denominations or movements: *Deobandi, Barelvi, Jamati* and *Salafi*. These factions appeared in the UK from the 1950s with the post-war

---

[70] See: Abu Jafar al-Tahawi, *Al-'Aqidah al-Tahawiyyah* (*The Creed according to al-Tahawi*).

[71] Shams Ad-Duha Muhammad, *Let's agree to disagree*, Islamique Magazine, Issue 4, February 2012.

migration of people from India and Pakistan.[72] The roots of these factions trace back to debates and unreconciled differences between religious leaders and contentious theological questions in predominantly 19th and 20th century India.[73] As a result, what we have in the UK is an inevitable constraining of religious identity by ethnic identity.

At least for first, second and many third generation British Muslims, these factions have been vital in imparting a basal level of Islamic learning and establishing mosque communities. This article isn't about that, but about contentious areas which, I would argue, unnecessarily hinder the rooting of future generations of Muslims in Islam in the UK.

## (a) *Deobandi-Barelvi* factionalism

While differences may not be noticeable to outsiders looking in, and aside from ethno-cultural differences, there are subtle differences in theology between all four factions. As Phillip Lewis[74] and other commentators have observed, these factions compete against each other in different ways.[75] For example, both *Deobandism* and *Barelvism* advocate the virtue of the

---

[72] *Understanding Muslim Ethnic Communities*, Change Institute, 2009: "Large scale Indian, Pakistani and Bangladeshi migration to Britain began in the post war years from the 1950s onward in response to the British Nationality Act 1948, labour shortages in the 1960s and active encouragement of immigration from the New Commonwealth countries."

[73] Barbara Metcalf, *Traditionalist Islamic Activism: Deoband, Tablighis, and Talibs*, http://www.ssrc.org/sept11/essays/metcalf.htm.

[74] Phillip Lewis, *Islamic Britain*, I. B. Tauris, 2002.

[75] It's worth highlighting that unlike *Deobandi* and *Barelvi*, *Jamati* isn't a distinct theological group in the strict sense of theology, but identify more in political terms. However, for convenience, while I've included them here because of their extensive contribution to the overall religious landscape of Muslim communities in the UK where they may take on various names, I haven't detailed out the identity dynamics that they're involved in. The Egyptian group *Ikhwaan al-Muslimeen* or "Muslim Brotherhood" can also be grouped into the same category. Both of these groups generally take part in mainstream political processes and are committed to non-violent means. However, with the increased securitisation agenda of governments around the world both of these groups have come under intense scrutiny and, for right and wrong reasons, have had to contend with political action to curtail their influence and organisation.

past with strong reference to scholarship of South Asia, whereas *Salafism* claims to purify religious beliefs and practices influenced by customs and mystics in order to return to "pure Islam" practiced by the first three generations. In turn, differences lead to subtle variation in religious identity and attitudes towards the community outlook, regeneration of tradition, globalisation, modernity, secularism, gender interaction etc.

Contextualisation is meant to play a crucial role in making Islam relevant across time and space. It should be possible to use the same Islamic scholarly methods and deliberations by a trained scholar whether in Pakistan or the UK and arrive at different answers because the contexts are different. However, I would argue this rarely happens. Instead, the vast majority of scholars and imams in the UK up and till now have tended to simply reproduce the same rulings (*fiqh*), the same analysis of society and the same programmes for social development (*tarbiyyah*) as if they were in South Asia or living in medieval times.

This isn't surprising. Most British imams were brought up and trained outside of the UK or trained by those who were. Naturally, they'll be caught up in the parochial sentiments and imagination of ethno-cultural belonging to some extent. Re-evaluating ingrained conformity to "old ways" of doing and thinking in light of the changed context was perhaps never going to be straightforward. Pressures to conform to community expectations can be quite debilitating at times. I would also argue that the *madrasah*-system training in South Asia has a hard time being relevant to conditions in South Asia let alone modern Britain.

Second and third generation Muslims born in the UK, who learn from local imams and teachers, or graduates of UK-based *madrasahs*, can often turn out to be more dogmatic in religion than their less religiously literate parents, and take little account of the ongoing evolution of *fiqh* in South Asia.[76] It's an emotional reaction that seems to overcompensate nostalgic rooting towards the East as a sure fast way of assuring the integrity of Islamic belonging in the West as it were. Others see themselves as "guardians" of Islam but the inadequacy of their Islamic training and anxieties about what the future might hold for Islam in the UK provokes fractured or tight-fisted responses.

Making matters worse, shorthand identity labels like *Deobandi* and *Barelvi* are used very loosely, often as throwaway labels, by both scholars and non-scholars alike. If an individual is seen frequenting a so-called *Deobandi* or *Barelvi* identifying mosque, they'll be perceived by others to belong to that group. Such reductive attitude means that believers don't necessarily see each other as believers at first glance but as categories of religious affiliation.

The historical basis of the *Deobandi-Barelvi* fracture (similar to denominational separatism in Christianity) can be attributed broadly to two basic factors. Firstly, with the advent of printing, increased urbanisation and movement of people in 19ᵗʰ and early 20ᵗʰ century India, there was a scattering of edicts (*fatawa*) and opinions of scholars, which became widely available to those who didn't necessarily have the requisite skills or knowledge to digest them properly.[77] Thus, people were exposed to differences while hitherto unaware that such differences could be valid, or indeed that ambiguity-tolerance had always a role in Islamic thought. The

---

[76] A good example of this is in absolutely insisting that stunned meat is not *halal* and cannot be consumed by Muslims. However, the *fiqh* has evolved elsewhere in the world (in line with improvements in stunning technology) to accept stunned meat and has its own set of *Shari'ah*-based legal requirements. See: *The Islamic Concept Of Animal Slaughter*, Islamic Fiqh Academy of India, 2005, pp. 40-41, http://www.download. ifa-india.org/download.php?f=Animal_Slaughter.pdf, retrieved 18 December 2018. The same ruling has been authorised by the Makkah-based Islamic Rabita al-'Alam al-Islami in Saudi Arabia, Al-Azhar University in Egypt, The Department of Islamic Development in Malaysia, as well as others.

[77] This is arguably similar to the confusion in the field of *hadith* today with modern Arabic printing houses including "modern ratings of *hadith* in their new prints," which according to Shaykh Mohammad Akram Nadwi, "stem from a shallow reading and application of the science of the narrators." Quoted here from Andrew Booso, *Principles of Interacting with the Sacred Texts with Shaykh Akram Nadwi*, 17 July 2010.

growing imperative was to make sense of this. But it was much easier to be seen to belong rather than to act based on rigorous study. For teachers, students and the general public alike, it was easier for them to just go along with, that is, more or less imitate, what others in "their group" were doing.[78]

Secondly, an exaggerated focus on linguistics developed in an effort to convey the finer details of abstract doctrinal meaning.[79] This was partly a reaction to society's shift from pre-modern to modern, the growth of *Wahhabism* in Arabia and the identity crisis posed by colonialism in India. However, the differences were not only inconclusive one way or the other they were also of little significance in the grand scheme of theology and what God requires of believers. Nor could they be removed of their intrinsic neuro-linguistic variation.[80] Rather than navigating these opinions and ambiguous meanings many scholars and laity alike, partly as a result of their own biases, escalated their commitment which served to sanitise fractious divisions. Variant ideas and practices were simply perceived to be illegitimate, going against established orthodoxy and authority vested in pre-existing positions and ways of doing things. To a degree this helped consolidate conformist behaviour; it was worthwhile belonging to something that vowed to protect against deviancy.

As religious self-assertion became more relevant under British colonial rule in India, differences became organised along differing textual interpretations (*dalil*) and attained widespread legitimacy. In identity politics, differences are of course exaggerated and heightened emphasis is

---

[78] Adapted quote of Shaykh Mohammad Akram Nadwi, 29 November 2014.

[79] The differences between *Deobandism* and *Barelvism* are on a small number of doctrinal questions primarily around the attributes of the Prophet. These are: (1) was the Prophet "celestial light" (*Nur*) or "human" (*Bashar*); (2) was the Prophet "knower of the unseen" (*'alimul ghaib*); was the Prophet "all seeing" (*haazir-o-azir*) or not; and (4) did the Prophet have choice/control over the workings of the universe (*mukhtar-i-kul*)? Other non-doctrinal differences exist in matters of practice. For further discussion see: Muhammad Yusuf Ludhianvi, *Differences in the Ummah and the Straight Path*.

[80] However, these differences are pale in comparison to what they actually agree upon. Both *Deobandis* and *Barelvis* adhere to the Hanafi *madhhab* and show allegiance to the same *Sufi* tariqahs and the scholars and mainstream scholarly works of Sunni Islam.

placed on them. However, the justification offered was that it was a duty for Muslims to ensure that they don't violate the Prophet's normative and prescribed ways of acting. Thus, what started off as perhaps a necessary dose of scepticism to safeguard against seemingly novel practices, quickly turned into a discourse of "my group is more authentic to your group." In turn, this created competitiveness, and instead of bonding based on shared Godliness, it led to institutionalised otherisation within Muslim communities.

The fault of some of the scholars (*'ulama*) in this, as Shaykh Muhammad Zakariyya Khandlawi (1898-1982) lamented, "is that they don't keep their differences in non-principle matters confined to the *'ulama*. No, in fact many of them go out of their way to solicit and canvas the support of the masses and to have them on their sides in their battles."[81] Indeed, such behaviour can also be seen on social media and ethno-religious TV channels in the UK. In scholars "deferring positions and even harsh and strong words (on both sides)," Shaykh Hamza Yusuf observes, "can be used by ignorant people today to confuse, divide, and even lead astray people who don't understand the nuances of juristic reasoning and the possibility of having more than one valid practice or position on any given matter."[82]

Commenting on the *Deobandi-Barelvi* schism, observers like Shaykh Habib Umar Ibn al-Hafiz of Yemen pointed out that for British Muslims, "it will be difficult for the older generation of both communities to do away with their differences,"[83] and so the "duty and responsibility" falls on the young from both camps to get together to create a plan to bring these schools closer. Similarly, Haji Imdadullah al-Muhajir al-Makki (1817-1899), a 19th century *Sufi* luminary from Makkah and prominent *Sufi* teacher in South Asia, advised protagonists in both camps to sidestep their apparent differences in order to be true to their shared goal of Muslim unity and progress.

Al-Makki based his advice on the understanding that divisions inevitably mutate into subdivisions, and breakaway groups form over

---

[81] Muhammad Zakariyya Khandlawi, *Al-E'tidal fi Maratibur Rijal*, p. 219.

[82] Hamza Yusuf, *The Content of Character: Ethical Sayings of the Prophet Muhammad*, Sandal, 2005, p. 57.

[83] Muhammad ibn Adam al-Kawthari, *10 Days in the Blessed Lands of Yemen*, http://www.daruliftaa.com, 22 November 2005.

matters of doctrine or practice which, to outsiders like him, appear minute and indistinguishable from each other compared to the general tenets that both sides shared.[84] Under such conditions, disputes and a "put-down" culture of deconstructing claims and counter-claims become normative learning outcomes and "edutainment culture" for ordinary non-scholar masses. Many instinctively feel compelled to defend "in-group" beliefs which they perceive is sacred or intrinsic to "saved sect" (*firqatun najah*).

Attempts to reconcile the two movements in the UK have been scant. The most recent was a high-profile event hosted by Shaykh Qasim Rashid Ahmad of the charity organisation Al-Khair Foundation and streamed live over IQRA TV. In recent years we've also seen a spate of public debates between preachers from rival camps on a range of issues which have all descended into factional show-boating. Other more private meetings between individuals involved in crescent moonsighting have also taken place. However, beyond light touch symbolism, the lack of progress on the ground has meant that *Deobandi-Barelvi* factionalism has continued unabated.

The constancy with which many British Muslims have to deal with the wider social fallout of the *Deobandi-Barelvi* fracture has increasingly led to calls for "de-linking" from the religious heritage of South Asia. Done in a managed way, it's an opportunity to leave a more positive legacy for future generations. As argued by advocates, substituting ethnic commitment to Islam for a British expression offers greater relevance to living in modern Britain, and away from the jarring ethnic experience of religion and wider ethno-cultural "baggage" of South Asia.

Such ethnocentric religion can be seen in a wide range of rituals and positions imported from South Asia, which take the veneer of being authentically religious. For illustration purpose, a selection of some of the more obvious examples are listed below. These are all examples of religious expressions that are justified by either a conscious ethno-cultural commitment to religion, or a passive acceptance of ethno-cultural norms as "the way things are."

---

[84] See: *No Difference between Barelvis and Deobandis* by Gibril Haddad and Muhammad Ibn Adam al-Kawthari's *Why do some Sunni Ulema—like the Deobandis—prohibit the Mawlid?* http://www.daruliftaa.com.

(1) The necessity of wearing particularly "ethnic," "Asian" or "Arab" attire to symbolise one's religiosity (e.g. wearing of the *salwar kameez* or the *kurta*, insisting on "Indian-style" turban, Saudi head gear etc.). Such clothing reflects more recent ethno-nationalistic traditions of South Asia or the Middle East rather than Islamic *per se*.

(2) The culture of commemorating the death of Muslim saints (*Urs*) and factional leaders of 19th and 20th century South Asia, imitating the rituals of popular religious culture in places like Pakistan (e.g. the insistence on consuming certain types of ethnic food, singing devotional songs in the genre of Qawwali music etc.). This is not a judgement on the theological (*fiqhi*) permissibility or otherwise of such commemorations. Rather, my contention here is with the fixation with popular religious culture specific to South Asia.

(3) A commitment to ethnic patriarchy that encourages "men-only" mosques and discourages or prohibits women from going to mosques for daily prayers. This often expresses as a lack of willingness to create equivalent facilities for women (e.g. lack of ablution areas, lighting, space, heating and generally poor design for women etc.), all of which is common in South Asia.

(4) Citing religious justifications for refusing to accommodate the growing needs of women in Muslim leadership circles, in mosque committees, as Islamic teachers and lectures etc., despite their increasing agency and bigger role outside of the home, in employment and empowerment through improved social mobility.

(5) Conforming to the negligent South Asian attitude towards *zakat* that not only advocates paying *zakat* hand-to-mouth (not institutionally) to the "poor and needy" abroad while overlooking local needs in the UK, but also overly-restricting many of the *zakat*-eligible categories.[85]

(6) The legitimisation of racism and colourism among Arab and Asian Muslims, holding prejudice and discrimination against individuals with dark skin tone (e.g. equating the concept of "*nur*" for spiritual light/illumination with skin tone). Such racism excludes non-Arab or non-Asians from participating in mosques run by Arabs or

---

[85] See later article: *UK zakat belongs in the UK.*

Asians, which in turn makes it more difficult to forge solidarity and alliances through shared religious outlook.

(7) Discouraging inter-ethnic marriage to maintain ethno-national identity and caste systems. Many men and women become trapped in a psychologically-traumatising cycle of ever-dwindling pool of prospective spouses to choose from.

(8) Mosques defined by their ethnic origin with congregants from Pakistani heritage predominantly going to "Pakistani mosques" and the same for those from Bangladeshi heritage. Little is done to recognise the need for mosques to become inclusive community hubs irrespective of the ethno-national origin of their founders or committee members. Consequently, black and white Muslim converts in particular struggle for inclusion.

(9) Maintaining the excesses and taboos associated with some religious events in South Asia. Most notable among them are "Eid Miladun Nabi" (also called "Mawlid an-Nabi") and the "night of 15th Sha'ban" (known as "Shab-e-Borat," "Lailatul Bara'ah" or "Nisf min Sha'ban") where many *Barelvi-* and *Deobandi*-identifying Muslims conform to the same excesses in rituals and taboos that are popular in South Asia. This isn't to discount legitimate theological (*fiqhi*) differences of opinion on the permissibility of these religious events which is broadly recognised. Rather, my contention here is with ritualising these events keeping to the same popular religious culture of South Asia (e.g. by cooking some special type of meal, or lighting up houses or mosques, holding religious meetings and delivering long speeches etc.). Other examples include: discouraging praying the *witr* night prayer in Ramadhan behind non-Hanafi imams; refusing to pray behind a *Wahhabi/Salafi* imam - particularly notorious among *Barelvis*; and refusing to co-operate on public affairs under the same religious organisation, leading to separate mosque councils for *Deobandi-* and *Barelvi*-identifying mosques in the same town.

(10) From amongst religiously justified taboos, these comprise of but are not limited to: getting daughters married as soon as they reach the legal age of marriage; not allowing trimming of nails in the

night; discouraging the use of "God" and insisting on saying "Allah" in every day conversations etc.

(11) Religious festivities like Eid are celebrated through displays of ethno-nationalistic symbols such as waving of the Pakistani or Bangladeshi flags. Similarly, when Pakistan plays India or England in cricket, or when a Muslim boxer fights a non-Muslim opponent, other Muslims are expected to support their fellow brethren not for sporting or cultural reasons but a shared religious outlook, which of course it isn't.

(12) The wearing of amulets (*taweez*) to ward off evil spirits and sorcery sometimes linked to mental illness taboos, or as part of wider "*pir*" or "*biraderi*" kinship/clan patriarchy culture. Most egregious of these are religiously-legitimised commercial enterprises that seek to exploit vulnerable people.

(13) Justifying nefarious practices such as forced marriages, honour-based retribution, female genital mutilation (FGM) particularly among British Muslims of North African descent, and witchcraft rituals/violent exorcism etc. as having a basis in religion, whereas they're perhaps the worst kind of cultural practices.

(14) Much like it is treated in South Asia, the concept of "abstention" (*zuhd*) and "religious devoutness" are vacuously linked to worldly mediocrity and overly-restrictive separatism from non-Muslim communities. However, rather than making devoutness about building confidence in the assumptions of the Islamic faith

intellectually and spiritually, such attitudes lead to self-imposed ghettoization and cognitive dissonance.[86]

---

[86] See: Ahmed Izzidien and Srivas Chennu, *A Neuroscience Study on the Implicit Subconscious Perceptions of Fairness and Islamic Law in Muslims Using the EEG N400 Event Related Potential*, Journal of Cognition and Neuroethics (ISSN: 2166-5087). February, 2018. Volume 5, Issue 2: "Cognitive dissonance is a negative drive state that occurs whenever an individual simultaneously holds two cognitions, be they ideas, beliefs, or opinions, which are psychologically inconsistent, whereby the opposite of one cognition follows from the other (Berkowitz 1978)." That is, it's a feeling of discomfort when one's actions or reality directly contradicts or opposes their beliefs or worldviews. In religious settings, it occurs predominantly due to: (a) theological misunderstanding; (b) teaching religious concepts and doctrines incorrectly in a non-holistic way; or (c) psychological issues specific to individuals or groups. A few examples are provided for illustration purpose.

(1) The belief that conviction in true faith means that Muslims will be protected by God from calamities or domination by others. However, the correct understanding is that, as God mentions, "tests" will always befall even if one has faith: "Do people think that on their mere claiming, 'We have faith,' they will be left to themselves, and will not be put to a test?" (29:2); and "And most certainly shall We try you by means of danger, and hunger, and loss of worldly goods, of lives and of labour's fruits. But give glad tidings unto those who are patient in adversity" (2:155). Moreover, the Prophet's life and the lives of all the prophets who were afflicted with a range of worldly problems (chronic ailments, family problems, problems of authority etc.) is testament to it. There are also specific *hadiths* where the Prophet directly explains the real nature of the world.

(2) The belief that sincerity in faith will lead to perfection in abstaining from sinning. However, the correct understanding is that behaviours and faith are both on a spectrum, which means that the idea that you're either perfect or not is an incorrect way of looking at faith. The Prophet clarified this, as reported in *al-Tirmidhi*: "All of the children of Adam are sinners, and the best sinners are those who repent." Some Muslims will interpret their "non-perfection" as a fundamental flaw in their faith, and may increase in their doubts about Islam and eventually reducing their subservience to God to avoid the anxiety being a "perfect Muslim" necessitates. This is sometimes exacerbated by eulogising the Companions of the Prophet as "superhuman" devoted worshippers, or by idealising past glories as "Golden Age" and in the image of heroes such as Khalid bin al-Walid, Salah Uddin Ayyubi, Sultan Fatih etc.

(3) Good and evil are ultimately to be determined through the *Qur'an* and by Muslims taken as meaning that only Muslims are capable of justice and goodness. However, the correct understanding is that, as God mentions, human beings generally do have some level of innate ability to recognise righteousness and wrongdoing: "And inspired it with the discernment of its wickedness and its righteousness" (91:8).

(15) The *Qur'an* is seen as a book for reciting and memorising by the general masses but with little emphasis placed on understanding its deeper meanings and learning about how it's a living guidance with persuasive power to influence society more generally. It's also treated with an otherworldly relevance in much the same way it is widespread in South Asia, ritualised through: (a) wrapping the *Qur'an* in a cloth and placing it on the highest shelf; and (b) prioritising entertainment culture in the genre of *nasheed* (vocal music) and na'at (poetry) singing in the Urdu language rather than studying the *Qur'an*.

The largest body of Islamic knowledge and scholarship which has come to the UK carries the outputs primarily of 19th and 20th century Hanafi *madhhab* scholarship of South Asia. It's therefore unsurprising that the religious cultivation of British Muslims often involves imams and scholars retelling the stories and achievements of the "Great Scholars" ("*Akabir*")[87] of *Darul 'Uloom Deoband* or the founders of the *Barelvi* movement in the likes of "'Ala Hazrat" Ahmad Reza Khan (1856-1921) and others.

While recounting the stories of past sages is useful for religious cultivation, listening to such sermons one can't help notice how scholarship and scholarly works of South Asia are tacitly pushed as authoritative over the Hanafi *madhhab* outputs of Egypt, Turkey or Central Asia. Counteracting this, Islamic studies students of the UK increasing have access to scholarly outputs beyond South Asia and beyond the Hanafi *madhhab*. This enables a more direct interaction with a wider range of scholarship giving access to potentially alternative viewpoints and methods compared to the more parochial ethno-cultural expressions of *Deobandism* and *Barelvism*.

As such expressions of ethnocentric religion become increasingly irrelevant for third generation Muslims, particularly millennials, it of course erodes the first and second generations' sense of being at home in their "mother tongue" and ethnic heritage as it were. In this sense, it's important to recognise that ethnic identity and culture in themselves

---

[87] "*Akabir*" are the most prominent scholars of *Darul 'Uloom Deoband*, which include erudite scholars like Muhammad Qasim Nanotavi (1832-1880), Ashraf 'Ali Thanvi (1863-1943), Mahmudul Hasan (1851-1920), Husain Ahmad Madani (1879-1957), Muhammad Shafi (1897-1976), Rashid Ahmad Gangohi (1826-1905) etc.

aren't necessarily contentious in the Islamic paradigm. Rather, what is contentious is having an ethnic commitment to religion that refuses to contextualise and productively mesh into the society one lives in.

## (b) *Sufi-Salafi* factionalism

Similar to *Deobandi-Barelvi* factionalism, another well-known polemic in the UK relates to *Sufi* excesses versus *Salafi* (also known by "*Wahhabi*") dogma.[88] Both of these traditions grew from different socio-religious contexts, whose relevance I would argue is often conveniently ignored by protagonists in either camp.[89]

In the case of the *Sufis*, the passing of the early generations of Muslims meant that Prophetic teachings pertaining to psychological "states of being" (*hal*) and inward purity of character known as *tazkiyyah* needed organising and preserving. Firstly, for some time it had been known that the intention or spirit of Islamic law could be violated with impunity such that, despite conforming to the law's outward requirements, one doesn't actually gain closeness to God. Outward conformity becomes merely the result of unconscious habit, social pressure or to keep the scorn of others at bay, rather than out of mindful awe of God. The purpose of Divine law becomes then just like the purpose of any secular system of law - a mechanistic behavioural code lacking metaphysical connection. By implication, spiritual purification and values like generosity, gentleness, patience and accommodating demeanour, which aren't necessarily the

---

[88] Some Muslims will contend that "*Wahhabi*" is a derogatory term, which was first used by British colonialists to apply to any Islamic reformist coming back from Makkah in the 19th century. The British vicegerents were afraid that the "*Wahhabi*" emphasis on "true Islam" and criticism of local customs, Western influence and so on would play a role in mobilising religious interpretation to a stricter sense, one that would motivate uprising and insurgency. In an attempt to differentiate and discredit such movements, the label "*Wahhabi*" was used for any reformist or politically active Islamic group with puritanical outlook. See: Barbara Metcalf, *Traditionalist Islamic Activism: Deoband, Tablighis, and Talibs*, http://www.ssrc.org/sept11/essays/metcalf.htm. Today, the loose use of "Islamist" results from the same line of thinking.

[89] For a wider discussion, see: Eva Evers Rosander and David Westerlund, *African Islam and Islam in Africa: encounters between Sufis and Islamists*, Hurst, 1997.

primary intents of law, struggle to be cultivated for individuals and society to flourish.

There was thus a need for something more esoteric (*batini*) that related not just to the external physical world (*dunya*) but to the inner life one's being. This was an utterly sincere and truthful submission to God, as demanded in the *Qur'an*, Prophetic examples and exemplified among people of erudition and righteousness. To achieve this, people had to look inward and attend to their inward state (*hal*).

Secondly, whilst not all believers could avoid being forgetful of God in every moment, they couldn't be excused of the obligation to keep away from what God explicitly forbids (*haram*), and thus the struggle (*mujahada*) against caving into one's whims and vices still remained. Once it becomes possible to avoid the forbidden, in order to maintain it or to achieve further perfection in one's persona and nearness to God, one is driven to abstain from doing things that despite being permitted (*mubah*) might impede their subservience to God. This kind of continuous struggle against one's inner motivations and poor character requires mentoring, encouraging (*targhib*) and training (*tarbiyyah*). Like the role of mentors or an older brother or sister figure, most people on balance appreciate someone they trust telling them when they err, when they need to be silent, or when they need to restrain themselves. Merely learning through reading books or personal intuition is seldom sufficient for purifying oneself of pride (*takabbur*), jealousy (*hasad*), ostentation (*riya*), wantonness (*batar*) etc.[90]

It was precisely for these reasons that scholars who became known as "*Sufis*" devoted themselves to the cause of cultivating inward states of

---

[90] See: Sheikh Masihullah Khan, *The Path to Perfection*, White Thread Press, 2005, pp. 26-34.

purity.[91] Ritualistic formulae[92] (*tariqah*) was to them the most efficacious way of constantly reminding oneself and immersing in one's striving (*mujahada*) against worldly desires (*zuhd*), cravings of their egos (*nafs 'ammara*) and blameworthy character traits like ostentation, pride, vanity (*'ujb*) etc. Through such striving, one increased their focus on God and with that came love of (*ma'arifah*) and obedience (*ta'ah*) to God, and transformation of themselves as sources of ease and benefit to others.[93]

By the 7th century of Islam, the knowledge of *tazkiyyah* became consolidated into Schools of *tariqah* or *Sufi* orders that came to be broadly known as the discipline of "*Tasawwuf.*"[94] Junaid Baghdadi (835-910), an early *Sufi*, defined it as: "to use every good character and to abandon every bad character." Each of these have since diversified into a plethora of sub-branches/orders in different localities. Since *Sufism* translates belief into feelings of contentment, emotional certainty in God and perfection of inner character, it quickly became a popular religious paradigm. As centuries passed, successive generations of scholars added their own contributions, forming elaborate *Sufi* practices and theology culminating

---

[91] Prominent among the early and most-renowned *Sufi* scholars were: Ibrahim Ibn Adham (718-782), Ibrahim Dhul Nun al-Misri (796-859), Junaid Baghdadi (830-910), Abu Bakr al-Shibli (861-946) and Abu Yazid al-Bistami (804-874).

[92] *Sufi* rituals typically consist of: reciting prayers, poems and selections from the *Qur'an*; calling out the Divine names of God (*dhikr*), *Qur'anic* verses or the *shahadah* etc. in a methodical repetitious way; and invoking praise on the Prophet and sending salutations to him etc. In most *Sufi* orders *dhikr* is performed aloud in communal gatherings. A specific format is practiced as daily devotional exercises, and their rules are set differently in each order, often by the founder as a special spiritual path that at least worked in their personal experience.

[93] One notes, for example, how contemporaries and friends of Imam al-Ghazali noticed a different man upon his return to teaching at the Nizamiyyah *madrasah* following his ten-year absence in which he is thought to have made acquaintance with *Sufism*. No longer was he the self-conceited distinguished professor but the sincere and humble one. See: Fazlur Rahman, *Revival and Reform*, edited by Ebrahim Moosa, Oneworld, 2000, p. 127, wth reference to al-Dhahabi's *Siyar*.

[94] The main ones being: *Qadariyya* - attributed to 'Abd al-Qadir Jilani (1077-1166); *Chistiyya* - founded by Qutub al-Din Mawdud Chisti (d. 1139); *Suhrawardiyya* - founded by Abu Hafs Umar al-Suhrawardi (1145-1234); *Naqshabandiyya* - founded by Baha al-Din al-Naqshaband (1318-1389); *Shadhiliyya* - founded by 'Abd al-Hasan al-Shadhili (1196-1258); *Rifa'iyya* - founded by Ahmad al-Rifa'i (1118-1182).

in a diversity of *tariqahs*[95] of varying methods and authenticity which we see across the world today.

*Salafism* on the other hand has a dual objective: (1) to shun *Sufism* altogether; and (2) to reform what it considers the "blind following" and over-institutionalisation of Sunni schools of law and creedal doctrines like the *Ash'ari* creed to return Muslims to a supposedly purist and literal way of the Prophet. Sadek Hamid points out that in the 1990s in particular British Muslims were attracted to the *Salafi* approach to religious commitment because of its seemingly "evidence based and stripped of the perceived corruption of folkloric religion as well as the less involved wishy-washy alternatives offered by political and cultural tendencies."[96] *Salafism* has of course a natural appeal in a globalising world where Muslims continually contact morally relative judgements, as well as divergent and contested religious practices.

The intentions of both *Salafis* and *Sufis* are tightly linked to these contexts. It's another dimension in the religious context whereby British Muslim communities struggle to bond and organise for mutual benefit. That they should clash is arguably a reflex of religious identity politics. Both *Salafis* and *Sufis* overwhelmingly desire beneficial change in the religious standing of Muslims and aren't necessarily opposed to one another as ultimate enemies. However, mutual cooperation is complicated with *Sufism* meaning different things to different people consistent with the fragmentation of religious learning on one hand, and on the other hand *Salafism* strengthens its presentation of a seemingly "no-nonsense" redress of modern ambiguities, consistent with an equally potent homogenisation of religious learning.

By consequence, a confrontational culture has developed despite the Prophet's warning that "tribulations are caused by speech."[97] Some *Sufis* have developed a dogmatic appraisal of all *Salafis* as "textual literalists" and even "enemies from within." *Salafis* have also had to contend with "the neo-conservative line that the whole conspiracy against America can be

---

[95] *Tariqah* (plural *turuq*) literally means way or path, the technical counterpart in English is "*Sufi* order," and each has its own distinct behavioural formulae.

[96] Sadek Hamid, *The Development of British "Salafism"*, Spring 2008, ISIM Review 21.

[97] Faraz Rabbani, *Sufism and Good Character*, White Thread Press, 2004, p. 23. Ibrahim al-Nakha'i is reported to have said this.

traced back to *Wahhabism*."[98] This defamatory line of attack, called "*Salafi/ Wahhabi*-bashing," is routinely exploited by hardcore advocates of *Sufism*, Muslim apologists, neo-liberals, as well as parts of the media and far-right nationalists' intent on demonising seemingly conservative Muslims or Islam. As an approach to religious commitment, *Salafi* puritanism is perhaps no more or no less inextricably linked to militancy than the wider population in general. However, outside of theology, when *Salafism* meets political ideology, such as in the cases of Al-Qaeda, Daesh/"ISIS" and radical jihadists, it has the potential to supply the ideological conditions for excommunicating Muslims (*takfir*) and religious violence on account of its intolerant and absolutist claims.[99] The same is true for militant groups like the Taleban and Tehreek-i-Labbaik which come from theologically *Deobandi* or *Barelvi* backgrounds, respectively.

To suggest, as some sociologists do, that *Salafis* are "extremists" overlooks the reality that for extremists possessing *Salafi*-like theology is merely coincidental.[100] Such sociological commentaries prematurely link puritanism or conservatism to violent extremism, seeking as it were as much "militant mileage" out of *Wahhabi-Salafi* bashing as possible.

In democratic settings *Salafism* remains predominantly politically quiet. Whilst this may have briefly changed with the emergence of assertive *Salafi* political parties in Arab countries since the so-called "Arab Spring," most observers recognise this to be a significant departure from the *Salafism* of the late 20th century that entered the UK and the West.

"Cultural *Sufis*" (described as "charlatan *Sufis*"[101] by Imam al-Ghazali and as "neo-*Sufis*" by Ibn Taymiyyah) in turn would do well to acknowledge that scholars celebrated for their spirituality have a long history of shunning chauvinism and isolation. Instead, they preferred a life of balance (*istiqamah*) between humility, teaching, research and campaigns

---

[98] Haneef James Oliver, *The Wahhabi Myth*, Trafford, 2008.

[99] Abu Aaliyah, *Political Violence and the End of Days*, The Humble "I", 20 September 2014. *Takfir* is to excommunicate Muslims.

[100] Quintain Wiktorowicz, *Anatomy of the Salafi Movement*, Studies in Conflict and Terrorism, 29 (2006): 207-239.

[101] Imam al-Ghazali terms such *Sufis* "charlatan *Sufis*" in *Ya Ayyuhal Walad (O Beloved Son/Youth)*, to distinguish *Sufis* who don't adhere to the *Shari'ah* in aspects of belief and law, and are not considered mainstream *Sufis*.

against tyranny. However, "cultural *Sufis*" contrast mainstream *Sufis* on many levels.

Firstly, for "cultural *Sufis*" "rituals are considered a veil," and hearts are rectified only through acts of "personal divination and mystical inspiration."[102] Religion is overly busy with rituals and personal mystical, esoteric experiences, leading to, as some would say, excessive privatisation of faith. Evaluated against the texts, as Ibn Taymiyyah (1263-1328) and others have, they broadly amount to ambiguous speculation or *"ta'wil"* in attempts to discover ultimate meanings and experiences. Muhammad Iqbal (1877-1938) noted that these were in fact "counterfeit experiences which creep into the circuit of the mystic state."[103]

Secondly, "cultural *Sufis*" often neglect the historic fact that the greatest *Sufi* scholars of South Asia, the likes of Shaykh Ahmad Sirhindi (1564-1624) and al-Dihlawi (1703-1762), led political activism in the 17th and 18th centuries. Medieval *Sufi's* of North West Africa (the *Maghreb*) such as Imam al-Jazouli[104] (d. 1465), whose famous poetic litany praising the Prophet, the *Dalail al-Khairat* (*The Proof of Goodness*) which is frequently read in *Sufi* circles, likewise stood up to tyrannical rulers of the 15th century. In fact, throughout history mainstream *Sufis* have been at the forefront of mobilising action to redress the excesses and injustices of their time through teaching, offering counsel and political engagement.[105]

Some *Salafis*, particularly at the extreme end known as *"Madhkali Salafis,"* counter *Sufism* by generalising all, or the greater number of, *Sufi* followers as polytheists. *Salafis* entrenched into this, much like hate-filled ideologues generally, go out of their way to spread a message of

---

[102] Ibn Rajab al-Hanbali, *The Heirs of the Prophets*, Starlatch, 2001.

[103] Muhammad Iqbal, *Reconstruction of Religious Thought in Islam*, p. 17.

[104] Imam al-Jazouli authored the popular poem eulogising prayers of salutation to the Prophet *Dhalail al-Khairat* (*The Proof of Goodness*), which is frequently read out in *Sufi* gatherings. For a review see: www.dar-sirr.com/Imam-al-Jazouli.html. Many scholars like Imams al-Ghazali (1058-1111), al-Razi (1149-1209), 'Abd al-Salam (1181-1262), Ahmad Zarruq (1442-1493), Ahmad Sirhindi (1564-1624), al-Dihlawi (1703-1762) to name a few, defended the core objectives and ways of mainstream *Sufism*, and where necessary sought to reform or check their populist developments based on what was permitted by the *Qur'an* and *Sunnah*.

[105] Abul 'Ala al-Mawdudi, *The Islamic Movement - Dynamics of Values, Power and Change*, The Islamic Foundation, 2007, p. 64.

*Sufi* innovation (*bid'a*) and falsely attribute to all *Sufis* what they did not necessarily say or practice in attempts to widen the gulf of dispute and opposition.[106] These perceptions are borne out of seeing the excesses of "cultural *Sufis*" in ostentatious celebrations, loud "screaming" music or the use of narcotics and the cult-like "*pir*" culture for example.

"Mainstream *Sufis*" contend that they adhere to the *Shari'ah* and therefore ought to be distinguished from "cultural *Sufis*." According to Zafar Ahmad al-Uthmani (1892-1974) mainstream *Sufis* "desire to direct people away from being deluded by this world, so incline towards the next life, to warn them of the enticing of the lower self and the deception of *Iblis* (Satan) the Accursed."[107]

Nevertheless, it would be naïve to deny complications by some *Sufi* scholars of the past that come into play. A dispassionate study of these complications reveals that they were mostly due to the perennial problems of language and speculative doctrines (*Sufi* theology) of the likes of Muhiyuddin ibn al-Arabi (1165-1240) for example, which arguably stretched mainstream understanding. Specifically problematic was the speculation about mystic powers of hierarchy (known as *Qutub*, *Gawth*, *'Abdal* etc.)[108] and the esoteric human union with the "Spirit" (*wahdatul wujud*) in the apparent "ascent to God"[109] which became a widespread paradigm for scholars generally in medieval times. However, in opposing self-claims of being "with God," a stand that seems hardened or unwilling

---

[106]  See: Muhammad Zakariyya Khandlawi, *Al-E'tidal fi Maratibur Rijal*.

[107]  Zafar Ahmad al-Uthmani, *Sufism and good character*, translated by Faraz Rabbani, White Thread Press, 2006.

[108]  For a brief discussion on *'Abdal*, which is perhaps the soundest of these categories see: Imam al-Qurtubi, *The Secrets of Asceticism*, Amal Press, 2008, pp. 85-87. Ibn Taymiyyah refers to the belief in the *'Abdal* in his *Al-'Aqidah al-Wasitiyyah* which *Salafis* contest the *Sufi* take on: "Those referred to in this saying, those who hold firmly to pure, unadulterated Islam, became the people of the *Sunnah* and the *Jama'ah*. Amongst them are the Siddiqs, the martyrs, the righteous, included in them are the cairns of guidance, the lamps for darkness, the masters of memorable merits, the ever-remembered virtues; Among them are the Abdal the Imams about whose judgment and understanding all Muslims agree."

[109]  For a brief view of Shaykh Ahmad al-Sirhindi's stance on *wahdatul wujud* (*unity of being*) see: *Maktubat-i Rabbani*.

to overlook for the greater good could hardly be in the interest of calling the same putative "deviants" as it were back to mainstream positions.

Instead, there should be moves to view such speculation more passively. Perhaps by accepting them as cryptic interpretations, or that they merely reflect the speculative influences of Greek thought or the prevailing norms of devotional culture at the time. After all, apart from the "cultural *Sufis*," most *Sufi* scholars were compliant to the *Shari'ah*. Ibn Tufayl (1105-1185) understood the subtleties of this and despite rejecting the doctrine of *wahdatul wujud* he generalised the problem by suggesting that the rationalist (*zahiri*) and mystic (*batini*) ways were both equally valid.[110] One might reasonably assume that his intention here was not merely to suggest that these differences weren't valid, but to point out that seemingly insurmountable differences can be put aside for the greater good of the community.

In recent years, protagonists of *Sufism* and *Salafism* have both increasingly recognised that past scholars championed in populist discourses for upholding the so-called "*Salafi* way" like Ibn Taymiyyah (1263-1328), al-Jawziyyah (1292-1350) and al-Shawkani (1759-1834), to name a few, whilst critical of some aspects of *Sufism* still held mainstream *Sufi* scholars in good esteem.[111] As is increasingly recognised today, these scholars wrote generally against the many excesses they saw among different groups including popular Islam,[112] not just "cultural *Sufis*," and didn't specifically hold out against mainstream *Sufism per se*. On account of this, and somewhat under pressure from external critique, more tolerant self-identifying *Salafis* in the West have opened up possibilities for mutual co-operation, rejecting the confrontational *Salafism* of the 1990s.

The prevalence of what might seem like a flourishing discourse of

---

[110] Ibn Tufayl explained most of his thoughts on political philosophy through the life of his functional character in the novel *Hayy ibn Yaqdhan* (*The Tale of Living Son of Vigilant*).

[111] See: Imam al-Jawziyyah, *Madarij al-Salikeen* (*Stations of Divine Seekers*) and Ibn Taymiyyah's *The Criterion between the Allies of the Merciful and the Allies of the Devil* both containing examples of esoteric anecdotes common in *Sufi* literature.

[112] There were many such abuses in popular Islam which arose because of a lack of moderation and knowledge, such as in the abuse of *tawassul*, *istigatha*, special relationships with "*pirs*," confusion over differences in theology and law, and doubtful matters (*shubuhaat*).

"cultural *Sufis*" and somewhat loose-labelling of ordinary non-scholar masses as "*Sufi*,"[113] nevertheless, tarnishes the credibility of what mainstream *Sufism* has to offer modern life. I would argue that for *Sufism* to become relevant and add value to British Muslims in a more meaningful way proponents would do well to expound a "British *Sufism*" contextualised to life in the UK. Such an expression would seek to: (1) evolve the overly-ritualised practices to holistic, cognitive paradigms rooted in *Qur'anic* and Prophetic examples, articulated in modern vernacular, incorporating the best of the knowledge of human psychology and British sensibilities; (2) remove ethnic commitment, secretive and cult-like in-group mentality of "cultural *Sufis*"; and (3) reinvent modern *Sufi* lodges or *khanqas* in the image of well-resourced training programmes delivered in environment-friendly centres or camps designed to cultivate people in the art of using faith to bring ease to human behaviours and intuitions in modern contexts.[114] However, it remains to be seen how feasible this is in practice, and whether or not it will gain any traction without triggering yet more fractious divisions.[115]

---

[113] For example: people who appeared to renounce the world (*zahid*); people who did nothing but engage in worship of God (*'ubbad*); people who claimed to have received inspiration in acts of devotion (*mulhamin*); people who spoke the truth in a way that may only be expected of an ascetic; travellers who lived without much possession (*sayyahin*); ascetics who deliberately acted in public in a way to be seen as blameworthy whilst being ascetics in private (*malamatiyya*); people who secluded themselves etc. all of these came to be loosely called *Sufi*. Personal notes from lectures with Shaykh Mohammad Akram Nadwi, 15 March 2014.

[114] Ibn Rajab al-Hanbali, *The Heirs of the Prophets*, Starlatch, 2001. See also: Zainab Istrabadi's PhD thesis on Ahmed Zarruq's *Qawa'id al-Tasawwuf* (*Principles of Sufism*) titled: *The Principles of Sufism (Qawa'id al-Tasawwuf): An Annotated Translation and introduction*, Indiana University,1988.

[115] See: Hamza Yusuf, *The Content of Character, Ethical Sayings of the Prophet Muhammad*, Sandala, 2005, p. 57. Writing about the ethical sayings of the Prophet, Shaykh Hamza Yusuf observes: "rightly guided scholars of the past resolved such matters and countless other debates centuries ago." But disinterested Muslims fail to recognise this, and seem entrenched in religious dissension in all matters of controversies such as: Ramadhan moonsighting debates; arguments over the *mawlid* (celebrating the birth of the Prophet), *Burda* (famous poem about the Prophet Muhammad), *inshad* (devotional songs), and recitation of the *Qur'an* for the dead or in groups etc.

"British *Sufism*" would contrast the numerous *Sufi* lodges or *khanqas* that are primarily found in *Barelvi* communities. These are shrouded in ethno-culture and consequently have little or no impact on British Muslims at large.

## (c) New trends in intra-religious identity politics

In recent years the divergent starting points and perspectives of Muslims has led to a mix of new trends. These have come about, arguably, as inevitable developments against the negative energies that are often associated with ethnocentric religious fervour, or the religious void in dealing with modernity created by *Deobandi-Barelvi* and *Sufi-Salafi* factionalism. A few of these are outlined below.

(1) Increased use of arguments of social liberalism, liberal democracy and the language of secularism to defend expressions of post-modern or ethnic commitment to Muslimness without necessarily validating them through *Qur'anic* and Prophetic paradigms. There is little checking-in as to whether or not, or to what extent, expressions (e.g. aggressive feminism, absolutist arguments in defence of *niqab*, secular-ethnic definitions of Islamophobia, approach to offence in public etc.) are rooted in sound theology.

(2) Adoption of a passive approach to religious differences pertaining to public matters with the intention to keep as much harmony as possible among Muslims. The phrase "unity is not conformity or uniformity" and the argument of "textual plurality" are advanced as coping mechanisms of sorts against very visible divisions (e.g. moonsighting controversy, patriarchal dominance over women, marriage within ethno-culture, mosques as centres of ethnic language and culture etc.). However, much of this is not well thought-out, and instead the underlying issues are unwittingly prolonged.

(3) Growing apathy towards local faith communities among the burgeoning Muslim middle-classes. Many of them feel let down by the leaders of their communities for not giving them a say in the way mosques or community centres are run, or the kind of amenities and platforms that they would like to see. That said, this kind of apathy often has more complex underlying reasons such as

social atomization and social mobility issues. As Muslims become more socially mobile, they move away from inner-town areas where mosques are usually located. Increased distance coupled to the lack of time due to work commitments and the burden of parenting reduces their ability to connect to the community that they would like to be a part of. One of the consequences of this is that there's an increasing void of leadership within communities, with the role of "authority figure" and capacity more geographically distributed and fractured among the third generation compared to the first.

(4) Public engagement has broadened to an array of topics outside of the typical controversies of the 1990s and 2000s (which were generally focused on *'aqidah, Salafism, mawlid* etc.) such as liberal thought, feminism, anti-racism, mainstream party politics etc. However, there is a lack of nuance, realism and political philosophy with which debates take place. In public engagement, Muslims in their capacity as believers struggle to advocate enlightening or original theocentric perspectives relevant to the real-life problem without being condescending or showing religious fervour. This isn't at all surprising. As people mix together, they naturally pick up the same good and bad aspects of the *status quo,* including perspectives, cynicism and skepticism etc. without necessarily thinking twice about whether it's God-centred. For whom, it's usually more about wanting to gain kudos, to fit in and not be seen as "out-group" by others. Moreover, Muslims engaged in the politics of cultural recognition aren't usually trained in Islamic theology. Yet, by virtue of being Muslim, their involvement is at least tacitly taken as representative of their faith when the reality is that it isn't necessarily.

These trends point to the fact that the problem of denominational factionalism isn't being addressed. Instead, Muslims in the public realm overlook the necessity of putting their house in order as it were, and yet feel confident enough to engage a completely new set of contentions. The nature of this engagement is quite reactionary and seldom from a holistic examination of what God intends for believers and what might be rational and productive for them. This is because the foundational vision and principles upon which to define the nature of British Muslim are themselves undefined. The consequence is that it creates even greater knots and fragments Muslim polities further. While this isn't unusual for modern open societies like ours in the UK, being reactionary and unable to formulate proper strategies, approaches and positions isn't a good place to be either.

Addressing *Deobandi-Barelvi* and *Sufi-Salafi* factionalism is thus an urgent matter. To address it properly modern theories on conflict resolution are instructive. Techniques like "consensus-promoting strategy" work by examining contradiction, attitude, behaviour, and resolution through awareness or "conscientisation."[116] Such interdisciplinary fields have developed to study and uncover ways in which people can transcend differences to build exemplary communities. In similar fashion, the Prophet's life can be taken as one of continuous conflict resolution of one kind or another, whether it's in the realm of international relations, social relations, relations between communities, families and individuals, with oneself, or between people and the environment.

For quarrelling groups, building relationships by coming together in mutual harmony and respect requires an attitude of "conscientisation," and a firm conviction in seeing benefit and goodness in other than one's own self-claims and perceptions. The challenge for third generation Muslims is to find ways to constructively leave behind the ethnic commitment to religion inherited from previous generations, and to forge new perspectives rooted in scholarship and Godliness contextualised to life in the UK.

---

[116] Hugh Miall, Oliver Ramsbotham, and Tom Woodhouse, *Contemporary Conflict Resolution*. Polity Press, 2005, p. 9.

# — 2 —

# Religion in society

## 2.1 Embracing the art of *khidma* (service)

Many of us have come across the term *khidma* at some point. It's pretty much the same word in Arabic, Urdu, Bengali and in many other languages too. Literally, it means to be "in service" to God, people and nature, through acts of devotion, virtue and benefit. To be a *khadim* (the one who offers *khidma*; plural *khudama*) one must strive towards the standard of *khulafa al-ard* (2:30; trustees/stewards of the earth). That is, to be of "people of incredible virtue, goodness and love, who give themselves wholly to the highest ideals and seek to create a world in which all people have the opportunity to actualise their fullest human potential in every domain of life, from the most mundane to the most transcendent."[117] Acts of *khidma* have the rare quality of leaving a sweet taste. It's not surprising why. *Khidma* takes well-meaning intentions to the level of truthfulness, selflessness and sincerity, for instance in "preserving peace," "improving conditions" and "holding people to account."

"Preserving peace" for the *khadim* is to reconcile between people and pursuing a discourse of justice, diplomacy and healing for those wronged or downtrodden. "Improving conditions" is to be a source of ease to others and helping them to meet their needs, overcome predicaments and struggles, whatever they may be. "Holding people to account" is to offer

---

[117] A useful definition by Fethullah Gulen, see: *A Dialogue of Civilization* by Jill Carroll, Tughra Books, 2007, p. 55. Wider reading of this concept in *tafsir* literature is worthwhile.

well-reasoned and unassuming honest words. Speaking truth to power, though necessary at times, can often be a bitter pill to swallow, especially for those directly called out. But the *khadim* has a graceful, correct manner (*adab*) and insight (*hikmah*) into the right time and place for things that makes feedback a little easier to absorb and act upon.

For sure the art of *khidma* can't be neatly taught in bestselling self-help manuals alone. Hope is not lost however. If our intention (*niyyah*) is to remember God, which should be the pivot at every step of the way for Muslims, naturally, we'll want to learn the art of *khidma* by mining the *Qur'an* and *Sunnah* or keeping the company of the *khudama*. If we struggle to make this connection, a leap of faith, reasoning and lived experience, it is perhaps to be expected that, in some way or another, we obscure God's command to tread gently on earth, to be forgiving, truthful and just, and to say "no" to the excesses of worldly life etc. We would also struggle to see how God commands us "to know one another," (49:13) or to understand that the *ahsanul qasas* ("beautiful stories"), as in the case of Prophet Yusuf and his brothers, "...are signs for anyone who wants to ask" (12:7).

Yet these are the very things that we usually overlook. And hence the narratives that quite possibly inspire us towards doing *khidma* often remain deeply buried. Instead, we feel that social, political or scientific rationalism are sufficiently empowering and solving. Whilst they're no doubt relevant, far from providing refreshing perspectives, it seems that we quite easily trap ourselves in their intrinsic limitations or, worse still, selectively use them to legitimise our own self-conceit. It's no wonder we struggle to even listen to others, least of all to take their advice. Nor do we realise that the words we use in being socially and politically engaged impact us both in this world and the next.

The unfortunate reality is that deep down we crave immediate results, thinking that on one hand we achieve through our own abilities, whilst on the other, somewhat lazily, remain unwilling to make the necessary sacrifices or be prepared to put the effort in. Here, power, money and idealism whisper seductively, and it's usually when we're least minded to serve others that we listen. In the course of which we struggle to see how our own journey back to God, and that of our "flocks,"[118] are interlocked into the very same existential spaces and contexts that we remain so detached from. The outcome is that we become far too reactionary. We convince ourselves that problems are "out there" and not "in here"; a case of seeing the speck of dirt in our brothers' eyes, but forgetting the splinter in our own.[119] Feelings of inadequacy or lack of trust and control lures us to confront power rather than seek ways to mutually work with it within our vast, though often largely unexplored, freedoms. What's more, we feel unbashful in complaining when the very power that we rushed to confront now exerts itself against us. Whilst we bemoan the very disheartening paradigm, we fail to see how we're so easily seduced by it.

The challenge for anyone working for positive change within their own spaces and contexts is surely to make that extra bit of space and time to at least contemplate taking things to the level of *khidma*. After all, the imperative to show compassion and to love people is a Prophetic one.[120]

---

[118] *Hadith* narrated by 'Abdullah ibn 'Umar in *Sunan Abu Dawud*: "The Messenger of Allah said: 'Each of you is a shepherd and each of you is responsible for his flock. The *amir* (ruler) who is over the people is a shepherd and is responsible for his flock; a man is a shepherd in charge of the inhabitants of his household and he is responsible for his flock; a woman is a shepherdess in charge of her husband's house and children and she is responsible for them; and a man's slave is a shepherd in charge of his master's property and he is responsible for it. So, each of you is a shepherd and each of you is responsible for his flock.'"

[119] *Hadith* narrated in *Sahih Ibn Hibban*: "One of you sees the speck of dirt in his brother's eye, but forgets the splinter in his own eye." Similar sayings can be found in Christian literature.

[120] *Hadith* narrated by 'Abdullah bin Umar in *Sunan al-Tirmidhi*: "Those who are merciful will be shown mercy by the Most Merciful. Be merciful to those on the earth and the One above the heavens will have mercy upon you. The womb is derived from the Most Merciful, thus whoever keeps relations with his family then Allah will keep relations with him, and whoever abandons his family, then Allah will abandon him."

# 2.2 Untrapping immorality on the web: *al-adab al-internet*

"Safer Internet Day" is a yearly campaign by a number of charities supported by organisations, including Internet Matters, Internet Watch Foundation and the UK Government to make the internet a safer place for children and young people. While it's not just the young and innocent who need protecting from inappropriate content (like violence, pornography, sites promoting alcohol, ransomware, identity theft, child grooming, cyber-bullying, hate etc.), it's children who are certainly most vulnerable. For Muslims, the nature of inappropriateness should extend to wider manners and conduct in the way we interact online and the implications it has for our spiritual, mental and physical well-being, which is relevant to both young and old alike.

According to a study in 2015 by the Internet Advertising Bureau UK, we spend on average three hours online every day. That's approximately 12% of the day or 18% of the 16 or so hours that the average person is awake. Over a lifetime it potentially amounts to around 11 years of an average 80 years of life expectancy, give or take.

Facebook is a very good example where all kinds of inappropriate and immoral activities take place. It's true that with so many updates you could easily drown in statuses. To work around this, Facebook uses sophisticated algorithms that assume we want to see more of the feeds from people whom we've most frequently "liked" or "commented" on. It's an assumption yet to be researched properly for the long-term psychological consequences to users, particularly across different personality traits. In turn, "public pages" are continuously scouring for new content and evermore ingenious ways to get people to "like" and "share"; volume is crucial to any good business model of course. While some content is definitely beneficial, there's plenty of time wasting, idle gawking, entertainment and frivolity too.

For some individuals the number of "likes" and "retweets" are a stamp of approval of their existential value and self-esteem. After all, an online profile implicitly demands recognition. However, unlike in conventional advertising where independent regulators with legal powers keep a watchful eye, there isn't anything as yet like it for social media.[121] Cue the scourge of "fake news"; the click bait culture that fuels online populism as a well-orchestrated, money-making or political interference scheme. When social media platforms first came out, the assumption was that they wouldn't need to be regulated, but with time they've also become popular vehicles for disinformation and criminal activity.

Others carefully curate online persona of themselves, which can often turn out to be completely at odds with their offline identity. For whom, a chance to remake identity of sorts can help escape from an otherwise mundane grind of daily life. For others, still, social media is a battlefield to defend ideas and beliefs from being ridiculed and hijacked, thinking that doing so is always necessary and productive, that it doesn't require much effort beyond typing some words. No doubt these things can lead to good outcomes, but too often they don't and simply add to the drama.

You can't help but notice just how obsessive, compulsive or neurotic these behaviours can be. Some of which is engineered by the way comments and shares are brought into view across people to provoke an opinion. The writing on the wall, as it were, can often be a cesspit. It also underlies the feeling of needing to connect with others, and satiating the feeling of one's self-importance can be quite difficult to placate too. Particularly, if one has amassed a respectable following there's an implicit weight of responsibility to say something worthy of being followed, trapping people into the very bubble of their own making.

Like Facebook, Snapchat and Instagram are sure fast ways of blurring private and public life. The need to show oneself in full technicolour with various filters makes it even more irresistible to show-off one's photos or to seek recognition by others (an estimated 2.5 trillion images were shared in 2016). However, what real value it adds is questionable. In the spiritual diseases of the heart, such expressions would be considered vanity (*'ujb*).

Then there is the vitriol, backbiting, racism, bullying, name-calling,

---

[121] Like the Advertising Standards Agency (ASA) for advertising and Ofcom for communications companies, both in the UK. At the time of writing, the UK Government has started consulting industry bodies looking at options for regulating the internet and social media platforms.

trolling and *ad hominem*[122] attacks that we come across daily on Facebook, WhatsApp, Twitter and in the comments section of online opinion articles. Of course, sitting behind a screen by its very nature invites people to express half-baked, unedited thoughts which they probably wouldn't have otherwise uttered in person, especially if it's directed at someone they've never met nor aware of their background and qualities. Yet this loss of manners (*adab*, correct conduct) is often seen as completely acceptable by many.

Unfortunately, though admittedly it's not surprising, few Muslim scholars have been clued-up enough to meet the great need of our time to expound and teach the finer details of the knowledge of correct online conduct, *al-'ilm al-adab al-internet* if you like. In the meantime, here's some basic advice.

(1) When interacting online check that your intentions are correct (*niyyah*). If we don't think about "why we're doing something," chances are we're acting out of mere impulse. However, the point of *niyyah* is to get us to focus on being subservient to God and doing things out of mindfulness. This technique can be applied to all actions, making our activities less wasteful and more purposeful and considered.

(2) Fact-check news or images for authenticity before sharing. The best way to do this is to pass the words (or content) through the "four gates of speech" before sharing, namely: (i) "is it true?"; (ii) "is it necessary?"; (iii) "is it kind?"; and (iv) "is it the right time?"[123]

(3) Even if information is factually correct, think critically about whether it'll be of any benefit to others, and if not don't share or spend time on it. Often things need explaining or interpreting by experts, otherwise people can easily switch off or form their own incorrect or confused conclusions.

---

[122] *Ad hominem* (Latin for "to the person"), is arguing in a manner to avoid genuine discussion of the topic at hand by instead attacking the character, motive, history, background etc. of the person making the argument.

[123] See: Lodro Rinzler, *The Four Gates of Speech: Is It Really a Good Idea to Call the Ex?*, The Huffington Post, 23 March 2012.

(4)  We shouldn't concern ourselves with something that doesn't concern us. It could be a conversation between others, or something we don't have expertise in or agency to influence. If that's the case, it's better to leave it.

(5)  Avoid sharing bad news stories from far places that have no relevance to people we're sharing with. This includes, for example, stories of shootings or car chases in America which have a completely different context to the gun laws in the UK.

(6)  Avoid sharing news that vilifies people or tout's pessimism and cynicism, as this is not the way of the believer.

(7)  Be kind by not saying things that might be hurtful, sly, derogatory or unfair. Try putting yourself in their shoes first. Where there is a need to call things out, be like an erudite scholar who thinks deep about the matter, takes time to reason properly before conveying them with due respect and language. It's always better to say something good or constructive and to remain silent if otherwise.

(8)  Finally, we need to find ways to actively disconnect from online to give ourselves the time to connect with God, people we love and our neighbours etc. This also means putting our phones and connected devices away to give people our full attention when speaking to them.

Admittedly, none of this stuff is easy in practice and we all get caught up in it from time to time. But our job is to strive against our own inner demons (*nafs lawwama*), compulsions and immorality. We must realise that online experiences play a big part in our lives and we don't necessarily possess the right skills and training to navigate its inherent trappings. And like medieval theological texts generally, if we're not trained with the prerequisite skills and competences, we risk being trapped by it. The World Wide Web is no different.

## 2.3 The trouble with "Islamophobia" 20 years on

Over the last two decades or so "Islamophobia" has become quite a common word in conversations about the experience of Muslims in the UK and elsewhere in the West. In conditions of runaway globalisation we've also become conditioned to importing news of "Islamophobia" from abroad, from places as far as Australia. News of an arson attack on a mosque or a Muslim man stabbed to death from a little-known place often arrives on our shores in near real time, naturally heightening the feeling of vulnerability nearer to home. Casting aside this subtle psychological amplification of our own local context, there is a fair amount of evidence to suggest that the volume of explicit hatred against Muslims and related incidents categorised as "Islamophobia" in the UK have increased in the last 20 years.[124] According to the Runnymede Trust's 20th anniversary report[125] published in November 2017, this has also led to a growing negative impact affecting Muslims and the direction of society at large.

It's worth bearing in mind that a number of macro variables come into play when comparing the size of "Islamophobia" over time. Firstly, awareness and reporting of "Islamophobia" has dramatically improved over this period. In 2015, the UK Government introduced a new category for Police forces to report anti-Muslim hate crimes.[126] We also have well-oiled organisations like Tell MAMA and MEND which do a huge amount of work to improve reporting and raising awareness.[127] However, in between

---

[124] According to Tell MAMA, there were 1,380 reports of anti-Muslim attacks and incidents in 2017, of which 1,201 reports were verified by them, of which slightly more than two thirds of verified incidents occurred "offline," or at street level, which represents a 30% rise in offline reports when compared with the previous reporting period. About 56% were on females. The perpetrators were 80% male and conviction rate is about 80% based on police statistics. See: *Beyond the Incident: Outcomes for Victims of Anti-Muslim Prejudice*, 2017, Tell MAMA, 23 July 2018.

[125] See: *Islamophobia Still a challenge for us all*, https://www.runnymedetrust.org/, November 2017, retrieved 13 November 2017.

[126] See: *Action Against Hate: The UK Government's plan for tackling hate crime*, 2016, https://assets.publishing.service.gov.uk, retrieved 8 August 2018.

[127] Other organisations include the APPG (All Party Parliamentary Group) for Hate Crimes, the "Hope Not Hate" campaign movements, interfaith alliances, and various initiatives within local communities etc.

these organisations there are questions about duplication of reporting, and alignment of standards, definitions and criteria used to validate reports.

Secondly, perception of what "Islamophobia" is has shifted over time. In the 1980s and early 1990s attacks against men or women on their way to a mosque or hurls of abuse like "Paki out" or "go back to where you came from" would have been counted under racism, not "Islamophobia." And so, arguably, it's not that the incidents in public or unfair discrimination in workplaces didn't take place, some of it was counted but under different categories.

Thirdly, with the advent of social media, it's become very easy to launch abuse and offend people sitting behind a screen. Much of it is just raw, nasty and impulsive emotions hurled at others, similar to what often happens in a football stadium. And equally, it's become very easy to share news of abuse and unfair treatment on social media.

Fourthly, as focus on Muslims has increased in the wake of 9/11, 7/7 and other attacks, many "Islamophobia" subject matter experts in public bodies and universities have tended to focus on the macro picture of: (1) political mobilizations against Islam and Muslims by far-right groups; (2) the government's focus on counter-terrorism; and (3) media-led discussions of them, which have played into people's already-held perceptions.

Perceptions and reporting issues aside, we call it "Islamophobia" despite the fact that the idea of "fearing Islam" neither conveys any sense of criminality, malevolent intent or immoral sentiment. Nor does it describe the actual phenomenon on several fronts.

Firstly, from an Islamic theological point of view, there is of course no Islamic legal (*fiqhi*) argument that makes it unlawful (*haram*) or even disliked (*makruh*) for non-Muslims to hold irrational fears about Islam. The general principle is that non-Muslims are afforded such liberties, as they are in any civilised society, about personal beliefs, anxieties, fears and values. Whether the context is Makkan where Muslims reside as a minority within a majority non-Muslim population with non-Muslim political authority, or in a Madinan context where Muslims have political authority and may or may not have been a majority, in either of them, there isn't anything documented in the annals of Islamic legal textbooks suggesting a moral value least of all criminalising the supposedly irrational fears or offensive opinions of non-Muslims.

In fact, in such a situation the believer is commanded by God to, "Repel evil by what is better" so that enmity between people turns to friendship (41:43). Thus, Muslims are commanded to be a source of ease, emotional intelligence and security to others, including those who fear Islam unknowingly. This is all the more relevant today given that: there is so much misinformation about Islam in the media; ethnic commitment to religion dominates among Muslims; 90% of the UK population has never visited a mosque;[128] and organised religion is generally perceived as unreasonable or an oddity in British society.

Secondly, for the sake of argument, if we set aside the above point and take the view that it's lawful for non-believers to say whatever they want about Islam but caveat it with the condition that "only if it doesn't lead to hatred," such as in the form of abuse, bullying, unfair discrimination in the workplace, or violence etc., we then have to question who it's directed at? If it's against Muslims on the basis of visible identity markers (such as a "Muslim sounding" name, clothing, refusal to drink alcohol etc.) it does lend support to the term "anti-Muslim hatred" given that it has a sense of clarity in specifically locating the object of hatred or "otherising," which is the person, and not necessarily the underlying religious doctrine or cultural symbol.

Thirdly, "Islamophobia" in the meaning of "irrational fear of Islam" seems to be somewhat unwittingly wedded to the cognitive dissonance (simultaneously holding two or more contradictory beliefs, ideas or values) that pervades the contemporary experiences of many Muslims. Holding the wider challenges in modernity as something done to them by others having a "phobia of Islam," arguably, it becomes easier to deflect criticism of questionable ethno-cultural activities or the uncontextualised conventions of Muslims that usually get passed off as "Islamic." Few would be motivated to see the need for self-reflective contextualisation, outreach and bridging activities, or re-evaluating the extent to which we can do more to engage and convey for the cultural imperative to root into British society out of what God says. Instead, there is a real risk that the institutionalisation of the term "Islamophobia" would lead to a specific

---

[128] See: *90% of people haven't been inside a mosque - change that this weekend!*, http://www.mcb.org.uk/90-of-people-havent-been-inside-a-mosque-change-that-this-weekend/, retrieved 18 February 2018.

kind of "privileging of victimhood" and inter-community otherisation by, say, Hindus against Muslims, or Asian Muslims against black Muslims.[129] Certainly Asian Muslims are well-known for their racism towards black Muslims.

Arguing "Islamophobia" as a valid term in the pattern of "homophobia" isn't helpful either. "Homophobia" is antipathy directed towards homosexual people and homosexuality, which is why the term is true to the actual phenomenon. "Islamophobia," on the other hand, seems to imply negative attitudes or antipathy directed against Islam, but what people actually mean here are Muslims. However, we can't assume that Muslim and Islam are one and the same. Human behaviours are always on a spectrum; Muslims don't necessarily act properly according to Islam and are at best considered to be "striving" to be accepted as "Muslim to God" (*muslimaini laka*).

In comparison to the Judaic tradition, which is perhaps most similar to the British Muslim situation, it's not surprising that the accepted and widely used term isn't "Jewdaism-phobia" or "Jew-phobia" but "anti-Semitic hatred" or "anti-Jewish hatred." These latter terms are much truer to the phenomenon: the object is Semitic people of the Jewish faith. In this sense, the Runnymede Trust's recommendation to call it "anti-Muslim racism" and giving it a rather nebulous definition,[130] whilst it adds something new to "Islamophobia" recognising the intersectionality of race and religion, and brings into focus structural and unconscious "otherising" and causes of socio-economic inequality, it goes down yet another pigeonhole of muddling race, religion and class by associating at

---

[129] See concerns submitted by Southall Black Sisters group to the APPG on British Muslims: *Islamophobia Defined: The inquiry into a working definition of Islamophobia*, https://appgbritishmuslims.org/s/Islamophobia-Defined.pdf, November 2018, p. 43, retrieved 28 November 2018.

[130] The Runneymede Trust in November 2017 published this wide definition of Islamophobia: "Islamophobia is any distinction, exclusion, or restriction towards, or preference against, Muslims (or those perceived to be Muslims) that has the purpose or effect of nullifying or impairing the recognition, enjoyment or exercise, on an equal footing, of human rights and fundamental freedoms in the political, economic, social, cultural or any other field of public life" See: *Islamophobia Still a challenge for us all*, https://www.runnymedetrust.org/, retrieved 13 November 2017.

face value people's liberty to dislike or hate Islam with the more popular vocabulary of "racism."

In doing so, it risks unwittingly undermining the significance of already widely-supported work to tackle core racism and race-related inequalities. After all, it's also possible to hurl hatred at Muslims of white ethnicities, particularly white women converts. Race isn't always necessarily implied. "Being Muslim" as a verb isn't a race but an act of servitude to God. However, there is a growing trend among sociologists to define "Islamophobia" as a form of racism on the basis that they see race not merely as the colour of one's skin but "a social construct incorporating a range of characteristics including skin colour, ethnic background and cultural identity." In doing so, they impose an external reading of what "Muslimness" is, constrained to ethno-cultural markers and not necessarily in terms of what God defines as Muslim. In this sense, taking up a secular public language of anti-racism represents a "racialisation of Muslims and the countering of it through anti-racism is also party to their secularisation."[131]

I would also argue that the cultural anthropological understanding of "being Muslim" dismally fails to recognise God as the central concern, and therefore doesn't seek to understand "Muslimness" on its own terms. In turn, it means that the cultural markers of "brownness" of British Muslims such as the languages they speak (e.g. Bengali, Urdu, Swahili etc.), or the clothes they wear (e.g. the *shalwar kameez, jilbab, turban,* or trousers cut above the ankles etc.) or the foods they eat (e.g. chapatti, curry etc.) are readily conflated with a theocentric view of "being Muslim." In the *Qur'anic* paradigm such ethno-cultural expressions have no intrinsic relation to "being Muslim" or "Muslimness." Such markers can of course be found among non-Muslims like Sikhs, Indian Christians and Hindus too, and are more relevant to people's ethnic identities rather than endogenous expressions of living Islam in Britain. This relation extends equally to nefarious results of ethnic commitment to religion, such as female genital mutilation (FGM), male patriarchy, forced marriages and abusive exorcist rituals to name a few.

The idea of defining "Islamophobia" as anything that takes up the language of racism to target "perceived Muslimness" has also been

---

[131] Yahya Birt, *Why this new definition of Islamophobia is bittersweet,* https://medium. com, 5 December 2018.

touted by the APPG on British Muslims. Such linking, I would argue, conceptually pushes the meaning of "racism" towards the idea of disliking or hating Islam as a religion or its ideas, and which isn't intuitive to racism as generally used in society.[132] Nor does it, at face value, imply that people's liberty to argue against Islamic ideas is protected. You could also argue that it's possible to construe almost anything as "perceived Muslimness."

The big elephant in the room which seems to be completely overlooked is the ethnic identities of people (the idea of being culturally Bangladeshi, Pakistani, Somali, Nigerian etc.) and their ethno-cultural polities on their own terms and contexts. British Muslims overall are far more rooted in their ethno-national identities and cultural conventions than a shared religious outlook. Under these proposals for a definition of "Islamophobia," racism for Muslims reduces to their being Muslim and not their ethnic identity and polities which are ironically much more dominant.

There is also the potentially confounding porosity in the discourse between extreme expressions of "Islamophobia" widely condemned in the media, and more normalised and insidious ones which politicians and the media may be tolerant to in comparison.[133] And, socio-economic disparities in the UK are not simply a function of race or about "being Muslim," but transfuse multitude of factors, as socio-economic problems naturally do, across religions, class, literacy levels, structural imbalances in the economy, immigration histories etc.

Whilst it's fair to say that we've all tended to use "Islamophobia" as the primary term, it is of course socially constructed and used in context. However, if we're proposing to change or redefine the label, then, as I have argued here, the compelling rationale would be to adopt the term "anti-Muslim hatred," not the broad definition of "anti-Muslim racism" or "Islamophobia" as "a type of racism that targets expressions of Muslimness

---

[132] Following a year-long consultation across the UK, the APPG on British Muslims released the following definition of "Islamophobia" on 27 November 2018: "Islamophobia is rooted in racism and is a type of racism that targets expressions of Muslimness or perceived Muslimness." See: *Islamophobia Defined: The inquiry into a working definition of Islamophobia*, https://appgbritishmuslims.org/s/Islamophobia-Defined.pdf, retrieved 28 November 2018.

[133] See: Aurelien Mondon & Aaron Winter(2017), *Articulations of Islamophobia: from the extreme to the mainstream?*, Ethnic and Racial Studies, 40:13, 2151-2179, DOI: 10.1080/01419870.2017.1312008, retrieved 8 August 2018.

or perceived Muslimness" that the Runnymede Trust and the APPG on British Muslims, and others, have advocated.

Those against using the term "anti-Muslim hatred" argue that it doesn't incorporate the array of broader structural racial inequalities that Muslims face, such as discrimination at work on having the name "Muhammad." However, "anti-Muslim" is a prejudice that, like prejudices generally, manifests in different walks of life, where the underlying causes aren't necessarily specific to Muslims. In the same way, to believe that "Islamophobia" is a type of structural racial inequality that deserves special treatment under a single overarching term, you would have to assume that animosity against Muslims or "perceived Muslimness" is the all-encompassing psychological driver. For example, the discrimination that Muhammad faces may well be faced by Srinivas too. Similarly, the lack of diversity in boardrooms is not an issue of animosity towards "perceived Muslimness" *per se* but wider variables and values in society. Much of these issues are at a basic level already covered in the Equality Act 2010[134] which protects people, including Muslims, from discrimination on grounds of age, race, colour, nationality, ethnic and national origin etc. in the fields of employment, the provision of goods and services, education and public functions. The idea that a broad definition of "Islamophobia" would somehow give new "meaning and substance to efforts to address conscious and unconscious forms of bias discrimination" overlooks the reality that remedy's such as name-blind applications, diverse interview panels and unconscious bias training for recruitment professionals can only be enforced through direct legislation (assuming that people are properly consulted in the first place), not the indirect route of legally enforcing a troubled definition of "Islamophobia" upon businesses. Doing so would only make Muslims feel even more uneasy and apologetic about their faith.

How the term "Islam," (bringing into view a moral, metaphysical and legal system and theocentric ideas) when juxtaposed alongside "phobia" could be expected to specifically refer to anti-Muslim hatred or racism towards ethnic minorities isn't straightforward. Thus, it's not surprising that the term "Islamophobia" almost always requires accompanying words such as "hatred," "bigotry," "prejudice," "discrimination," "racism" or

---

[134] See: *Equality Act 2010*, http://www.legislation.gov.uk/ukpga/2010/15/contents, retrieved 28 November 2018.

some other descriptor depending on the realm in which the hatred or discrimination occurs. As the politics of defining Islamophobia rumbles on, failure to propose a minimal workable definition will only add to the problems Muslims face.

# 2.4 UK *zakat* belongs in the UK

As the month of Ramadhan nears, many of us increasingly think about paying *zakat*. Ramadhan presents itself with immense rewards which multiply many folds, and hence it's opportune that we find ourselves fixing the anniversary of what is in effect a yearly tax-like return in the month of Ramadhan. Except it's not quite like a normal tax since *zakat* is a minimal obligation to God for the upkeep of society. God is most compassionate for there is a threshold (*nisab*) before *zakat* becomes due, many types of wealth and basic necessities are exempt and we're only liable to pay 2.5% based on the net position of our wealth on a fixed point in time.[135] And, just in case we forget, be sure we'll be reminded by the ensuing frenzy of fundraising activities across online, in mosques, through direct marketing and on TV channels, where the clamour of "*zakat* eligible" or "give your *zakat, sadaqah, lillah*" will peak for the year in Ramadhan.

There was a time when not a single British Muslim charity was remotely interested in spending *zakat* in the UK despite collecting it from British citizens. Muslims saw it as just like any other charity with the added fuss of having to take stock of one's wealth. It was perhaps understandable for first generation immigrants to send *zakat* abroad to the countries of their birth since they still had close family ties and a strong sense of obligation to the poor in those countries, especially without an organised way of distributing it in the UK. Unless they personally knew of someone eligible for *zakat* here in the UK, chances are it didn't warrant any consideration at all. Moreover, for reasons of ethno-cultural taboo, unlike today, many struggling British Muslim educational establishments didn't have the courage to publicly declare that their students were eligible for *zakat*. There was also an uncontested assumption that *zakat* was only to help the "poor" and "needy" (and nobody else) since that's who our parents and grandparents gave their *zakat* to.

But with the establishment of NZF (National Zakat Foundation) in 2011 this changed. We now have a professional and institutional capability that can strategically intervene to fix and transform some of the most pressing barriers to Muslims flourishing in the UK and with it bringing

---

[135] *Zakat* is not a transactional tax like Value Added Tax (at 20% in the UK) nor is it a monthly income-based tax (between 20%-45% in the UK).

the hope of helping society overall to prosper. Given the changed situation, then, spending *zakat* in the UK can be seen as a litmus test of whether as various communities we've woken up to our context.

Certainly, there are lessons to be learned from the moonsighting rupture of the 1990s which has since blighted communities.[136] Primarily, it's the dilemma of agreeing whether it should be local (UK/Morocco sighting) or global moonsighting (usually fixed to Saudi declaration). What resonates most is that while *fiqhi* reasoning overwhelmingly establishes local moonsighting, much like local spending of *zakat*, global telecommunications and a lack of local moonsighting processes led many to unquestioningly accept global moonsighting fixed to whatever happened in Saudi Arabia, much like what's happened to *zakat* until recently. Deferring to Saudi Arabia was of course the easy way out with the increasing influence of Muslim TV channels, just as it happens with *zakat* when there is natural disaster in the Muslim world.

However, with that came also the ignorance of astronomical data for negating false or improbable "sightings" and an engendering of laziness and lack of ownership to collectively fix problems that, after all, affects us here in the UK and not people living in Saudi Arabia. I can't see Saudis, Pakistanis, Bangladeshis, Indians, Somalis etc. being concerned about when we start Ramadhan in the UK nor would they be willing to spend their *zakat* on poverty-stricken Brits. And why should they since it's completely inconsequential to them? Besides, British Muslims would do well to understand the principle that God limits our individual responsibilities to our own spaces, contexts and spheres of influence (2:286). The Prophet

---

[136] Mamnun Khan, *Towards a unified approach to Crescent Moon Sighting in the UK*, www.wifaqululama.co.uk/unified-crescent/, 2015.

exemplified it as a general principle,[137] and specifically in the example of *zakat* he indicated that the starting position is to spend it locally.[138]

One difference perhaps is that while foreign *muftis* almost unanimously wrote edicts (*fatawa*) in favour of local moonsighting which, as it so happened, far too many British Muslims simply ignored, for *zakat* there is a tendency for some *muftis* (both in the UK and abroad) to argue for globalised distribution. It turns out there is inherent self-interest: foreign *zakat* represents a rich source of inward investment to fund foreign *madrasahs* and orphanages etc. Arguably, the fact that British Muslims living as minorities have to contemplate this is an indictment on the level of importance Muslims give to *zakat* in majority Muslim countries. In the language of economics, what such *muftis* actually argue for is perhaps akin to a "free rider" effect,[139] which is made all the more unpalatable since in the UK: (1) around 3000 Muslim children come into foster care every year[140]; (2) there are thousands of destitute Muslim families and women every year; (3) hundreds of *maktabs* (afterschool Islamic studies classes) struggle to achieve quality and scale; (4) Islamic scholarship is yet to truly inspire Muslims in the British experience to achieve a moral, Godly plane; and (5) there is a need to pick-up the pieces in exceptional tragedies like Grenfell Tower where there is failure of the state and local authority etc.

This kind of uncontextualised reasoning completely ignores *zakat's* highly specialised, philosophically socio-political, role. The role of *zakat*,

---

[137] See *hadith* narrated by 'Abdullah bin Umar in *Sunan Abu Dawud*: "The Messenger of Allah as saying: 'Each of you is a shepherd and each of you is responsible for his flock. The *amir* (ruler) who is over the people is a shepherd and is responsible for his flock; a man is a shepherd in charge of the inhabitants of his household and he is responsible for his flock; a woman is a shepherdess in charge of her husband's house and children and she is responsible for them; and a man's slave is a shepherd in charge of his master's property and he is responsible for it. So each of you is a shepherd and each of you is responsible for his flock.'"

[138] For details See: Mufti Faraz Adam, *Our Zakat Distribution Strategy - Juristic Evidences and Explanations*, NZF, May 2018. See also: Mamnun Khan, *Contextual development of the Hanafi Madhhab: implications for UK Muslims sending zakat abroad and the eight zakat-eligible categories*, 2018.

[139] "Free-rider" effect occurs when people can benefit from a good/service without paying anything towards it. It also occurs, if people can get away with making only a token contribution (something less than overall benefit).

[140] Source: The Fostering Network.

translated into modern vocabulary, is to ensure that those who aren't beneficiaries of employment, commerce or social policy can be attended to in the localities in which *zakat* is collected. This is what is meant by the reference to "wealthy among them" (*agh-niya-i-him*) in the *hadith*, "...It is to be taken from the wealthy among them and given to the poor."[141] It doesn't in any way negate any of the other multi-dimensional objectives of *zakat*, such as being an act of disciplining and purification of the soul, which some scholars emphasised.[142] *Zakat* is in some respects like investment decisions which we make on the basis of "gap/needs analysis," which we then prioritise based on the size of the impact in terms of its benefit or avoidance of harm. This isn't a modern concoction; many classical and post-classical scholars such Imam al-Qurtubi (1214-1273) held *zakat* to be fulfilling the needs of Muslims as well as assisting and strengthening Islam.[143] On a societal level we can only do this properly if we have a holistic bird's-eye view of the ground. Otherwise it's like seeing someone in mild poverty who struggles to make ends meet from time to time and, as individuals distributing our *zakat* independently, we give all our *zakat* to this one person, but the news of a second person in a worse situation never reaches us, but if it were to, we would probably think twice about being more efficient in how we distributed our *zakat*.

Extending this logic to the eight *zakat*-eligible categories of spend mentioned in the *Qur'an* (9:60), it's very clear how disorganised and

---

[141] *Hadith* narrated by Ibn 'Abbas in *Sahih al-Bukhari*: "The Prophet sent Mu'adh to Yemen and said, 'Invite the people to testify that none has the right to be worshipped but God and I am Allah's Messenger, and if they obey you to do so, then teach them that Allah has enjoined on them five prayers in every day and night (in twenty-four hours), and if they obey you to do so, then teach them that Allah has made it obligatory for them to pay the *zakat* from their property and it is to be taken from the wealthy among them and given to the poor.'"

[142] See discussion in Ahmad al-Raysuni's *Imam al-Shatibi's Theory of the Higher Objectives and intents of Islamic Law*, IIIT, 2005, pp. 175-176.

[143] See: Mufti Faraz Adam, *Our Zakat Distribution Strategy - Juristic Evidences and Explanations*, NZF, May 2018.

negligent we've become.[144] These categories aren't mutually exclusive; God doesn't overly restrict their definitions or relative priorities, and there are already plenty of highly varied and valid differences of interpretation within and across legal schools (*madhahib*). It's clear that those with sectarian zeal exaggerate the authority of medieval legal texts to the extent that they overlook actual social realities and conditions on the ground today where *zakat* is relevant. Yet, arguably, the God-conscious act is to rationally and reasonably decipher how best to discharge responsibility based on the needs of our time and space. Of course, keeping *zakat* local doesn't mean that we stop giving other forms of charity (*sadaqah*) to whatever cause we choose anywhere in the world. But if we fix our own neighbourhood and *zakat* is distributed in a transformative way, imagine how much more *sadaqah* we'll be in a position to give collectively.

---

[144] *Qur'an* 9:60 mentions: "*Sadaqah [Zakat]* are only for the poor (*fuqara*) and for the needy (*masakin*) and for those employed to collect [*zakat*] ('*amilin*) and for bringing hearts together [for Islam] (*muallafat qulubuhum*) and for freeing captives [or slaves] (*riqab*) and for those in debt (*gharimin*) and for the cause of Allah (*fi sabi lillah*) and for the [stranded] traveller (*ibn sabil*) - an obligation [imposed] by Allah. And Allah is Knowing and Wise."

# 2.5 Removing "decoloniality" of its post-colonial hangover

In recent years we've heard much about decolonialism or decoloniality. This is the idea that with European colonisation, a hierarchy of human beings has operated which has organised and justified the subordination of people of colour and women. And now, restitution in modernity requires decolonising knowledge, education, symbols, ideas, social systems and so on that retain the worst aspects of coloniality. This article isn't about undermining the general value of decoloniality movements but to argue that they're often emotionally too caught up in post-colonial hangovers to have the clarity of mature thought, diplomacy and virtue necessary to deal with the issues. As painful as it might be for activists of populist decolonial movements to accept this, my argument is that a critical rethink of the problem space is essential for forging new liberation strategies. Not least because attempts to put right historical wrongs cannot be achieved through mere rhetoric, point scoring or campaigning to remove historical symbols, and the moral motive needs to move beyond idealism and vendetta to embracing the productive attitude of understanding the situation for what it is and being prepared to deal with it accordingly. It matters because it could be the difference between prolonging the *status quo* versus accelerating the removal of barriers for people of colour both at home and around the world.

A central question which decoloniality activists pose is: "What would have been the history of colonised people in the absence of colonisation?" Since we cannot turn time back, we have to recreate scenarios and apply assumptions to explain what could have happened. It is here that a posterior look back can be quite subjective (for academics and social justice activists alike) opening up room for all kinds of fair and unfair claims and counterclaims. What should, instead, interest us as believers of the Islamic faith is to find constructive and efficacious ways of moving things forward.

With this in mind it's important to realise that for the discerning Muslim there are problems with how decoloniality is approached today. For a start, the language of populist decolonial rhetoric can often essentialise people today into identities based on the historical wrongs of previous generations. Such populist attitudes can be quite irritating to ordinary people and doesn't help them to see how they can be part of the solution.

It's already well-recognised, for example, by the likes of Johanna Gotfried Herder (d. 1803) as early as the 18ᵗʰ century that culture is the product of innate human creativity and ought to be approached through their own lenses. Today, it's less about people being at war with one another, and we live in more diverse communities than ever before. And, power-implying interactions are much more subtly juxtaposed; no longer are we talking about military colonial rule, human zoos or slaves being whipped in the field.

In this context, use of shorthand labels like "white man" or "black man," used consciously or otherwise, speak about motives and worldviews on the basis of people's skin colour which is simply far too crude, polarising and unwittingly fuels culturally-specific stereotypes. Similarly, the terms "white-washing," "extremist" and "racist," which are far too casually thrown around, struggle to encourage people to take a look at what's actually going on in the minds of those accused. The point is, using loaded descriptors, while offering a shorthand way of talking about things or even in some cases short-lasting cathartic relief, inevitably deters a "let's fix it" mentality where stakeholders are seen as part of the solution, and key for collective liberation to be possible. The net effect of today's attitude protracts the *status quo*, rather than curtailing it.

A mature approach to decoloniality ought to be willing to bracket out subsidiary ideas, positions or minutiae without having to dispense an overarching direction of effort. Indeed, this kind of ambiguity-tolerance should be one of the lessons of Islamic scholarship for Muslims. For example, despite the author of the famous *tafsir* work *Al-Kash'shaaf* being a chief Mu'tazilite, Abul Qasim al-Zamakhshari (1074-1144), later scholars appreciated its tremendous usefulness for probing the Arabic of the *Qur'an* while bracketing out its alleged "over-rationalising" tendency in parts. The same reasoning was used by Imam al-Bukhari (d. 870) whose insight led him to accept well-known narrators (*rawi*) belonging to the Khawarij sect for whom lying was tantamount to disbelief (*kufr*). Imam al-Bukhari didn't agree with the beliefs of the Khawarij sect, yet accepted some narrators from among them since they more than satisfied his conditions for considering narrators of *hadith* as trustworthy (*dabt*). The same can be said of Abul 'Ala Mawdudi's (d. 1979) *tafsir, Tahfim al-Qur'an;* which, while arguably littered with political ideology, it still holds educational

103

value as a historical socio-political reading. Moreover, being offended by or not agreeing with something weren't sufficient reasons to warrant removal. Imam al-Tabari (839-923), for example, knowingly collected all kinds of weak information in his works for its historical value. Similarly, al-Biruni (973-1050) counselled the ruler Sultan Mahmud Ghazni (971-1030) to preserve the non-Islamic, indeed idolatrous, ancient cultural and religious heritage of India. Many works and events like these can be cited throughout the ages. The point is, when it comes to populist decoloniality movements, such a nuanced attitude is seldom seen. But this is precisely what's needed to identify real pain points and to focus on areas where progress can be made.

When we look back in time to examine the ghastly consequences of colonialism that unfortunately linger on today, it's worth remembering that we're not innocent of today's cultural filters, attitudes or ideologies. As an example, we often parade the phenomenal history of Muslims of Spain, yet from a Christian perspective it was seen as a foreign imposition, enough to provoke even the Muslim Nasrid rulers of the time into what could be arguably interpreted as a guilt-ridden act of carving the interior of the Alhambra palace with the words, "There is no victor except God" (*la ghaliba il-lallah*). Another example would be the East India Company which gained foothold through a divide and conquer strategy because provincial leaders of India were fractious and co-operated with colonialists to gain leverage over local rivals.

How do decoloniality movements reconcile such historical events and where in history should we draw the line? Why should decoloniality stop with the start of colonialism if there were plenty of pre-colonial tyrants and corruption already in evidence in colonised lands? And, how do decolonialists reconcile the moral worth of the many mutual or power-implying interactions between civilisations and cultural exchanges that have productively taken place, even during colonialism?

According to the sociologist Peter Berger's analysis of culture, we project our own experiences onto the outside world (externalisation), then regard these projections as independent (objectification), and finally incorporate these projections into our own psychological consciousness (internalisation). Of course, we're constantly adjusting ourselves in this way, and more often than not we do so reasonably. To validate our assumptions and claims it would be appropriate, then, to ask similar questions of decoloniality as we do of coloniality.

Unless we do so, we risk falling into traps like the recent and now infamous report of "Allah" embroidered on a Viking textile. Where, a small bout of journalistic hype and academic stretch was enough to fool many people. It wasn't until an independent Islamic art historian and archaeologist, Stephennie Mulder, debunked it that others realised what had happened.[145] Popular narratives of decoloniality can be very similar. Today's institutional racism and historic injustices are ready made frameworks for retrospectively attributing failures of the modern world only to the past while ignoring present causes. Little attention is drawn to the things which we can do within our own sphere of influence to fix things today.

Activists also risk relying on mass media to galvanise public pressure, but in doing so trap themselves into the media's lack of nuance and investment to solve complex problems of society. This was very clear in Priyamvaka Gopal's assessment when Cambridge University unfairly came under attack by decolonial activists, where substantive issues became, she observed, "…obscured in this facile attempt at stoking a keyboard race war with real-life consequences at a time when hate crimes are on the rise."[146]

A diversified media would no doubt help, but it's not a guarantee. There will always be a need for erudite, nuanced and caring journalism, regardless of gender, race or belief. Equally, there is a need for greater introspective and pragmatic decoloniality movements.

---

[145] Stephennie Mulder, *The Rise and Fall of the Viking "Allah" Textile*, 27 October 2017, https://www.hyperallergic.com/407746/refuting-viking-allah-textiles-meaning/, retrieved 8 November 2017.
[146] Priyamvada Gopal, *Yes, we must decolonise: our teaching has to go beyond elite white men*, The Guardian, 27 October 2017.

# 2.6 Caliphate: a saviour for the Rohingya or a distraction?

Amidst the continuous stream of harrowing pictures of the displacement of the Rohingya people, in the UK we've seen a resurgence of calls for the re-establishment of the *Khilafah* (or Caliphate). It's an eerie feeling of *déjà-vu* reliving the 1990s when groups, largely made of youth in their late teens to early 30s, appeared touting Caliphate ideology as a means to restoring Muslim identity to its past glory.[147] Following 9/11 and 7/7, greater counters by Muslim communities and increased public scrutiny partially arrested the growth of Caliphate ideology. Many of course matured and simply moved on with their lives. Some continued touting, but took a less confrontational and rabble-rousing approach. However, in what looks like a more recent development, a few in their capacity as "spiritual preachers" have now quite publicly joined the call, albeit on what they reckon are theological grounds rather than out of mere membership of a so-called "Islamic" political group. So, what's actually changed to bring this about?

No doubt, social media has a larger-than-life role in amplifying fringe voices and opinions, voices which didn't exist in the 1990s as they do now. What's more, opinions and news items decay as quickly as they become popularised on social media. The sheer volume of recirculating information, data points and opinions hitting us every day seldom contribute independently and meaningfully to the world outside. To cite an example, in a conference held at the London Muslim Centre on the Rohingya situation, there was a show of hands to see who had contacted their MP to urge the UK Government to act. Out of perhaps a thousand attendees less than 50 had. In other words, when it comes to the hard graft of actually doing something meaningful, even as simple as sending an email, few will overcome barriers of laziness, inability, time or other constraints. My point is, calling for a Caliphate, in the end, amounts to little more than hyperbole.

Oddly, none of the "spiritual preachers" and activists calling for the Caliphate are known for their experience in international law and

---

[147] Prominent groups were Hizb-ut Tahrir, Al-Muhajiroun and to a lesser extent Jamat-i-Islami.

diplomacy, or expertise in *al-siyasah al-shar'iyyah* ("political Islam"),[148] or for their involvement in local or national government, foreign policy bodies, or have any track record in academia. Yet, the seeming authority with which some preach about how to resolve geopolitical problems through political intervention would have many believing otherwise. Preaching such idealism on social media, or from the pulpit, perpetuates a great disconnect with the way Muslims actually experience life. As Imam al-Ghazali noted in his *Ihya' 'Ulum al-Din* (*The Revival of Religious Knowledge*), many jurists (*fuqaha*) of his time were too engrossed with the minutia of legal practices that they became disconnected from what really mattered to people. Fast forward to the late Ottoman period and, yet again, we find the same: the authors of the *Ottoman Courts Hanafi Manual of Law* (*Majallah al-Ahkam al-'Adliyya*, 1877) criticised the lack of grounding in the practical propositions of the *Shari'ah* among jurists. Those "spiritual preachers" who call for the Caliphate today arguably fit into this category.

Even a simple reading of the Prophetic example (*Sunnah*) indicates that in the public realm the objective is always to offer workable solutions as appropriate to circumstances. This begs the question, what exactly is a Caliphate today? Is it fulfilled only if the "entire" Muslim world lives under a single contiguous central political authority: one presidential-style leader and a single *Shar'i* legal code implemented in its "entirety" and what is "entirety" in this context? Or is it sufficient if it covers a single region or country? What if the country is as small as Qatar, or as poor as Ethiopia, or as sprawling as the Maldives? Does it have to include an axis of Egypt-Saudi Arabia-Turkey, and if so, why should it be these countries which account for only a fifth of the world's Muslims and don't share borders with each other? What's so different about Iran's theocracy with its own implemented Islamic legal code and a supreme spiritual leader? What makes the Caliphate of ISIS any different to the one espoused, beyond their theological excommunications? Is it a federal republic like the USA, built on a single constitution? Will the constitution simply be the *Qur'an* and the *Sunnah*, and if so, whose interpretation will be authoritative?

The point is, there is no hard and fast rule. At best, there is a lot of

---

[148] *Al-siyasah al-shar'iyyah* captures the general meaning of public policy for good governance based on Islamic law, for governing territories under Muslim rule.

conjecture and conceptions remain highly subjective. Given this, can it be expected of the average Muslim to evaluate such subjectivity in pursuance of the Caliphate's formation? Is it even Prophetic to pursue such a vague expression, especially where it is at the cost of actually doing something meaningful in the now? The point here is not to discount governance as a means of Muslim self-determination, nor political philosophy found within revelatory texts (*nass*), nor to downplay the role of Islamic law, but to highlight the simplistic rhetoric that serves for little except chest-beating and compensating for one's lack of meaningful action.

Of course, pundits will claim to have got all of this worked out. They will mine classical texts on the matter of Caliphate, linguistically and politically rooted in the exigencies of the medieval era, and present it doctrinally as a particular manifestation and in a specific vernacular, taken as a determined theological tenet. Some advocates have suggested that the most important action for us is to realise the importance of re-establishing the Caliphate in the Muslim world by firstly studying its economic and military benefits. Yet, if most Muslims haven't even studied economics to GCSE level, can it be expected of them to know where to begin? The farce that the Brexit vote became, with the absurd expectation that the masses might evaluate economic pros and cons should be informative here.

As for military benefits, to believe that a Caliphate would simply intervene in Myanmar is to assume that the norms of modern international law would not be a barrier, and that other nations will simply cast away their own strategic interests. The reality is that Muslim countries co-operate poorly with each other, and have a hard time overcoming their own political wrangling. Just look how dismally the GCC (Gulf Co-operation Council) members have railed against Qatar to get them to comply with some rather strange demands. Worse still, look at how Saudi Arabia and Iran struggle to come to mutual understanding and instead continue to be invested in a proxy war in Yemen, while one of biggest man-made humanitarian catastrophes so far this century goes on.

My question then is, if most Muslims cannot even write to their MPs what makes activists so sure that under a Caliphate they would be so willing to wage war? Besides, where would the fiscal budget for such military prowess come from if at least 25% of the world's Muslim population is in abject poverty, youth unemployment is at 33% in places like Egypt, and the rate of investment in infrastructure can hardly meet the needs of growing populations. The point is, preaching the idealism of a super-state, supreme-leader ruled, with basic legal codes referenced as the *Shari'ah* and that only seems to manifest with the linguistics of violence (*jihad* and *hudud*), lacks a shockingly basic awareness of the environment we live in, or to know what God is asking of us.

The brunt of the nationalist xenophobic resentment meted out by extremists intensified after Myanmar was no longer administered as a province of the British Raj in 1938. But when colonialists first entered Myanmar, where was the Caliphate of the time? Are calls for re-establishing a Caliphate a sign of unconscious bias among the new breed of "spiritual leaders" (as it was for political activists of the 1990s) that views the 1400-year history of Muslim "unity" and political union through rose-tinted glasses?

In all of this, what is most disconcerting is that social media broadcasts encouraging Muslims to embrace Caliphate ideology are a step back into the 1990s which evidently got Muslims nowhere and significantly stunted a mature political outlook. What activists and "spiritual preachers" fail to recognise is that when preaching to thousands of people on social media they take on a scattergun approach; there is no way of knowing if what they're saying is being internalised with the right nuance or if it's simply igniting emotions. Rousing calls to the Caliphate in the 1990s led to a whole generation of activists becoming distracted by an unrealisable rhetoric from unsubstantial doctrinal commitments. And this, in turn, caused a great deal of pain for Muslim identity. Knowing this, we are at liberty to challenge such rhetoric in order to safeguard future generations from such simplistic ways of thinking and imbue them with attitudes that are revelation-based guidance. It will be possible then to understand what is feasible and reflect what God wants of believers true to their capacities and situations.

## 2.7 Undoing the damage of "non-violent Caliphates"

The notion of "Islamist extremism" to many commentators is a spectrum which at one end has "violent fanatics," the likes of Daesh/ISIS and Al-Qaeda, followed by "sympathetic fanatics," through to the other end, the so-called "non-violent Caliphates" seeking to re-establish a *Khilafah* or Caliphate using non-violent means. Government policies have for some time assumed, at least tacitly, that non-violent extremism leads progressively to violence. How, if, or to what extent that happens is of course much debated and many explanations of radicalisation theory and, indeed, contentious definitions of "non-violent extremism" have been offered. Exactly why the government chose to take such a course, it could be argued, was at least partly because of what seems like an elephant in the room: the confrontational activities of British non-violent Caliphates who from the 1990s did much to cement an idealised image of Islam and Muslims.

For nearly a decade before 9/11 non-violent Caliphates were by far the most active political voices among Muslim activists in Britain.[149] They were young and articulate, but had a very naïve take on what is otherwise a complex relationship between society, religion and politics. It meant that they were quite easily seduced by the "endism"[150] of a "pan-Islamic State" or Caliphate as the *bona fide* answer to grievances and socio-political problems in the Muslim world.

In return, new Caliphates got answers. They became aware of a political dimension of Islam (*al-siyasah al-shar'iyyah*) which they seldom heard in mosques, albeit grossly decontextualised and misappropriated. They also acquired a new-found identity as exponents of Islamic politics and a greater sense of belonging to a group that had meaning for their existence. Moral relativity became at once banished. All that mattered was the triumphalist rhetoric of separation between them and what they saw were Western neo-colonial impulses, dystopia and contradictions.

Unfortunately, the damage was done. This period spread among some

---

[149] Sadek Hamid, *Sufis, Salafis and Islamists - The Contested Ground of British Islamic Activism*, I.B. Tauris, 2016, pp. 33-50.
[150] Endism is "the belief that something of significant scope and duration, particularly something negative, is coming to an end."

a narrow, politicised take on Islam, where Islam was reduced to a mere political ideology (*mabda'*[151]). It became necessary to see world events through narrow, political filters. The mother of all root causes to problems of society, international conflicts, poverty etc., was almost always retro-fitted to the lack of a Caliphate. As time went on, some in Britain splintered into a violent streak in the form of "sympathetic fanatics."

Mosques for their part took to banning Caliphate literature. Many Islamic teachers and imams did much to refute non-violent Caliphates, though most struggled to deconstruct their arguments intellectually. And with that, despite sporadic effort, a well-organised, robust, alternative narrative and strategy was lacking. On the side of policy makers, and some sections of British media too, this period did much to hard-wire a particularly sweeping take on political imperatives normative to Islam, one that would have found salience in intolerant Orientalist images or post-colonial expressions.

Eventually, as is often the case with extreme tendencies, counter reactions are born. The Quilliam Foundation, a prime example, was founded by those who were themselves once non-violent Caliphates. They now positioned themselves as bludgeon-cum-saviour: the apparent voice of liberal rationalism to counter non-violent Caliphates. But their lack of connection with Muslim communities was very telling. And to top it all off, alliances forged with sinister organisations who it turned out were more interested in stoking anti-Muslim hatred,[152] meant that they quickly lost credibility and became an inverted mirror image of the very extremists they were trying to oppose.

The damage, however, was unrelenting. In all of this the relationship between Muslims and also of the Islamic faith, with the government and parts of the media became progressively less and less about the sincerity of faith (*iman*) and people coming together in mutual respect and harmony.

---

[151] *Mabda'* is an Arabic term for "principle," and when used in context to today's politics it lacks assumptions to do with modern democratic conventions of coming into power, the development of party politics, the modern "nation state system" or international conventions of citizenship and rules-based order etc.

[152] Nafeez Ahmed, *How Violent Extremists Hijacked London-Based 'Counter-Extremism' Think Tank*, https://www.alternet.org/world/how-violent-extremists hijacked-london-based-counter-extremism-think-tank, 28 April 2015.

Beneath the surface the problem with the non-violent Caliphates is their lack of erudition, immature attitude and clumsy use of language. What non-violent Caliphates meant by *din* to describe Islam as "a way of life" was brazenly synonymised with the term "ideology" in an effort to contrast against other political and economic systems like democracy, capitalism, socialism etc. But in doing so they lost the very spirit and holistic form of Islam.

In his book, *The End of Ideology*,[153] the sociologist Daniel Bell describes ideology as "reification, a frozen mimicry of reality, a hypostatization of terms that gives false life to categories. And that it is also its fatal flaw, its Achilles' heel, which leaves it vulnerable in the end to other forms of cognition and faith." It's "frozen" because it lacks an adaptive quality. However, the *Qur'anic* paradigm, as a living speech, asserts that help is there "for anyone who wants to ask" (12:7). The word of God (*kalam Allah*) meets people's own spaces and contexts as guidance-in-the-making if the right attention is given to it.

In fact, God and Prophetic ways (*Sunnah*) speak about knowing God as a process realised through striving with good action. And Muslims believe that people are naturally predisposed (*fitrah*) to believe in God, and to prefer good and virtue. In practice, whether one achieves this or not is another matter. However, to call Islam an ideology implies that Muslims can act unnaturally or irrationally yet still remain normative to the religion. Moreover, the idea that ideology follows when power is exercised without some ideas or beliefs that justify support, implying that submitting to God is not something self-evident or natural, is not at all as linear or mechanistic in the life of a believer.

Islam has never been viewed historically as a "political solution" that avoids the element of test or conditionality, or the ever-present need to refine one's character (*adab*), to strive for sincerity (*ikhlas*), to act with excellence (*ihsan*), or to remain in need of God (*faqr*). The word "solution" is often appropriated by non-violent Caliphates to give the impression of "definitive/final political outcomes" even though nothing before the Hereafter can be deemed absolutely final, and politics certainly doesn't even come close to it. In the Islamic paradigm people are tasked to continuously seek to improve and finesse their character, responsibilities and subservience to God. To

---

[153] Daniel Bell, *The End of Ideology*, Harvard University Press, 2000.

the extent that even good actions are necessarily qualified by a state of imperfection, striving and seeking God's acceptance. Thus, to label Islam as an ideology is to grossly overlook all of these aspects.

Moreover, the motivations of non-violent Caliphates are set against a number of reality checks, as interpreted by well-known scholars and thinkers. Some argue that the so-called "Islamic world" is only a place where Muslims live, where Islam is followed as a culture but not as a faith. And certainly, where they "are not able to come into contact with one another and constitute a union, to work together to solve common problems, to interpret the universe, to understand it well, to consider the universe carefully according to the *Qur'an*, to interpret the future well, to generate projects for the future, to determine their place in the future."[154] It thus seems somewhat fanciful to talk of a *bona fide* "Islamic world."

Others argue that the Prophetic model of Caliphate ended with the *Khulafa al-Rashidun*, the four rightly-guided Caliphs (632-661). In the words of the great historiographer, Ibn Khaldun (1332-1406), with the rise of the Umayyads the Caliphate system turned into one of "Royal Authority." Leaders gave "preference to their own sons and brothers, [and] in that respect depart[ed] from the *Sunnah* of the first four caliphs."[155] It was the restraining influence of Islam, Ibn Khaldun argued, which gave way to people's worldly motivations. The knowledge and interpretation of Islam, including in the public realm, by consequence depended increasingly on independent scholarship which quickly became the mechanism through which the integrity and legal authority of Islam came to be preserved.

Yet others argue that Muslims aren't able to articulate a normative conception of Islamic government for today's world. This is partly because the nature of modern government isn't the same as what's been articulated in medieval books of Islamic law, like al-Mawardi's *The Laws of Islamic Governance* (*Al-Ahkam al-Sultaniyyah*). The nation-state system and democratic conventions of coming into power, social mores, as well as the expectation of conforming to international conventions of citizenship and rules-based order etc. have all vastly changed.

Some scholars also argue that because "we do not fulfil the

---

[154] M. Fethullah Gulen, *Essay - Perspective - Opinions*, The Light, 2006, pp. 130-131.
[155] Ibn Khaldun, *The Muqaddimah*, translated by Franz Rosenthal, 2005, pp. 167-170.

commandments of Allah and refrain from the forbidden in our [own] personal lives over which we have full control and there is no obstacle or compulsion," it follows that if that's not possible, how would it be possible that we are entrusted with governing? Thus, it is argued, "when we are not doing this in the sphere of our own choice (in our individual lives), how can it be expected, when tomorrow we are given the reins of government, we shall do so?"[156]

In practical terms, too, ordinary Muslims right across the world see the value of Islam, but rather than be told by an authoritarian-like group or state to "conform or else," they would prefer to embrace faith out of their own inner devotion and love for God in a mutual relationship with the state. The non-violent Caliphate narrative thus comes across as telling ordinary Muslims who may not know much more than the basic rites of Islam that the complete way of life of being subservient to God requires political activism as a priority. You can expect at this point of course that the rebellious, aggrieved, vulnerable or overzealous take most notice.

Given these reality checks, one cannot help but notice just how reactionary and misguided non-violent Caliphates were. And they, alongside other sociological factors,[157] did much to obfuscate many from establishing deeper theocentric cultural roots in Britain.

The government for their part would do well to see that the Muslim communities' failure to respond to non-violent Caliphates was not because they tacitly supported it, but far from it, it was because they lacked the right civic structures, leadership and institutions. Thus, counter-extremism policy must somehow take this into account to be seen as fair, targeted and proportionate. It also means that today's ideological threat of radicalisation ought not to be over-conflated with the more sociological challenges of integration.

For their part, Muslim communities would do well to go back to the future, as it were, to dispassionately reflect, study, and find answers to past failures and missed opportunities. The term *muhasabah*, a type

---

[156] See: *Malfoozat : Discourses of Maulana Ilyas*, Islamic Book Service India, 2000.

[157] Factors include: the lack of scholars and institutions; generational gaps; lack of opportunity in society and subsequent marginalization; lack of standards and platforms for accelerating Muslim communities to thrive and achieve their potential etc.

of self-criticism, when at a convenient time one critically evaluates one's actions until finding oneself failing judgement and being motivated to doing better next time, is something Muslims should be habitually tuned into.

## 2.8 Saving our mosques

The UK has around 2000 mosques ranging from mega-complexes like the East London Mosque with space for over 10,000 people to small terraced buildings like the mosque on the corner of Chapel Street on the Isle of Wight which has space for perhaps no more than 100. As an overall ratio, there's roughly one mosque in the UK for every 1350 Muslims.[158] If we remove the under 4's (12%) and over 65's (4%) who we perhaps wouldn't normally expect to frequent mosques so much, the ratio improves to one mosque for every 1200 Muslims. If we then remove the 48% women, the ratio becomes one mosque for every 550 Muslim men.[159] The latter stat suggests that aside from an increase in the rate of male mosque-goers or from a natural increase in the Muslim population, future growth in mosque numbers and sizes would depend heavily on women's attendance or expansion in the provision of community services. Excluding outlier days like Eid and Friday when congregations are always the biggest, elementary after-school Arabic classes (*maktab*) and the occasional "*iman* booster"[160] talk, the proportion of regular congregants (attending mosque for at least once a day) is probably no more than 2-3% of the UK's Muslim population. That's roughly a mean average of 30-40 attendees in every mosque at prayer time (*salah*).

That said, 2000 mosques is a significant achievement. After all, it's only been about 60 or so years since the start of mass migration of Muslims from the old British empire. And it's a fair number considering that the first mosque, the Abdullah Quilliam Mosque on Mount Vernon Street in Liverpool was established in 1887, or the "Turkish-style" replica built by William Chambers on a whim in Kew Gardens in 1761. However, these stats aside, there are good reasons to believe that many mosques are struggling on a number of fronts. In light of this, it's brilliant and courageous to see the MCB (Muslim Council of Britain) launch a groundbreaking

---

[158]  Based on 2011 census data, includes male and female.

[159]  For more stats, see the MCB's very useful summary, *British Muslims in Numbers: A Demographic, Socio-economic and Health profile of Muslims in Britain drawing on the 2011 Census,* January 2015.

[160]  See: Mohammed Nizami, *Boosters and Softeners: Replacing proper religion*, April 2017.

"Our Mosques Our Future" conference to explore solutions to systemic, underlying issues. So, what are some of these issues?

A look at the impact of demographic changes is usually a good place to start, where a number of trends are emerging. Firstly, in many towns, Muslims are living further away from mosques and often establishing new smaller mosques, mainly for *maktab* services and convenient communal prayer spaces. Consequently, in many towns, resources (finance, expertise, skills etc.) are spread thinly across mosques making the economics of scale and quality (of imams, community services, general experience etc.) less likely. It doesn't help that the management committees and trustees of mosques generally aren't good collaborators prepared to share best practices and resources due to sectarian or ethnic differences, lacking professional standards, and interpersonal politics. Cue the lack of inspiration to attract the right kind of "thinkers" and "doers" as volunteers for the upkeep and spirit of "community hub" that a Prophetic model for a mosque demands. It's made worse by a lack of confidence among those running mosques, fearing external influence and questions will only lead to a dilution of religion.

Secondly, an overwhelming majority of mosques still don't adequately cater for women despite their huge socio-spiritual potential. However, we're not short of edicts (*fatawa*) explicitly arguing the lawfulness of unfettered access for women. Notable examples include Shaykh Mohammad Akram Nadwi's translation and annotation of Ibn Hazm's 10th century *fatwa*,[161] and Dr Jasser Auda's *fatwa* titled *Are Women Welcome in the Mosque?*[162] Nevertheless, I have yet to come across one that offers a compelling holistic approach to the issue, combining *fiqh* with considerations about the practical dilemmas and challenges on the ground that require non-*fiqhi*

---

[161] Ibn Hazm, *The Lawfulness of Women's Prayer in The Mosque*, translated & annotated by Shaykh Mohammad Akram Nadwi, Interface Publications, 2015 and 2018.
[162] Jasser Auda, *Are Women Welcome in the Mosque?*, http://aboutislam.net/shariah/contemporary-issues/are-women-welcome-to-the-mosque-part-1/, 1 June 2017.

interventions.[163] Overall, this can be distilled into four contentions as I see them.

(1) The issue is largely a South Asian religio-cultural expression. Turkish, Arab or African Muslims don't in the main have this problem, and I'm certain that if the majority of British Muslims didn't descend from South Asia we would be having a different discussion.

(2) It also reflects the cultural patriarchy of these places which continues among women of first and second generation in particular, who conform to norms that largely make them absent from public religious discourses. This means that in practice there is as yet only a nascent internal demand (among third generation and particularly millennials), and certainly actual demand is geographically sporadic. As third generation and millennials aren't yet in positions of authority, calls for change will likely be an uphill struggle on the ground.

(3) There is a lack of willingness and courage by exclusively male management committees to recognise the changing lifestyles of Muslim women and families and therefore to be more accommodating. While some recognise the absurdity that "women are free to go shopping" yet aren't given space to pray to their Lord in what is after all the "House of Allah," they then lack the necessary courage to step out of their comfort zones, and to go against the social pressure to conform.

---

[163] Marion Holmes Katz, *Women in the Mosque - A History of Legal Thought and Social Practice*, Columbia University Press, 2014. Although this book provides a very good overall analysis of legal thought, on the Hanafi texts section the author hasn't considered what it would take to contextualise to today's standards of equality of access to buildings specific to the British or Western contexts, and in view of the changed needs of third generation Muslims. There was a general hardening in the Hanafi *madhhab* against women going to mosques over time which coincided with changing conditions in societies outside of the West, but those conditions may not apply at all anywhere let alone in the West, or the risk of thinking that it still applies would have far greater harms to Muslims seeking to firmly establish their faith as something reasonable in Western societies.

(4) Many mosques are heavily constrained by physical space or financial burdens and so spending to build separate toilet and ablution (*wudu*) facilities, privacy, and possibly crèche facilities can be a tricky case to make.

Thirdly, the lack of progress on English-speaking and British-trained imams who can contextualise Islam for us in the UK is another major area of improvement. A study by Professor Ron Geaves in 2007 found that out of 300 British imams, 83.7% were from South Asian origin and 91.9% weren't born or educated in the UK. While a number of recent policy reports[164] have also made similar references, in practice there are more fundamentally-rooted issues. (1) There are few institutes in the UK that professionally train imams for public service with the insight to contextualise meaningfully in modern Britain, overcoming cognitive dissonance for instance. (2) There is generally a lack of foresight and courage by Muslims to perceive mosques as places of vigorous intellectual pursuits of "What does God want of us?" and "What is the Prophetic guidance for us?" (3) Mosque culture in some places is caught up in the sentiment of preserving what is usually a mish-mash of low-grade Pakistani/Bangladeshi/Somali ethno-culture, as opposed to perhaps a "high culture" typified by an acquaintance with literature, learning, philosophy, history, arts etc. This, in turn, acts as a barrier to mosques becoming inclusive community hubs.

Now, there has been a flurry of activity in many mosques in recent years to sort out some basic housekeeping like DBS checks for those involved in teaching kids in mosques, instituting policies for safeguarding, health and safety, and fire etc. However, training and upskilling of management committees and trustees has struggled to be prioritised.

In all of this, perhaps the single biggest factor which is arguably already impacting many mosques is the rampant apathy and disinterestedness of third generation Muslims. Partly this is because there is a wider process of society becoming more socially atomised. With more third generation Muslims becoming middle class, they're living busier and more

---

[164] For example: Citizens UK's report, *The Missing Muslims: Unlocking British Muslim Potential for the Benefit of All* published in June 2017, and Dame Louise Casey's report, *A Review of Opportunity and Integration*, published December 2016.

community-independent lifestyles. Finding committed and competent volunteers has become increasingly challenging as a result. Mosques are no longer the only opportunity to volunteer (*khidma*) or to work in service of God. A plethora of choices exist between diverse charity organisations, at hospitals, at work and so on. All of which must somehow be accommodated alongside the demands of a career, raising children, looking after elderly parents etc. Given this trend, unless the mosque scene changes for the better the next generation will have little confidence in them, and there will be a filtering process by which the least able will remain associated with them. But if Islam is to bring value to British society, our mosques will have to play a pivotal role, and more will have to become thriving community hubs.

# 2.9 "Visit My Mosque"

For many of us the "Visit My Mosque" day in 2018 will be remembered as a day when we opened up our mosques to those who may never have been in one. Up and down the country there was a sense of excitement, a buzz, for not just the seemingly hurried mosque volunteers but also non-Muslims who attended them. As one visitor explained, "I just didn't know what to expect, but I've been made so welcome." Many others left feedback where descriptors like "amazing," "excellent," "countering hate with love," and "really enjoyed it" were abound. It gained the attention of Theresa May and Jeremy Corbyn, both of whom showed solidarity by visiting their local mosques. And at one point #VisitMyMosque was trending in the top 10 hashtags. So, to what extent was it a success?

Looking at the headline stats to start with, we can see a significant increase in the number of participating mosques, up more than 50 year-on-year in 2017 to more than 200 or so in 2018 (and over 250 in 2019). That's an increase by a third with roughly 10% coverage of all mosques in the UK. If we believe a mean average of 35-50 visitors to each mosque, the total across the UK was perhaps somewhere in the region of approximately 7000-10,000. Considering that this is only the fourth year the initiative has run, these numbers are quite reasonable and momentum is certainly building with each year. Many mosques which took part for the first time were from traditionally non-MCB affiliated segments. This level of cross-sectional involvement with mosques embracing the "Visit My Mosque" branding is a sign of slowly loosening patterns among hitherto entrenched herding by sectarian, political or ethnic affiliations. What it proves is that the MCB's strategy for engagement is working.

A breakdown of visitors shows a more mixed and varied picture across mosques and between towns and cities. One common theme is the sizeable contingent of non-Muslim visitors who were already familiar with mosques and have well-established relationships with them. Among them were the police and fire services, politicians, councillors and faith groups, all of whom, you could argue have roles in fostering cohesion and community building which necessitates turning up to these events in show of support. Of the previously unmosqued non-Muslim visitors, which accounts for 90% of the British population according to a YouGuv poll,[165] the demographics, anecdotally speaking, look somewhat skewed towards older people. The portion of younger non-Muslims, who are arguably mostly passive to organised religion, and those from volunteering sectors, professions and the private sector were disproportionately few.

It's important to have a well-thought-out engagement strategy for this latter unmosqued group. The divergence between the seemingly "religious setting" and the seemingly "not so religious setting" is arguably at the heart of the public's perception of the value of being Godly and organised religion. This dichotomy also strengthens the perception of "cultic religion" among non-Muslims and for Muslims it drives cynicism with an unhealthy focus on risk and protection rather than gratitude and confidence in navigating the modern world. Breaking the back of this requires speaking of God in the modern vocabulary that provides a deeper, more meaningful and enlightening insight which many arguably struggle with.

There's good practice in some mosques which organisers would do well to share. Mosques where volunteers went out canvassing people door-to-door not just with flyers but pausing to have a conversation were more successful in attracting visitors. But it wasn't all about simply canvassing in the run up to this one event. Successful mosques already had outreach activities without all the showboating that goes on. This indirectly comes back to the problem of location. Unsurprisingly, most of our mosques are in areas of large Muslim populations, and so the engagement becomes more challenging while the need for opening up increases.

So, if Visit My Mosque 2018 was good, how can it be better next year? Here are some ideas to think about. (1) Mosques should invite local news reporters from print and television and focus on putting out good news messages. (2) Mosque volunteers who work in major organisations should seek corporate sponsorship or PR similar to the very cool Ben and Jerry's tweet. (3) Volunteers should upskill themselves in articulating faith in a way rooted in real-life, showing their human side, and not overly focus on romantic notions of past glory. (4) All mosques should invite members from the local charity sector, particularly from those

---

[165] See: *90% of people haven't been inside a mosque - change that this weekend!*, http://www.mcb.org.uk/90-of-people-havent-been-inside-a-mosque-change-that-this-weekend/, retrieved 18 February 2018.

charities which are well-known to wider society - Barnados, Oxfam, Red Cross etc. (5) Mosques should co-ordinate activities with local Scout/ Guide groups. 6) Mosques should make it a matter of routine to carry out productive outreach activities throughout the year in areas where there are few Muslims, though sensitivity applies of course. (7) In the run-up to the event, each town should take out a collective advert in their local newspaper or on social media. (8) Each mosque volunteer should take it upon them to invite a minimum of ten visitors and compete with each other to see who can bring in the most visitors. (9) Mosques should make it an interesting experience by organising a variety of activities from tours, providing food, presentations, displays of art, to showing prayer in action etc. (10) Volunteers should explain that it isn't necessary for non-Muslim women visiting mosques to wear a headscarf in order to make the point that Islam doesn't compel non-Muslims. (11) Mosques should give out welcome packs containing not just a good translation of the *Qur'an* but also literature about the positive contribution of Muslims to Western society in the past and today, as well as literature about common misconceptions. (12) Mosques should practice open days by doing them in Ramadhan too.

To conclude, you might wonder why we should go to this length to champion mosques. Of course, there are many good reasons, but perhaps the one that stands out for me is about being "Muslim to God." In the broad sense this entails being steeped in the virtue of high aspiration (*'uluwwul himmah*) built on knowledge (*'ilm*), sincerity (*ikhlas*) and desire (*irada*) to achieve excellence (*ihsan*). Our mosques need to embody all of that.

## 2.10 *Nikah* versus civil marriage?

Following Myriam François-Cerrah's Channel 4 documentary *The Truth About Muslim Marriage*,[166] there's been a fair amount of discussion on the lack of legal rights that women expose themselves to if they enter into *nikah* (religious marriage contract) and not, additionally, a civil marriage contract. The survey of 923 respondents across 14 cities showed some startling findings. 61% didn't have a legally-binding civil ceremony. About 10% were polygamous *nikah* marriages. 3% were polygamous *nikah* marriages where consent was lacking. For anyone close to community goings-on, these stats aren't at all surprising, but they do shed empirical insights into a plethora of issues for women. Of course, almost anything to do with "Muslim" and "women" has the potential for notoriety in our current climate of social media-driven identity politics. However, that aside, I don't think there's any denying of the need for practical solutions in situations today where women looking for legal protection can feel incredibly let down. Thus, the documentary primarily called for British law to recognise *nikah* as a legally-binding marriage contract. But is it as simple as that, and is this the right call to make to address the problems women face effectively at this point in time?

*Nikah* is a contractual agreement between a husband and a wife based on principles of Islamic law (*Shari'ah*). While for a very small number the *nikah* is an interest out of social expectation, for most it's an act of virtue of following the Prophet's *Sunnah*. However, it isn't without social intrigue and family politics, which isn't unusual for weddings generally, not least since friends and family are involved. For third generation Muslims of the UK, deciding how much the dowry should be, should it include jewellery, should it be paid upfront or in instalments, or should the bride's-side exercise their right to demand a sizeable dowry as a deposit for a house for the newlyweds, or should the *nikah* ceremony take place at a mosque or in the home, and who should act as the "guardian" (*wali*) if the father has passed away can all be tricky dilemmas to negotiate.

All of that before the cultural taboo with the bride expected to avoid being seen uttering her consent ("*kabool*") too quickly. In some cases, this

---

[166] *The Truth About Muslim Marriage*, Channel 4, https://www.channel4.com/programmes/the-truth-about-muslim-marriage, aired on 21 November 2017.

can end up being a long-drawn-out saga where "*desi* aunties" gather around to hear the bride officially accept the marriage proposal, and shedding tears together. This sometimes happens even though the bride may have already happily taken part in a prenuptial engagement party (known in Bengali as "*pan-cini*"). Part of this reflects bashfulness (*haya*) and ethnic customs. Part of it perhaps also reflects anxieties with arranged marriages compared to, say, a socially liberal situation where the bride and groom have some experience of cohabiting or dating. While such ethno-cultural conventions and family politics might not have much to do with the letter of the *nikah* law, they are nevertheless experiences which prospective couples go through.

These kinds of experiences can be greatly amplified if the marriage breaks down. Divorce (*talaq*) is seldom free of emotional scars or acrimony, at least in the short-term. And just like in any legal system where people look for ways to protect their own material interests or refuse to co-operate, this is no different when it comes to the *nikah* in Islamic law. In divorce proceedings most Muslims tread a commonsense line. They must do so because the *nikah* contract isn't regulated by any credible overseeing body as such. Conformity to the letter of the original *nikah* contract varies greatly too. Divorce mediation can be fraught with its own politics, where often the biggest obstacle for women is identifying who they can "go to" to redress grievances. Divorce is still socially perceived to bring shame on parents which doesn't help. Moreover, since the nature of the *nikah* contract is religious and religious institutions in the UK today are generally male dominated, it's not women who divorce-seeking women must typically interact with to realise their rights.

It remains to be seen as to what extent any of these issues will be solved simply by recognising the *nikah* as a legally-standing contract under British law. Here are some more complications. Firstly, the *nikah* contract doesn't seek to prevent an already married man from marrying again, unlike British marriage laws against polygamy. This means, unless the *fiqh* (school-based Islamic laws) of *nikah* evolves to mandate monogamy or polygamy is decriminalised in British law, which is unlikely, we'll have completely unworkable directly contradicting laws.

Secondly, to recognise *nikah* properly it would be necessary to recognise the process for annulling the contract through the *talaq* process, but this would open up yet more issues. As applied in the UK, the *talaq* process lacks standards and compliance checks. After all, it's usually done through imams, mosque committee members or elderly members of the family who aren't necessarily trained professionally to do so. In the most whacky cases, it's possible for complete quacks to perform *nikah* ceremonies. Both *nikah* and *talaq* processes, as currently implemented, thus aren't nearly as robust enough as they need to be for a civilian court of law.

These contentions are now becoming better recognised. In a landmark divorce case brought to the High Court in 2018, the presiding judge applied English law to a *nikah* marriage and dismissed the husband's attempt to block his wife's civil divorce petition based on his argument of being married only under *Shari'ah* law. While it was the first case law of an English Court recognising an Islamic marriage, it certainly didn't positively defend *nikah* as an institution. Rather, the Court declared the *nikah* as a non-marriage and delegitimized the *talaq* system, with the judge arguing that this was necessary in order to, at least in this case, prevent abuse and to establish the rights of the wife.[167]

Putting these considerations aside, isn't the big elephant in the room one of education and awareness? How is it possible that the civil ceremony doesn't come into discussion for so many third generation Muslim couples? And why is there a lack of standards and bodies overseeing *nikah* contracts? Surely, these are more pressing questions, solutions to which are far more workable and likely to alleviate the problems identified.

---

[167] Harriet Sherwood, *English law applies to Islamic marriage, judge rules in divorce case*, The Guardian, 1 August 2018.

# 2.11 Why the "post-truth" age is "fake news"

With the election of Donald Trump and in light of arguments over Brexit on both sides, some have claimed that we're now living in a "post-truth" age. It is implied that we've somehow shifted from an apparent age of "truth" where objective facts were more influential in shaping public opinion than appeals to emotion and personal belief, to an age that comes after truth, where objective facts are less influential. Whilst use of this rhetorical device dramatises a certain effect in politics or to make a point about the nature of people, electioneering, or today's media culture, digging a little deeper reveals an elaborate conscious dishonesty in the term "post-truth."

If I am not mistaken "two plus two" still equals four, and we still experience feelings of hunger and tiredness if we go for long periods without food. Since this is the case, we must recognise that truths are surely not beyond human beings. Is, then, the use of the term "post-truth" a failure to obtain knowledge about the complexities of modern socio-political phenomena because we're caught up in concurrent events which we don't fully understand yet? Is this resolved through merely brandishing a new term like "post-truth?" What about taking, instead, a look at the nature of truth itself? Are we moving into an age where information, ideas, opinions, and in fact just about anything meets and interpenetrates anything to the extent that what we know or expect to be "true" is now being challenged in previously unimaginable ways?

As with many things in life, answers to these questions aren't straightforward. For a start, "fake news" which gave caesarean birth to "post-truth" is not a new phenomenon. This is partly because in the meaning of a sentence, as Bertrand Russell (1872-1970) noticed, "there are three psychological elements: the environmental causes of uttering it, the effects of hearing it, and (as part of the cause of utterance) the effects which the speaker expects it to have on the hearer."[168] Thus, what can be "fake news" to some can be received as truth by others, and each perspective can of course proliferate through mass media.

As human beings we're usually quite casual creatures who like embellishing stories by adding a little spice or taking rhetorical shortcuts when pitching our message. Whilst meanings may not change substantially,

---

[168] Bertrand Russell, *An Inquiry into Meaning and Truth*, Routledge, 2005, p. 27.

saying a few things here and there to appeal to people's emotions and personal beliefs is actually an inviolable facet of human utterance. After all, we speak to communicate and others can hear us, which in turn means that we can influence them, and there could also be power interactions and wider human psychology at play too. To a degree, we're biologically wired in this way since recognition by others stimulates confirmatory, albeit transitory, feelings of self-importance. This might all seem harmless, and it probably is in most everyday situations, thank God.

However, if what I've described is the basic pattern that operates across political influence too, it seems a little odd that it is only now that we think we've arrived at a radically new age of "post-truth." What is it about politics that's so new? Elections, for example, have always been about political parties and candidates vying with each other to convince ordinary people that only they will deliver new futures, tapping into people's emotions, hopes, worries, cultures and pre-existing political-economic philosophies and assumptions. And naturally, they focus on things that give them advantage, which also necessitates sidestepping around inconvenient truths or facts that might go against their viewpoints. In fact, hasn't it always been the case that policy decisions are based on prevailing values, ideology and political philosophy, which are all subjective and not necessarily data or fact-driven.

The subjective nature of photos and moving pictures, too, work to powerful effect in influencing people based on the selective truth on display in-between the four corners of a screen. This is partly why the art of soundbites and choreography in politics has become so important. There is also a long list of major political decisions that have been socially or politically engineered against the body of "objective data" which the media and ordinary public have chosen to ignore for decades (e.g. gun crime, health impacts of smoking, gender and racial inequalities, loss of biodiversity, climate change etc.).

There are subtle differences in how we use data in everyday decision-making. Being "data-driven" means making decisions entirely based on evidence, and which encourages information to be examined and kept up-to-date. However, it's possible for people to blindly trust data without interrogating it or failing to make it coherent to the wider context, both of which require competence and skills. Moreover, relying on incomplete or inaccurate data can lead to misinformed decisions, particularly if the variables involved have complex interrelationships.

By contrast, "data-informed" decision-making means using data and evidence as part of wider considerations (political, instinct, cultural, budgetary, religious etc.) rather than relying on it entirely. Human beings aren't simply rational actors, and we need to avoid applying conclusions from data literally, and to allow intuition- or gut instinct-led decisions. However, it may lead to less efficient outcomes. The reality is that we're both "data-informed" decision makers on many things, while being "data-driven" on others, and the relative mix of them changes depending on both the issue at hand and people's perspectives.

As it has come to light now, one could argue that the use of Facebook and Twitter bot accounts to flood anti-Hillary and pro-Brexit messages at key moments of campaigning merely amplified latent populist sentiment, but crucially didn't engineer the outcome because the deciding vote had already passed the winning line. It isn't unheard of for the US Electoral College system to throw up unexpected results well before the advent of social media. Similarly, for the EU Referendum, it's somewhat of a stretch to think that 1.3 million people could have all been unduly influenced to give the 3.78% winning margin for Vote Leave.[169] After all, Euroscepticism has been a growing trend ever since the UK first joined the EU, and it has proved particularly painfully in hindsight seeing just how risky the Referendum design was, which played into the hands of the Eurosceptics.

Equally, the availability of information in the 21st century certainly has vastly increased transparency in how the media, governments, corporates and powerful people operate, and shed light into the way they go to great lengths to deny inconvenient truths. Yet, none of this is considered relevant to the definition of "post-truth."

As for spin-doctoring, it's become a necessary tool for managing the

---

[169] There are also consistent patterns in the leave-remain distribution of votes across the UK which would add further weight here. For example, in England, outside of Greater London and large university cities like Manchester, Bristol, Bath, other places saw a winning margin in excess of 5% of the votes cast. See also, concerns about immigration and disenfranchisement with politics as explanatory factors: NatCen Social Research, *The vote to leave the EU - Litmus test or lightning rod?*, http://www.bsa.natcen.ac.uk/media/39149/bsa34 brexit final.pdf.

business of journalism. Journalists ask difficult questions to get to the truth of a matter. However, in the process they also act as gatekeepers of information, and produce carefully crafted content intended to sell or get noticed. Both spin and gatekeeping can at times conceal subtle truths (try reading tabloid newspapers, for example), yet they aren't interpreted as "post-truth" conditions.

"Truth" as a process works often in mysterious ways. It's a "composite awareness" that pushes and pulls in different directions of inquiry, usually in a creative, sometimes contradictory, restless tension. The pursuit of truth, nevertheless, requires us to question and to have our own viewpoints (whatever they might be), until we're enlightened by new knowledge or awareness that convinces us.

Whilst we naturally conceptualise things in our own, rather subjective, cognitive and experiential bubbles, the satisfaction of our egos, ideologies, false consciousness, political and socio-economic polarisations, tribal perversions and unconscious biases etc. are natural traps that we can easily fall into. Such traps can of course be overcome. However, here's the challenge: it requires open-mindedness, being receptive to challenge, having awareness of one's limits, having sincere attitude, striving for Godliness etc. Thus, Trump's counter-claims of "fake news" directed at media outlets as crass as they were, can't be in and of themselves a sign of having arrived at some kind of a momentous "post-truth" age.

There are perhaps clues as to why some consider this to be a "post-truth" age in retaliation to Trump and Brexit, where the alleged lack of objectivity of some sections of the media and politicians has been exposed like it has rarely been before. However, instead of taking the moral high-ground by helping to reconcile the divisiveness of the world and doing something about the current exposure to disinformation on social media as the Cambridge Analytica and Russian examples of political meddling have shown, in the final analysis, those called out took to faking a new age.

# 2.12 Men in crisis?

The recent centenary celebrations of the Suffragette movement hit home the sobering reality of just how much we take the historic and ongoing struggles of women for granted. It's also highlighted something subtle yet quite significant, but doesn't get the attention it deserves. This is the idea that much of the gender justice focus, whether in mainstream media, on blogs or on Twitter, is expressed through the lenses of the "plight of women" and their experiences. While this is necessary, and must continue as a social justice movement, typically, it's in a vacuum of being a "women only" issue, one that as a society we tend to think that it's only up to women who must voice their concerns. My argument here is that if we step back a little, we find that at the root of gender injustice is, arguably, an endemic crisis in men and "masculinity," which we perhaps don't acknowledge nearly as much, both historically and today. I would therefore like to flip the focus on men here and explore some home truths, as the *faux pas* cliché "it's a man's world"[170] goes, which men must deal with in their responsibility for gender justice. Not least since the Prophetic model compels men to be sensitive to the needs of women,[171] and to work towards healing the discontents of our world.

Much of today's gender injustices are of course inherited in the fundamentally patriarchal historical social constructions which are not just peculiar to the West but by and large found across the world, with some exceptions, perhaps. In other words, setting aside subtle issues to do with post-enlightenment concept formation which is of course not free of problems of its own, "patriarchal" denotes power relations wherein women's interests are subordinated to those of men.

In pre-modern times biological sex differences gave rise to a basic complementarity arrangement of the relative roles of men and women in society. Men with their raw physical strength were perceived to be naturally better-equipped for the physically-intensive world out of the home, while

---

[170] Soraya Chemaly, *What Exactly Does 'It's A Man's World' Mean?*, The Huffington Post, 27 May 2015.
[171] In a *hadith* narrated by Abu Huraira in *Sunan al-Tirmidhi*, the Prophet said: "The most complete of the believers in faith is the one with the best character among them. And the best of you are those who are best to your women."

women were perceived to be naturally better-equipped for child-rearing and meeting the needs of the family in the home. It would be unfair to retrospectively judge such historical social arrangements through the prism of current notions of patriarchy. To reduce historical patriarchy to simply a narrative of male aggression towards women, for instance, would be a gross oversimplification. Pre-modern conditions were vastly different, and the integration of society (public versus private life, urban versus rural, trust frameworks etc.) had limitations for which there were no solutions. Patriarchy was much more a function of the social environment e.g. for farming, dealing with tribal feuds, communal violence and ever-present threats from bandits etc. Something which we might view as patriarchal today may well have been necessary to protect society or to make the world work as productively as possible given the inherent constraints of the pre-modern world.[172]

Aside from this kind of pragmatism, there were nevertheless darker sides too. Narratives around "Eve's fall from Grace" had a tendency in large parts of medieval Christendom to symbolise women as normatively "sinning" and "witch-like." Similar references existed in other parts of the world. In India, Hindu girls were often buried alive, and even in arguably more legally-advanced Muslim societies, women's rights struggled to be enforced - far from the standards in the examples of Mary, Khadija, A'isha and so on. Whatever the conditions, they helped legitimise and reinforce the idea that men had a moral power over women, which was an accepted societal norm that went unchallenged.

However, following the industrial revolution in the 18th century everything changed. For the first time, women took up public spaces and worked alongside men *en mass* and it became increasingly apparent that men and women could do the same jobs but be held to different standards of rights and recognition. The hegemony of "male outlook" began to be noticed as a "dehumanising gap."

However, recognition and equal rights were only part of the picture. Since the industrial revolution, human social and economic activities had grown exponentially and, under patriarchal conditions, women had

---

[172] Other constraints in pre-modern settings include: the lack of modern communication technology; electronic devices; the internet; modern systems of law and order; big private enterprises; modern industries etc.

to negotiate their "discovery," or "making," of new roles and definitions of "female identity." And with structures of male privilege increasingly challenged by courageous movements like the Suffragettes in the 19th and 20th centuries or the "second-wave feminism" in the 1960s, or the appearance of "gender-neutral" office and IT-related jobs etc., we've ended up with all the intricacies of gender politics today.

These intricacies broadly fall into four categories today, as I see them. (1) Men increasingly feel "squeezed" by the growing public presence of women which has challenged their sense of privilege and identity. (2) Structural barriers hinder society's corrective polity (e.g. lack of aligned political will, lack of protective legal frameworks, unfavourable commercial commitments etc.). (3) Gender-justice is also a moving goal-post which reflects the dynamism in the subjective notions of under- versus over-feminisation. (4) There is fierce ongoing evolution of perspectives and debates about femininity among women, including Muslim women. In the interest of brevity, my focus here will be related to the first category.

The stats at the egregious end of the spectrum suggest that quite a few men are sexual predators of one kind or another. A staggering 85,000 women are raped every year (on average ten every hour), and 4000 help calls a week are made about attempted or actual cases of rape in England and Wales, of which 93% are by women.[173] We're also all too aware of near-daily reports of Harvey Weinstein-style exploitative "hit on" women. More recently it's come to light that even among charity workers at Oxfam male opportunists have long exploited vulnerable women in disaster zones. Metrics on other types of male violence and intimidation against women, trafficking and prostitution, abusive marriages, honour-based violence etc., aren't any better.[174] These behaviours aren't exclusive to the West, but prevalent across the world.

Some men will often compare themselves against a "gold standard" which prizes power, control and invincibility. Men are often socialised to aspire towards a "hegemonic masculinity" based on traits such as having

---

[173] *Rape Crisis England and Wales statistics 2017-18*, https://rapecrisis.org.uk/statistics. php, retrieved 15 February 2018.

[174] Data on violence against women and girls, https://www.endviolenceagainstwomen. org.uk/about/data-on-violence-against-women-and-girls/, retrieved 15 February 2018.

power, dominance and aggression etc. For others, being a man means "behaving badly" - the occasional drunkenness and disorderly behaviour. Yet these standards belie men's actual fragility as evidenced in the rise in their obsession and addiction to pornography.[175] In some cases, according to observers, it's contributing to an actual downturn in men's overall sexual and psychological well-being.[176] It's also a far cry from studies showing that men in midlife, ironically, remain overwhelmingly dependent on a female partner for emotional support.

Studies also point to an increase in the lack of self-confidence in men, usually because they avoid talking about their feelings and anxieties. Suicide rates in men aged 35-54 in the UK are more than twice that of women, while female suicide rates in comparison have declined over the last 50 years. According to the Samaritans, this is partly due to emotional illiteracy among men and a loss of masculine pride and identity due to the decline of traditional male industries and the rise of gender-neutral jobs.[177]

If truth be told, many of these trends are no better for Muslims. While I've resisted focusing on Muslim men since much of the crisis is generic to men, there is no doubt that British Muslims fall way too short on gender justice measured against the Prophetic model of what God commands. Muslim sexual predators and misogynists who take uncaring, blasé attitude towards women would do well to remember that God is ever-Watchful and most Just.

---

[175] Had GM, *Gender differences in pornography consumption among young heterosexual Danish adults*, Arch Sex Behav. 2006 Oct;35(5):577-85, https://www.ncbi.nlm.nih.gov/m/pubmed/17039402/, retrieved 15 February 2018.

[176] Elwood Watson, *Pornography Addiction Among Men is On The Rise,* The Huffington Post, 9 December 2014.

[177] Research report: *Men, Suicide and Society*, 2012, https://www.samaritans.org/sites/default/files/kcfinder/files/press/Men%20Suicide%20and%20Society%20Research%20Report%2051112.pdf, retrieved 15 February 2018.

# 2.13 Muslim dilemmas when choosing a baby's name

Choosing the right name for a newborn matters in both life and death. At the very least it's a way of ensuring continuity of a nominal Muslim identity from one generation to another. For parents, it's also a test of stepping up to the responsibility of honouring their children with the best names possible. But along the way to choosing a name there are plenty of dilemmas for parents to navigate.

We might purposefully choose to avoid names that when rendered into English makes them vulnerable to name-calling at school. The school playground can often be a place of nightmares for parents. Names have a tendency of taking shorthand forms, and whilst most times the results are benign, the use of "Mo" for "Mohammed" or "Zak" for "Zakariya" are good examples, they can also result sometimes in unedifying forms. All languages no doubt have their fair share of this.

Similarly, names can be pronounced differently when spelt in English. The name "Ishaaq," for example, can be read both "Ish-aaq" and "Is-haaq." This seemingly slender resource of language is not exclusive to English. Languages are not designed with transliteration in mind of course. For example, there isn't a "p" sound in Arabic, so Indian names like "Patel" get pronounced differently, in this case quite amusingly as "Batel." As for grammatical structures like particles used to combine words in Arabic (such as "*ur*," "*ar*," "*ul*" etc.), they do seem to further complicate things in the English language.

There's also the matter of proper Arabic names versus names indigenised into a different language. The names "Ridwan"/"Ridwana" are typically expressed as "Rizwan"/"Rizwana" in Urdu or "Rejwan"/"Rejwana" in Bengali. Similarly, if we're living in a predominant Muslim country like Turkey, such indigenisation doesn't matter so much when it comes to "Mehmet" or "Ahmet" which to native Turkish speakers are as good as "Muhammad" and "Ahmad." It's much more of a dilemma for those keen to remove "cultural baggage" of sorts. Recent surge in the use of *kunya* names beginning with "Abu" ("father of") or "Umm" ("mother of"), particularly on social media, suggests an "Arabisation" of Asians or a "hipster-like" fad might be in full swing for some parents when it comes to their own names.

135

Spelling and pronunciation matter too. As second and third generation British Muslims we're mindful of keeping spelling easy for those unfamiliar with Muslim names. Some parents focus on finding names familiar to Christian and post-Christian English speakers whilst retaining their Islamic identity - "Hannah," "Adam," "Sofia," "Sarah," "Rebecca" are good examples.

Whilst some will call for maintaining a greater degree of "Muslim distinction" when naming their children such calls can often be shrouded in identity politics rather than the real substance of "being Muslim" through a knowledge culture, good character (*husnul akhlaq*) and giving value to society (*fa'idah*) from a theocentric premise. In any case, by no means is this a phenomenon exclusive to British Muslims. The same indigenisation process that transformed "Ridwan" to "Rizwan" and "Rejwan" in South Asian languages is at work in English and European languages too.

Keeping to classical Muslim-only names that have variant spellings can be tricky too. Just look at the plethora of different ways we spell "Muhammad." Incidentally, "Muhammad" isn't just the most common Muslim name but is arguably and consistently the most common of all baby names in the UK.[178] However, when it comes to "foreign-sounding" names, sadly, at the back of our minds is the anxiety that, as things stand today, newborns may face unfair discrimination just because of their name.

Frustratingly, we can often find that the more preferred "best"[179] names beginning with "Abd" ("servant of…" such as "Abdullah," "Abdur Rahman" etc.), or of the Prophets such as "Muhammad," "Dawud," "Yusuf," "Idris," "Sulaiman," etc. have already been taken by family and friends for their own kids. In which case, social convention, family politics or one's own desire for a unique name for their offspring, may dictate that we avoid choosing them. Speaking of family, whilst it's nice for grandparents, uncles and aunts to pitch in with their suggestions for names, expectations do need to be managed.

There are some names which remind us of unsavoury characters we've

---

[178] Lizzie Dearden, *Why Muhammad may be the most common baby boys' name in England and Wales*, The Independent, 2 September 2016.

[179] Among several Prophetic statements on this, the *hadith* narrated by Ibn Umar in *Sunan Ibn Majah is*: "The most beloved names to Allah are: Abdullah, and Abd-ur-Rahman."

come across or we've associated the name with unpleasant experiences, which might make us slightly allergic to them. That said, whist other names might be perfectly reasonable in themselves, we might find the odd scholar has expressed some reservation with our chosen name, often for personal reasons or to conform to the particular social conventions of their time. Getting one's head around this or explaining it to others isn't easy.

Of course there are names that are clearly to be avoided such as "Abu Lahab" ("Father of Flame," 111:1-5) and "Abu Jahl," ("Father of Folly," 96:9-14), which are synonymous with the most famous antagonists of the Prophet; or "Qarun" ("Korah" in the Bible), the hoarder engulfed by a sinkhole like structure for his ingratitude and self-pride (28:76). And there are some non-*Qur'anic* historical examples of tyrants which Muslims avoid (like "Hitler" or "Judas") such as "Hajjaj" (Ibn Yusuf). It wasn't long ago that in some Muslim countries the name "Saddam" became a swear sword hurled at shopkeepers who refused to budge on price. In similar vein, parents might think twice today about keeping the name "Usama," even though it's a beautiful name.

Lastly, all parents want to avoid regretting the name they chose. However, "An online poll of more than 1,000 parents carried out by Mumsnet found that 18% of parents regretted the name they chose for their offspring."[180] This is more than buyer's remorse; it can be an indictment of a lack of managing the wider family's expectations, research and advice-seeking (*nasihah*) on the part of parents.

Above all, whatever name we choose for our children, our prayers are one and the same: "My Lord, enable me to be grateful for Your favour which You have bestowed upon me and upon my parents and to work righteousness of which You will approve and make righteous for me my offspring. Indeed, I have repented to You, and indeed, I am of the Muslims" (46:15).

---

[180] *Nearly a fifth of parents regret baby name - survey,* BBC News website, 31 August 2016.

## 2.14 Our love of dates

There is surely no food that symbolises Ramadhan more so than the humble date fruit. The English word "date" comes from the Greek "daktulos" describing their seemingly finger-like shape.[181] Every Ramadhan dates make their presence in a huge variety of colours, tastes, shapes and textures. Sold in all types of shops, from the local corner shop to online retail outlets, and even in our supermarkets - the Tesco's and Sainsbury's of the world all stockpile on dates. Places that might rarely see dates get inundated with them as Ramadhan nears. It's an annual global phenomenon, and come to think of it, worthy of some contemplation. Particularly, given that our consumption of dates and its indelible mark on our food tables today is an example of a food tradition that grew out of Arabia at the time of the Prophet.

Dates come from the date palm tree (*Phoenix dactylifera*), which can grow to an average height of 23 metres.[182] From pollination, it takes six to eight months for dates to ripen in desert-like conditions. In the first stage of their development (*khimr*), they're quite small and unripe. The second stage (*khalal*) begins by about four months when dates become hard and crunchy. By around six months (*rutab*), they start becoming sweet and soft. It then takes roughly another two months to reach the fourth and final stage (*tamar*) for the dates to fully ripen, sweeten and become sticky.

The worldwide production of dates is estimated to have increased almost threefold over the last 40 years, reaching 7.68 million tons in 2010.[183] To put it in some context, this is roughly the same as strawberries.[184] Though, farming dates is significantly more labour intensive, needing hand pollination and, for some dates, the tall trees need to be climbed to thin them down to allow room for the dates to grow. And once ripened, they

---

[181] See: http://www.thefreedictionary.com/date, retrieved 26 May 2017.

[182] See: https://www.britannica.com/plant/date-palm, retrieved 26 May 2017.

[183] *Date fruit: chemical composition, nutritional and medicinal values, products*, J Sci Food Agric. 2013 Aug 15;93(10):2351-61. doi: 10.1002/jsfa.6154. Epub 2013 May 3.

[184] See: *Global fruit production in 2016, by variety* (in million metric tons), https://www.statista.com/statistics/264001/worldwide-production-of-fruit-by-variety/, retrieved 26 May 2017.

then need to be hand-picked. Some farmers harvest dates after the *rutab* stage and ripen them off-tree or sell them on as the dry, sweet variety.

According to one study, dates are made up of 70-80% carbohydrates (or sugars), 2-4% protein, 1% fat and the rest water and trace amounts of minerals.[185] Three types of sugars can be found in dates (fructose, glucose and sucrose), of which fructose varies the most between different types of dates. The high sugar and low water content give dates a relatively long shelf life. The protein content contains essential amino acids (which the body cannot make) and there are also minerals like (in order of amount) potassium, calcium, magnesium, phosphorus, sodium, as well as trace amounts of vitamin C, B1 thiamine and others.

In short, dates are super foods that can be eaten even when unripe. Thus, it's not surprisingly that for thousands of years they've been staple food in the Middle East and elsewhere. It's thought that the Moors introduced dates to Spain and Spanish travellers later brought them to places like the West Coast of America.

Many types of dates can be found in our shops. The Medjool dates, with their large size, soft texture and sweet taste, cultivated from places like Palestine and Jordan have become quite popular in recent years. Prior to them, what probably dominated was the Deglet Noor type. Then there are dates like Khalas from Saudi Arabia. But perhaps the most sought after are the Ajwa dates with their soft, dry, fruity, dark-coloured appearance, cultivated in and around Madina. Today, the growing numbers of cake bakers in our families will also seek just about any type of date to make things like chocolate brownies and sticky toffee puddings and so on.

Dates are mentioned in the *Qur'an* in multiple places. For example, in the chapter on Maryam we learn that God commanded Maryam to eat dates (19:21). As it turns out, according to published research, consumption of date fruit in the last weeks of pregnancy can help with labour pains. From the Prophet's *Sunnah*, too, we find culturally-rooted practices like rubbing a small part of a date into the mouth of a newborn baby (a process known as *tahnik*)[186] which has known medicinal benefits.

---

[185] *Nutritional composition of fruit of 10 date palm (Phoenix dactylifera L.) cultivars grown in Saudi Arabia*, https://doi.org/10.1016/j.jtusci.2014.07.002.
[186] Narrations by different Companions about *Tahnik* can be found in *Sahih al-Bukhari* and other books of *hadith*.

And of course, we open fasts with dates to follow the *Sunnah*. Of the trees mentioned in the *Qur'an*, the date palm tree, called *Nakhlah*, is one of them (24:25). The tree in the famous parable describing the nature of faith (*iman*) with firm roots and trunks that break high into the sky, refers to none other than the date palm tree. The Prophet's Mosque was first built using the trunk and leaves of the date palm tree, reflecting its versatility too.

Perhaps, then, the less obvious story of the date fruit is the deep trans-historical blessings of the Prophet. Contemplating it, one is certainly left awe-struck and asking the question: if it wasn't for the Prophet, by God's grace, who would have acquainted us with this most nutritious of fruits?

# 2.15 When *"al-kohl"* becomes alcoholic

When Arabs first perfected the art of making *"al-kohl"* (cosmetic eye make-up) some one thousand years ago,[187] little did they think that *"al-kohl"* would one day become a cultural phenomenon. That *"al-kohl"* would morph into "alcoholic" as a commonly used noun for those who sadly succumbed to its inherent chemical seduction. That once elusive quest by Arab alchemists to isolate purified hydroxyl (OH) compounds through the process of distillation, today takes on the distinct cultural meaning of "having fun," "letting loose," "getting hammered," and of course various other descriptions that could be mistaken for being expletives.

The sad news of the death, and as many have said, a life "taken early," of the former Liberal Democrat leader Charles Kennedy has rightly put the media focus back on the dangers of alcohol abuse, even if only temporarily. The post-mortem analysis concluded a death by haemorrhage linked to alcoholism; in other words, years of consuming large amounts of alcohol meant that the liver's capacity to carry out its function, indeed, to maintain its own structural integrity, had been critically damaged. In a healthy person the liver functions as the body's "salvage factory," catalysing all sorts of detoxification reactions, including stripping old red blood cells of the brown colour that we see in our faeces. Thus, alcohol is a poison to the liver and it kills.

Unfortunately, what often seems innocuous or occasional conformity to cultural norms linked to casual drinking ends up for some, for one reason or another, in a serious life-threatening liver condition. People develop, in the words of alcoholics themselves, a "physical compulsion, coupled with a mental obsession" to consume alcohol.[188]

To make matters worse, the economic consequences of drinking alcohol as a cultural phenomenon aren't any good either. Alcohol causes

---

[187] The English world "alcohol" is derived from the Arabic word *"al-kohl."* The *Cambridge World History of Food*, 2000, Volume 1, p. 655. See also: *The Arabs discovered how to distil alcohol. They still do it best, say some*, The Economist, 18 December 2013.

[188] See: *Alcoholics Anonymous* website, http://www.alcoholics-anonymous.org.uk/About-AA/Newcomers/About-Alcoholism, retrieved 7 June 2015.

4% of cancer cases in the UK.[189] Come Friday nights and disorderly drunk behaviour takes over many of our public places. In fact, David Cameron rightly said, "Every night, in town centres, hospitals and police stations across the country, people have to cope with the consequences of alcohol abuse."[190] Over 200,000 hospitals admissions are related to alcohol each year, up 40% compared to 2002/3. In 2012, the NHS spent £2.7b on alcohol related admissions, a staggering £90 for every taxpayer. The wider cost to society from alcohol is considered between £17b and £22b each year.

Socially, too, there are serious negative consequences. As normal civilising inhibitions are lost, unkind words about work colleagues and friends and family become standard exchanges between drunks, frequently ending up with hurling abuse at passers-by. There is also the stigmatisation and struggle of loved ones who feel helpless when alcoholism gets out of hand even if only on that odd occasion. A chance to learn from hangovers, vomiting, alcohol-induced blackouts, frequent or otherwise, it seems is not enough for some to resist the temptation. Of course not everyone who drinks a couple of beers here and there, the so-called "responsible drinking" or "drinking in moderation," becomes an alcoholic over time. However, even for them there are health consequences and socio-economic costs.

Interestingly, the inherent addictive properties of alcohol lie in its intoxicating effect. Unlike nicotine, for example, alcohol is addictive without necessarily offering the same level of euphoria and mood enhancement. Whilst a disposition to alcoholism can owe itself to quite complex interrelated factors, genes and physiology to name a few, experts say that too often a dependency on alcohol comes from craving its rewarding effects. Back in the 9th century, Arab chemists might have ironically called this "alchemy of happiness" (*kimiya al-sa'ada*). For consumers of alcohol it means temporary relief, perhaps helping to momentarily forget one's problems, suppressing painful memories, confiding into oneself by

---

[189] See: *Drinkaware* website for facts about alcohol, who work with an independent panel of medical experts to bring reliable information and advice about alcohol, http://www.drinkaware.co.uk/check-the-facts, retrieved 7 June 2015.

[190] *PM highlights impact of alcohol on NHS*, https://www.gov.uk/government/news/pm-highlights-impact-of-alcohol-on-nhs, 15 February 2012.

drinking alone, or fulfilling a desire to artificially boost one's moods and euphoria etc.

Thank God for the likes of Alcoholics Anonymous (and others), without whom it is difficult to see how so many alcoholics would cope, even with the significant growth in teetotalers among millennials.[191] But for those affected by alcoholism the real solution surely lies not in dealing with symptoms, but to have at hand a different medium to fall back on when all else seems to fail, before that first recourse or dependency on alcohol sets in. There was a time when, for many, this very safety net was faith and religion, in the hope and trust in God. But in today's increasingly post-Christian society, that alternative recourse has become obscured, for which Charles Kennedy's death will sadly not be the last one. We should perhaps ask ourselves, have we as a society done enough to understand the meaning and role of faith in combating the problems of alcoholism?

---

[191] Kate Samuelson, *The Millennial Teetotalers Upending the Stereotype of Boozy Britain*, http://time.com/5356272/millennial-teetotalers-boozy-britain/, retrieved 9 August 2018.

# $\,3\,$

# Integration and identity politics

## 3.1 It's not Muslims who need integrating but Asians

It was a privilege to attend the MCB's launch of the report *Our Shared British Future*,[192] hosted by Naz Shah MP at the Houses of Parliament. The report is an anthology of perspectives from people from different specialisms on the challenges of Muslim integration in the UK today. Well-timed, it coincided with Sajid Javed's[193] announcement of a public consultation on integration. In all, the event seemed well-organised and Miqdaad Versi's hard work in compiling the report as well as chairing the event was good. However, I left with mixed feelings, for the report fell short of presenting an accurate and nuanced picture. A better structure for the report would have been to: (1) positively make the case for how far communities have actually come along in only 60 or so years as a baseline before (2) addressing both (a) internal and (b) external challenges. In fact, the speeches and case studies presented at the event seemed fairer in comparison to the written publication. James Fergusson's[194] early presentation, for example, brought an air of positivity to the event pointing out that there is already "terrific social mobility" and that "overall the outlook is much more encouraging

---

[192] *Our Shared British Future: Muslims and Integration in the UK,* launched on 14 March 2018.

[193] Sajid Javid was the Secretary of State for Communities and Local Government at the time.

[194] James Fergusson is the acclaimed author of *Al-Britannia, My Country: A Journey Through Muslim Britain*, Transworld Publishers, 2018.

than the orthodox view suggests." Aside from this, it was quite perplexing to see that God was only mentioned in ten out of the 130 pages of the report. In fact, you have to get to the end of the report, at page 114, to find the first mention of God. This made me question if there was a deeper, more troubling effect at play?

Much of the report highlighted socio-economic conditions within pockets of communities, referred to as "Muslim." However, it remains unclear as to why religious identity should be considered the significant factor in the debate on integration. The conditions to which the report refers reflects issues around social mobility in inner city post-industrial towns where, in the main, poorly educated, working-class immigrants settled to meet the demand for manual labour. Subsequently, immigrant groups formed close-knit communities out of a shared culture, and partly also as a reflection of the housing policies of successive governments.

However, these "social microcosms" have over time become opportune for segregation and cultural inertia. What is evident is that the shared identity of such communities is far more rooted in their ethno-cultural identity than a shared religious outlook, and often, rather than being one large community, an area may be made up of various ethnic communities, whilst sharing the same faith, with their own particular interests. These communities are, however, superficially judged by those on the outside to be alike due to their ostensibly shared "brownness." Interestingly, non-religious organisations that serve a particular ethnic identity (be it a Pakistani cultural association or an Asian business association etc.) have largely evaded focus and shirked their fair share of responsibility towards enabling a more cohesive integration. Arguably, by consequence, they've unnecessarily amplified heat on bodies that are ostensibly to do with religion such as mosques and Islamic schools etc.

As individuals, we have various identities which we navigate including those related to our faith, but wind back to the 1990s and the underlying basis for public engagement centred on ethnic identity: we were "British Bangladeshis," "British Pakistanis," "British Somalis" etc. So how have we become a "religious community" and the focus centred on it? There are possibly three factors playing out. (1) A security focus in the last decade has turned issues of integration from a socio-economic and cultural issue to one with both tenuous and indirect links with religious extremism. (2)

Communities that also happen to be Muslim have not responded with any strategic intervention often because their ethnic interests and faith-based interests are either considered as one and the same, or because it remains useful in order to rally a wider cohort from society behind their own cause. (3) At play is also the poorly documented phenomenon of cognitive dissonance whereby many simultaneously hold two or more contradictory beliefs, ideas or values, which is conveniently pacified through self-claims of being a "religious community."

Second and third generation descendants of immigrants who came to the UK for economic reasons are at a crossroad between divesting transnational belongings of diverse ancestry and dealing with Britain as home. The confusion this creates and the resulting conflations made, come to the fore when, it is argued, we're not "encouraged to participate in national conversations in a way that isn't directly in relation to [our] religious identities." For a group of citizens who seemingly come together on the basis of their faith, which other identity are they meant to participate with as a religious group? Ostensibly, such lamentations spring from using religion as a source of "ethnic protest," where God sits squarely outside of the conversation. The report explores the sentiments of Muslims as an ethnic group (which of course they aren't) and speaks for those who lifestyles and culture might be informed by a "cultural Muslimness" rather than the primary objective of being subservient to God.

What becomes clear is that the term "Muslim" is readily appropriated without much thought given to what God wants today of those British people who primarily seek to be truly subservient to Him. We tend to market ourselves under the identity of "Muslim," yet we relegate God in "how we do subservience" (Islam) and "be appropriately subservient" (Muslim) in the wider context, particular in the politics of identity and public engagement. The fact that you have to flick to page 114 to see the first mention of God is simply a reflection of this. The point came across by someone in the Q&A session, who questioned whether as Muslims we can legitimately consider ourselves to be religiously literate, let alone define ourselves as a "religious community."

Putting aside this problem of conflating religious identity with ethno-culture, the social mobility issues come from a mix of failures. (1) First and second generation immigrants, for sentimental reasons, were often lured by a "myth of return" to ancestral homes at the expense of building a thriving home and future for them in the UK. It meant that, over decades, they sent billions of Pounds of remittance money outside of the UK, usually to support close relatives which was proper and understandable, but quite often also to build huge mansions and acquiring land in ancestral countries, much of which fails to attract the interest of the third generation. (2) There have been many policy failures such as not encouraging and supporting immigrants to learn English and new skills, and not intervening to facilitate a kind of multiculturalism that encouraged endearing and meaningful mixing of communities, and avoiding the phenomenon of "white flight." The push for the integration of society based on "British Values" in recent years comes perhaps a little too late for those who went to school before it became part of the national curriculum, or for those beholden to post-colonial or post-modern tendencies. (3) There has been a lack of well-executed strategies for economic regeneration of post-industrial towns. This is similar to the issues which the movement for a Northern Powerhouse is seeking to address. Some minorities, including various Caribbean communities alike, happened to be caught up in the historical fact of this.

Solving complex social problems require understanding and accepting the spheres of responsibilities that can be distinct as well as shared between citizens, public institutions and government. Only then is it possible to practically and productively focus on delivering outcomes. It's actually much subtler than calling for a "two-way street," as the report did, for the simple reason that while some things require government to take a lead on, it would still require citizens to comply, shape or engage with an open mind. Hence, it's not like a street where you stay in your lane, but you need to crisscross and work across them in both ways. Similarly, other things may require citizens to step-up and own their narratives to do justice to themselves, or perhaps to help the wider public and government see the opportunities in a particular initiative. A "street" analogy is also quite ironic from the point of view that we know for a fact that streets can be jammed, where pot-holes exist, road rages occur and have tolls and lanes at different speeds etc.

Interesting, the lack of emotional intelligence[195] was very telling in a poem towards the end of the report which questioned, "Will I Always Be An Outsider?" This poem was read out at the beginning of the event, and follows a growing genre of spoken-word poetry. However, it's not like unearthing the subtleties of human nature or societies in the genre of Rumi or Wordsworth for example, but rather in the style of post-colonial rhetoric, outrage and "immigrant frustrations" taken up as a hammer that threatens to treat all government social policy and Westernism generally as if it were a nail. But strangely, the author, as a Cambridge and LSE graduate and a working solicitor, is herself the product of the social mobility of the current system which she bemoans. Such voices lack emotional and political intelligence and end up protracting the *status quo* rather than productively contributing to an efficient and feasible way out.

With the above said, I want to end with a note of hope. Naz Shah MP explained how she and others have influenced Sajid Javed. Similarly, the director of the Khayaal Theatre, Lukman Ali, and the CEO of Muslim Aid, Jehangir Malik, who presented case studies showing that Muslims and public institutions alike need to reach out and do more to fulfil their own responsibilities. The question is do we have the right insight, political and emotional intelligence, and religious literacy to do so?

---

[195] Emotional intelligence can be defined as: "the ability to identify and manage your own emotions and the emotions of others. It is generally said to include three skills: emotional awareness; the ability to harness emotions and apply them to tasks like thinking and problem solving; and the ability to manage emotions, which includes regulating your own emotions and cheering up or calming down other people," Psychology Today, https://www.psychologytoday.com/gb/basics/emotional-intelligence, retrieved 17 March 2018.

# 3.2 The new *"apna"* ("our people")?

Many British Muslims when abroad have some experience of facing the question, "Where are you from?" Normally, we shrug off such questions with some banter or a straightforward reply with "UK" or "Britain." However, quite often we then find ourselves with the slightly awkward question: "Where originally?" In other words, our looks can be perceived by others to have a different origin to the country we claim to be from. Such passing conversations, while it's usually nothing more than genuine curiosity based on prior assumptions or even people just being friendly, do raise some interesting questions about our identity and belonging. These questions may have been brought to the fore watching *The Chronicles of Nadiya*.[196]

Back in the UK, "Muslimness" is frequently put under the spotlight by some sections of the media, and in the process misrepresented, not to understand the nature and value of faith, but for crass suspicion of "otherness." What comes out in the wash are all kinds of prejudices, lack of familiarity with diverse cultures and traditions, as well as in some cases healthy tensions that are to be expected in the continual making of any pluralistic society. When it gets out of hand it antagonises others, resulting in a two-way process of hate, ridicule and feelings of siege mentality.

Chauvinistic nationalism is frowned upon not just in Islam, but rightly whenever we learn about the history of wars when men capitulated to the excesses of their egos. "Patriots could display over the centuries many memorable and useful virtues, but gentleness and sympathy towards outsiders are not prominent among them," says the sociologist Zygmunt Bauman.[197]

However, chauvinistic nationalism is quite different to expressing one's identity, having pride in a national identity or belonging to a group of people geographically closer to home. Our basic human instinct is to

---

[196] *The Chronicles of Nadiya* was a two-part series in which The Great British Bake Off 2015 winner Nadiya Hussain explores the recipes that have shaped her love of cooking, which involved a trip to her parent's homeland in Bangladesh in 2016. This series was then followed by an eight-part series on BBC Two in July 2017 titled *Nadiya's British Food Adventure*.

[197] Zygmunt Bauman, *Liquid Modernity*, Polity Press, 2008.

form greater communion with those living closer to us. It's also necessary for practical and psychological reasons. We achieve through collective effort and shared experiences, as spouses, families, friends, communities, clubs, business partners, political groups, trading blocks, nations etc. We're socially interwoven into groups and multiple levels of sharing, which result in different levels of interactions between people. Naturally, they give us identity and solidarity with some more than others. Different levels of empathy and concern may follow as a result too. Even if we look at economic transactions, the "gravity effect" dictates that trade and foreign direct investment (FDI) reduces at an accelerating rate as the distance between trading partners increases.

At the same time, this kind of close communion doesn't imply that we automatically ignore or deny the rights of others who fall outside of these communions. Being born into different families, for instance, doesn't make us spontaneously dislike others or arbitrarily exclude them from things. Such prejudice, if it grows, does so for other reasons. Instead, there are social norms, laws, Prophetic guidance and indeed inherent human goodness, that helps us to form mutual friendships with others, to uphold fairness and justice etc.

Questions about identity and belonging get yet more interesting when, for example, we visit the home of our ancestors in Pakistan or Bangladesh etc. The chances are, particularly if we've not been for a while, we'll be met with curiosity and stares, confirming us as *"desi"* (native) outsiders.

It seems our sense of "who we are" has actually moved on in the eyes of those whom our fathers' and grandfathers' generation would have called "our folk" or *"apna"* in Urdu and *"amrar manush"* in Bengali. The *"apna"* or *"amrar manush"* for us are in our "back home" in the UK and has widened to include people of white, black, faith and non-faith backgrounds etc. Proof of this can be found in our response to randomly meeting a fellow Brit of a different background to us while on holiday abroad.

Mind you, the old sentiment hasn't become completely irrelevant. Many second and third generation British Muslims still have family and assets in ancestral countries. And of course, the heritage of our roots is in one sense forever etched into our DNA. So too the folkloric tales, languages, stories, cultural idioms and songs that have been passed down to us.

However, where such nostalgia becomes overbearing is when it's overtaken by seemingly unresolved post-colonial attitudes that unnecessarily skew us towards pessimism and cynicism here in the UK. For those hungover in this way, criticism of the West and efforts by Muslims to express an indigenised "British" or "English" Muslim culture can be all too quick and automatic. At the sharp end, it's a kind of isolationist, culturally predatory view that questions overt loyalty to the British establishment and institutions, and often feels devoid of core qualities of faith (*iman*), being a source of ease (*ihsan*) and showing gratitude (*shukr*) to others. Similarly, the sharp ends of the left- and right-media and politics generally have vested interests of their own when it comes to the diverse strands of Muslim identity of Britain. For whom on the question of assimilation, "resistance may be futile" and there is an expectation that we must look, speak and behave in a certain way to be unconditionally accepted as *bona fide* Britons.

It is at this juncture that as believers we ought to study and reflect on how Muslims historically absorbed themselves into the diverse cultures that they lived in. Islam has an accommodating spirit that directs believers to mesh in, to establish warm relations, and to be of real value and service (*khidma*) to others. Sadly, the self-reflective focus on "being Muslim" and the responsibility that it entails is often the least worry for far too many Muslims. However, this kind of self-awareness is essential for creating a contextualised, post-ethnic realisation of Islam in the UK.

Human beings have been created not as a monolithic race devoid of different nations (49:13), colours and languages (30:22). The Madinan society, formed on the Prophetic motto "spread peace amongst you" (*afshus salama bainakum*) was as good an example as any. For the *Muhajir* (Muslims of Makkah who emigrated to Madina during the *Hijra*) the diverse *Ansar* (helpers of Madina) became the new "*apna*," and vice versa. God interchanges the way He addresses the reader, in some cases referring to them as "children of Adam" (*banu Adam*) whilst in other cases as "humankind" (*an-naas*) or "all that exists" (*'alamin*). How terms like *Qawm* and *Millat* used in the *Qur'an* and *hadith* literature can be applied to our times are worth exploring too.[198] In fact, interestingly, in Islamic

---

[198] Yahya Birt, *Between Nation and Umma: Muslim Loyalty in a Globalizing World*, https://yahyabirt1.wordpress.com/2007/03/18/between-nation-and-umma-muslim-loyalty-in-a-globalizing-world/, 18 March 2007.

scholarship such as in the works of logic (*mantiq*) it was customary to classify human beings as "the rational animal" (*al-hayawan al-natiq*). In other words, human presence went beyond nations, colours and languages, to a relation with the animal kingdom, contemplating the fuller *sunan* (Divine patterns) of creation.

Finally, the deeper question of our identity and belonging is much closer to us than we perhaps realise. Our lack of knowledge and conformity to self-claims of being "British," "English," "Muslim," "Pakistani," "Bangladeshi," "Nigerian," "Arab" or "Indian" and their various combinations etc. is quite telling of the differences between "who we think we are" from "who we want to be" from "who others perceive us to be" from "who we actually are." Not being true to what we claim creates, perhaps, far deeper spiritual and psychological problems. And with that comes yet more inner questions about identity and belonging than we perhaps realise.

## 3.3 The focus on Muslim women's clothing is complicated

The construction of femininity in the modern world is vastly different from pre-modern, and the politics of the *hijab* (head scarf) is arguably right at the centre of it. The heightened focus on Muslim women's sports clothing in Rio 2016 and, nearer to home, in French politics and the Cannes Film festival, comes in a long line of calls over the years to ban the *hijab* and *niqab* (full face veil, also called *burka*). Much of this muscular assertion is historical Orientalist imperialism flowing through or racism that some in the style of tabloid journalism entertain to this day. Few people seem to realise that up until recent centuries it was custom for women in Britain to cover up modestly, including all of the hair on their head. Thankfully, Western societies have generally resisted calls to ban clothing worn by millions of women around the world, though increasingly as the case of the *burka* in Denmark, Austria and France, and even in some Muslim countries like Morocco have shown, there can be a red line. But one thing is for sure, the politics of women's clothing is complicated for Muslims, non-Muslims and society at large.

From the moment Muslim women are seen wearing the *hijab* or *niqab* in public, they're often met with the *prima facie* perception of being victims of some kind of forced claustration. If it's not a case of patriarchy denying women their freedoms, it's because they're somehow unworthy of, or a threat to, Western liberal society. Whatever the case, the implication is that either they or society need "saving." With that, everything about Muslim women, their hopes, anxieties and experiences, become reduced to a piece of cloth. But, time and time again, studies have disproved such perceptions.[199]

Unfortunately, these perceptions have deep-rooted foundations. The way many societies across the world today expect women to dress purports to have "nothing to do with pleasing men and everything to do with self-identification and self-gratification."[200] However, it's not a secret that the female body is an object of fantasy for many men, and of course it's

---

[199] Dalia Mogahed, *Perspectives of Women in the Muslim World*, http://media.gallup.com/worldpoll/pdf/perspectivesofwomeninthemuslimworld.pdf, 6 June 2006.

[200] *Feminisms*, edited by Sandra Kemp and Judith Squires, Oxford University Press, 1998. Spanning nearly two decades (1980-1996), the six sections of this book investigate the debates which have most characterised feminist theory to date.

a central ingredient in the commercial commitment to "looks sell." In turn, when some women feel the urge to mould themselves to the desires of men, to be "sought after," as perhaps implicit when some feel the need to make themselves "look good," modern society often disguises this instinct as the outcome of female self-confidence and freedom. In this sense, "women's readiness to buy into the myths of sexual desirability" is socially constructed as the "ultimate source of female potency, as if for women the only power they can wield is sexual power,"[201] as some argue.

This is not the only narrative at play. Much as women, including Muslim women, generally do in everyday conversation, the media takes an interest in women's body and clothing. It's not surprising given that fashion is "a means of symbolic display, a way of giving external form to narratives of self-identity."[202] Thus, what celebrities and public figures wear or don't wear, or the size of their hip or other body parts fills newspapers and TV shows. Talk of what Muslim women wear, then, can be interpreted as a continuation of "things" the media like to talk about.

However, where it gets a little sinister is when talk of these "things" lead to actual intent or proposals to criminalise Muslim women's clothing. How that isn't itself misogynistic or authoritarian is perplexing; a point which many feminists, tabloid journalists and aggressive liberals often struggle to come to terms with. Moreover, the claim that Muslim women need liberating simply because they wear the *hijab* or *niqab* without first understanding Muslim women as they would like to be understood is surely evidence of a self-centered superiority complex.

Perceptions and debates across different countries are far from uniform too. France, for example, has had a fetish-like fascination with women's clothing for centuries, culminating perhaps in today's concepts like *haute couture* ("high fashion" as custom fit clothing) and *prêt-à-porter* ("ready to wear" clothing). Different countries differ in the nature and boundaries they set for state secularity. Governments are under different pressures from modern terrorism and changing definitions of national identity. The public also have different understanding of Muslim clothing and tolerance for "otherness."

---

[201] Ibid.
[202] Anthony Giddens, *Modernity and Self-Identity: Self and Society in the Late Modern Age*, Polity, 2006, p. 62.

The situation in Muslim countries isn't straightforward either. There are long-standing differences between scholars about the necessity of the *niqab*. Many women today choose not to wear the *hijab*, too, sometimes because they simply choose not to, or because they feel they haven't reached a certain level of religious observance, lack courage, or due to anxieties about what others might say. A few governments like Saudi Arabia and Iran prescribe public dress code, whilst others, the overwhelming majority, leave it up to individual Muslims to decide for themselves.

In the context of third generation Muslims of the UK, the question of cultural self-assertion is also relevant. It is of course human nature that if we stand out in a crowd, the chances are, others will look at us. Usually, this is nothing more than human perceptual senses at work, reflecting curiosity on the part of those perceiving something slightly out of the ordinary. Over time, as people get more used to seeing things, they take less notice, until perhaps, eventually, it's all part of the same view. In the meantime, however, it can go badly wrong when fairness, respect or a caring attitude is neglected by onlookers.

In this respect I would argue that "Islam's ancient cultural wisdom"[203] is instructive. Historically, Muslims tended to adapt their clothing to whatever cultures they were part of. Like the *saree, salwar kameez* or the African head wrap and blouse and skirt, all of which are indigenous to non-Arab peoples, they can be designed or worn with the requirement for modesty intact. And so, the experience of third generation British Muslims can be interpreted as one of negotiating clothing that meshes them into British society while still fulfilling the requirement for modesty. The so-called "burkini" is perhaps a more recent attempt, and other examples can be seen in the growing Muslim women's fashion industry. Where, the value of Muslim women's clothing extends to more than modesty, as an antidote to the harms caused by objectifying women,[204] and girls growing up accepting that how they look is more important than how they feel or who they are. As for men, independent studies have shown that simply seeing pictures of

---

[203] Umar Faruq Abd-Allah, *Islam and the Cultural Imperative*, Nawawi Foundation, 2004
[204] Mairi Macleod, *What's Really to Blame for Our Skinny Obsession?*, https://www.psychologytoday.com/gb/blog/sexy-science/201602/what-s-really-blame-our-skinnyobsession, 26 February 2016.

glamorised skinny women on TV conditions their attractiveness towards such forms. Even though, as the actress Emma Watson noted, "With airbrushing and digital manipulation," we create "an unobtainable image that's dangerously unhealthy."[205]

Thus, ongoing indigenisation means that clothing forms will evolve. In the meantime, it's natural that some Muslims will feel let down when others complain that they don't integrate more, and yet when they do join in they get the feeling that it's not right either. Here, patience and continued education of the public is needed. Thank God for the emergence of some Muslim women who have begun to competently argue their case. However, I sense also the need to make friends with tabloid journalists and holding emotionally intelligent dialogues.

There are also gender imbalances specific to Muslim communities that need urgent attention (as there are with society at large). Such issues are easy fodder for maintaining stereotypes and ill-formed perceptions, not to mention the way they limit the potential of Muslim women in society. Many causes can be cited, some to do with economic disadvantages, cultural taboos, lack of education and aspiration deficit, narrow interpretations of religious texts, lack of female scholarship etc.

Finally, it's worth noting that the underlying principle for Muslim women's clothing is the concept of *haya*, which is acting out of self-respect, virtue, modesty, bashfulness, decency and scruple. *Haya* conditions people's behaviour with the anticipation of uneasy feelings of embarrassment in acting out something indecent or breaking a commitment to a social standard. The Prophet said, "modesty is a part of faith."[206] The Prophet also said, "Every faith has an innate character. The character of Islam is modesty."[207] "Lowering the gaze," then, is as eminently a part of *haya* for men as it is for women to dress modestly.

---

[205] Maev Kennedy, *Emma Watson criticises 'dangerously unhealthy' pressure on young women*, The Guardian, 20 March 2014.

[206] *Hadith* narrated by Abu Huraira in *Sahih al-Bukhari* (and similar variations are recorded in other books of *hadith*): "The Prophet said, "Faith (Belief) consists of more than sixty branches (i.e. parts). And *Haya* is a part of faith."

[207] *Hadith* narrated by Zayd Ibn Talha Ibn Rukana, in the *Mu'atta* of Imam Malik: "The Messenger of Allah, may Allah bless him and grant him peace, said, 'Every deen has an innate character. The character of Islam is modesty.'"

Modesty in dress is meant to move the focus both for men and women from the external to the internal, "making the beauty of the inner self the most important focus."[208] That's also part of the complication when it comes to Muslim women's clothing.

---

[208] Syima Aslam, *To hijab or not to hijab - a Muslim businesswoman's view*, The Guardian, 10 December 2012.

# 3.4 The Casey Review: what are we to make of it?

The much-awaited "Casey Review"[209] has already been dubbed by some as "white-washing" whilst others have praised it "excellent." Either way, it was always bound to ignite passionate debate, for it would ask difficult questions; reviews of this kind are of course seldom completely free of political or ideological bias, even if unconscious. Not least, this was always going to be a subjective review: it's Dame Louise Casey and her teams' perspective and intellectual proficiency to cut through the complexities of society using interview technique (with over 800 interviews and written submissions considered). The battle lines between the left- and right-media have already taken place, tainting or exonerating the review. Here are a few take outs.

Many of the diversifying trends that Casey identified are not new. In fact, they're actually ongoing experiences in many countries and are not necessarily specific to the UK, reflecting the wider socio-geographic impacts of new technologies, globalisation and immigration policies in support of post-colonial, post-war transitions and modernisation. Much of it is also simply reflecting the natural ebb and flow of how human societies have always developed culturally since perhaps as far back as the semi-permanent village civilisation of the late Stone Age. The composition of the UK's Anglo-Saxon-Celt history is itself a very good example. And the fact that British society is becoming more secular is hardly a new insight.

Some of the trends that Casey focuses on seem to be somewhat outdated perception or they lack rigorous demographic segmentation. For example, it is well-known that compared to earlier generations, third generation Bangladeshis and Pakistanis are less interested in going back to Bangladesh or Pakistan to look for a spouse. However, the lack of more granular segmentation means that the transitory, intergenerational nature of social attitudes isn't reflected, giving erroneous conclusions like Casey's

---

[209] Dame Louise Casey, *The Casey Review: a review into opportunity and integration*, 5 December 2016, https://www.gov.uk/government/publications/the-casey-review-a-review-into-opportunity-and-integration. In July 2015, at the request of the then Prime Minister and Home Secretary, Dame Louise Casey was asked to undertake a review into integration and opportunity in our most isolated and deprived communities. This report sets out the findings of that review.

overemphasis on "first generation in every generation" phenomenon. Yet we know that when it comes to understanding forward-looking social attitudes appropriate demographic segmentation is absolutely vital.

Sometimes the lack of appropriate segmentation can be at least partially compensated by a rigorously thought-out structure. But that's also not quite there in parts of the review either. For example, discussions on immigration haven't been broken out into different periods. Casey somewhat sloppily doesn't differentiate immigration from Eastern Europe post-2004 EU-enlargement and post-war from South Asia. Yet we know they bring different challenges and arise out of different socio-economic and political environments which in turn require different policy treatments. This pattern is repeated in many sections of the review which unwittingly leaves the reader with the impression that it's a case of the "trouble with Muslim communities" wrapped up within some broader observations about "immigrant communities."

The language used seems to be at times quite loose too. In one place, somewhat lazily, suggesting "too many cases..." without then substantiating it. And generally, the problem statement hasn't been properly scoped out at the beginning, so from the outset you don't quite know what should be in or out of scope in the report. On that note, one other glaringly obvious omission is the lack of review on working-class white communities, even as a brief look at their intercultural exchanges with Muslims. This is a large segment of our society that, as the Brexit vote has indicated, feels hugely marginalised, which quite frankly isn't surprising given the socio-economic and structural consequences of post-industrialism. However, they've not yet been addressed properly by any political party.

Whilst these aren't the only weaknesses in Casey's review, it would be wrong to dismiss the report in its entirety as some critics have suggested. The tendency to uncritically accept the critique of the left in its ideological tussle with the right is one that requires temperance and originality if we're ever to come up with compelling policies and narratives. For example, if we claim that it's about Muslim communities for whom the Islamic faith is meant to be important, surely, it's also a space to contribute through an understanding of what Islam (being subservient to God) has to offer?

Hence, it's worth reading the review dispassionately, to see that it does highlight useful matter-of-fact stats and insights about Muslim communities and areas that need discussing in order to form workable policies. Fears about immigration among some Muslims, for example, require reconciling given that British Muslims are themselves overwhelmingly descendants of immigrants; and there are Prophetic values of self-less tolerance which we need to be mindful of especially in light of what Brexit has revealed about immigration concerns. Casey's review also highlights pockets of comparatively low levels of educational attainment and employment. Here, what more can we do to support and nurture our young to aspire and achieve more? Do we have role models and mentoring programmes in place, for example? The fact that hate crime has increased 19% on last year is another good callout in the review. But how do we engage this space? Is it a question of simply reporting to the likes of Tell MAMA and thinking that our job is done? What about also recognising that 90% of the UK's population has never entered a mosque and therefore cannot be expected to fully understand Islam or Muslims, requiring us to respond with empathy when they do hold misconceptions? What about reaching out to those who might hate us in an emotionally intelligent way that tries to win their hearts and minds? What lessons are there for us when we learn that the Prophet was someone in whose presence even his enemies felt more secure? And, there are as yet difficult discussions on approaches to sexuality, honour-based crimes, clothing, access to female education, etiquette of speaking English when around others, the role of our mosques and institutes etc. that Muslim communities would do well to take a more institutional approach to.

Casey also makes some good recommendations about the need for additional funding, using data to promote integration and finding best practices, as well as developing approaches for overcoming cultural barriers to employment etc. These are quite sensible and targeted recommendations that if implemented properly will help with a more successful integration and well-being of communities.

To conclude, it's clear that whilst this review will be debated intensely, the real challenge is of course translating the recommendations into the right mix of policy interventions that can effectively address problems in the way that they "need to" rather than the way they "ought to." It's a subtle point about the need for government and communities to work together. Getting it right is important. It could be the difference between a more cohesive UK that flourishes and becomes an example to the world, commanding moral authority, versus a UK that withdraws into the narcissistic appeal of the human psyche.

## 3.5 Citizens UK report: clues to finding the "Missing Muslims"

The Citizens UK report *The Missing Muslims - Unlocking British Muslim Potential for the Benefit of All*[210] chaired by Dominic Grieve QC is overall a welcome study that should help form policies to strengthen and progress civil society in the UK. It has many excellent recommendations, albeit at high level, for local authorities, businesses, statutory bodies, government and Muslim communities, keeping to a shared collective responsibility whilst identifying well-weighted actions for each of them. The report highlights some of the great contributions of Muslims of the UK in all sectors, as well as calling out the evolving challenges on integration, employment, political and civic participation, government policy, in mosques and Muslim institutes. In this sense, I would argue that it builds on aspects of Dame Louise Casey's Review in December 2016. That said, given that this is the culmination of 500 or so hours of testimonies and evidence gathering across the UK (by experts and active members of civil society), there are bound to be gaps and nuances which haven't been properly factored in, a few of which are worth calling out.

One of the challenges of this kind of report is getting away from speaking of a "Muslim" social category whilst recognising that "being Muslim" is not necessarily the identity marker which believers of the Islamic faith would always want to purposefully and solely interact with the rest of society. And it would be equally misguided if the rest of the society assumes this always to be the case or seeks to only interact on this basis. For example, a Muslim football enthusiast who wishes to get into coaching might reasonably want to on the basis of their passion for football,

---

[210] *The Missing Muslims - Unlocking British Muslim Potential for the Benefit of All*, Citizens UK, 2017, http://www.citizensuk.org/missing_muslims. This report known in shorthand as "Missing Muslims report" is the result of the Citizens Commission on Islam, Participation & Public Life. Conducted over 18-months, the Commissioners, comprising high profile names from the world of business, academia, politics and faith travelled to hearings across the UK to listen to more than 500 hours of testimonies and evidence detailing the experiences of Muslim and non-Muslim individuals. The report includes a series of recommendations, primarily to be actioned by community and faith institutions themselves, as well as a call on business to play its part and some key areas for action by the government.

not necessarily on the basis of "being Muslim." In cases like this, use of the category "Muslim" is completely irrelevant and misleading. Moreover, whilst the report recognises the heterogeneity of the category "Muslim," it seems to have missed the wider point about educating Muslims and society at large that self-identity is reflexive and constituted in the actions of the individual.

The report rightly recognises how the toxic climate of "us and them" as well as growing anti-Muslim hatred and prejudice in society leads to a cycle of separateness, and Muslims feeling that they're being unfairly targeted for their faith. The report offers workable recommendations for the media and IPSO.[211] Particularly useful is the commonsense "triple-check" to avoid conflating faith with extremism (relevance, statistics and terminology). However, the report hasn't identified sources of "otherising" and suspicion that some Muslims get away with, which are not in response to the more recent toxic climate (predating 9/11), but borne out of worldviews that undermine civil society and shared values.

It's also good to see, perhaps for the first time in a report of this kind, the influence of "*biraderi*" kinship/clan patriarchy called out, which it rightly says, in some communities, frustrates women and the young from greater civic participation. The report suggests that members outside of the Muslim community (MPs, councillors, statutory agencies etc.) could help remedy this. The question of "*biraderi*" kinship/clan politics is a good example of how a cultural phenomenon reflecting practices imported from Pakistan is perceived to overlap with the category "Muslim" in the UK. This intersectionality between cultural and religious identity markers requires more rigorous research and development of nuanced frameworks to avoid cross-implanting issues of genealogical ethno-culture with those of faith. Particularly given that the extent to which third generation Muslims should insist on actively, or passively, retaining their genealogical culture into the next generation remains an ongoing exploration both for parents individually and collectively as communities. The report's call for well-paid, professionally trained "British imams" who are tuned into the British experience and given Muslim women access to mosques are subtle indications that there comes a point when it becomes necessary to evaluate

---

[211] IPSO (Independent Press Standards Organisation) is the independent regulator for the newspaper and magazine industry in the UK.

the continuity of genealogical ethno-culture or uncontextualised religion and consider if it requires institutional intervention.

The "Prevent Policy" is also called out for being ineffective in tackling extremism and radicalisation, which the report recognises as being seen by Muslim communities as a "very real problem" and requires a more trusted framework, for better buy-in and collaboration. Whilst not calling for an outright scrapping of Prevent, it joins growing calls for an independent review, offering ideas like an Independent Ombudsman, involvement of Advisory Groups of local stakeholders etc. However, the report doesn't identify how it's "a very real problem." Nor does the report identify how Muslims might overcome the current climate of cynicism and victim mentality to any notion of institutional intervention, or the historical reluctance of sectarian groups and rival national organisations to work together for mutual benefit. Particularly, given that interventions encouraged by government (even if independently) are likely to be seen by some as colonial and tainted with suspicion. The history of malpractices of Prevent and politicians' unhelpful use of "inflammatory rhetoric" doesn't help, which has been called out in the report as "the broken relationship" between the government and Muslim communities "on both sides." Moreover, conditions of runaway globalisation, fragmented authority and post-modern consciousness can be challenging barriers to effecting policy regardless of which political party is implementing it, though by no means is it insurmountable.

The report does well to highlight "unconscious bias" in attitudes towards employability. According to BBC research, a Muslim-sounding name is offered three times fewer interviews than an English sounding name. It's even worse for women, the report claims, often passed over for jobs that they're well-qualified for. Overall, such realities damage confidence and exacerbates "aspiration ambition deficit," income inequalities and social mobility issues in Muslim communities. Sometimes to the extent that women have to resort to "removing their *hijab* to find work." Given these issues, the report recommends better mentoring schemes and outreach programmes, and calls on employers to act, amongst other things.

The report recommends that scouting should be used to consciously bring together young people of different cultures and faiths. However, on the ground, scouting has in many places become stratified into "Muslim scouts" as opposed to enabling kids from different communities to mix together. This traces to a more fundamental question about the way we design initiatives for civil society and whether we give enough thought to wider society for fear of "betraying our own traditions." It's a bit like policies that didn't encourage first generation immigrants to learn English, and a couple of generations on we're seeing the consequences of it in the older generation's struggle to communicate with the young in English.

Finally, there are many gaps in the report. It's surprising that there's hardly any mention of online strategy not just in respect of preventing radicalisation, but for creating fruitful narratives for consolidating shared values and strengthening civil society online. Moreover, there's no mention of best practices for religious education and curricula in after-school Islamic studies classes (*maktab*). Nor are there any recommendations for: overcoming religious factionalism which struggles to contextualise to British life (mentioned only in context to "persecution" in the report); racism by Asian against black Muslims; and the lack of intra-community integration between those of, for example, Bangladeshi and Pakistani heritage.

One of the running themes of the report is for diversifying voices and engagement. However, uncoordinated diversification doesn't automatically guarantee quality or the right outcomes for civil society. And, at least in the short-term, may only attract the already "activated" or "politically-aggrieved" rather than the currently disinterested who, given the right encouragement and platform, may nevertheless possess great potential to contribute meaningfully towards civil society. Thus, for this report to be useful overall, it requires greater planning, institution-building, strategic roadmaps and funding - all of which is in scarce supply. But one thing is for sure, it's in the UK's interests to unlock the potential of British Muslims as the report recommends.

# 3.6 Race Disparity Audit: what next for government

Standing outside of Number 10 Downing Street on her first day as Prime Minister, Theresa May called for a Race Disparity Audit.[212] Whilst it was highly commendable that the structural race-inequality question was once again coming back into government focus, there was a fair amount of scepticism of what exactly it would tell us that we didn't already know. Perhaps more to the point, there was genuine scepticism about how the government would intervene given the decade-long policy of fiscal tightening ("austerity"), keeping tax and spending low and more recently the heavy preoccupation with Brexit. So, what are we to make of the Race Disparity Audit published in October 2017, and what should we lobby for to undo the burning race-inequality injustices?

To start with, it's quite encouraging that the government has sought to bring greater transparency by putting the many disparate metrics into a single portal. Not only does this give everyone a relatively easy and one-stop convenient access (as opposed to being scattered in a multitude of reports across many civic bodies and university studies), but the fact that it's a government department which has effectively laid out to bare a revealing state-of-the-nation view does potentially give greater legitimacy and urgency to the cause.

That said, it's worth noting that statistics don't have the power in themselves to explain why things are the way they are. Hence, we shouldn't simply jump to conclusions faced with seemingly stark differences in areas of public life, as unpalatable as they may seem at first. For example, in education, while 71% of British Chinese achieve expected results, among white British it's 54%, and for white Gypsy and Roma pupils it's as low as 13%. The fact that Gypsy and Roma pupils hugely underachieve in education relative to others may simply be a natural consequence of the migratory cultural choice that these communities rely on for their cultural identity. The question primarily becomes then not necessarily one directly about race-inequality injustices. Equally, there's opportunity to benchmark other communities against Chinese pupils. Again, it may come to a complex intermix of cultural and structural factors.

---

[212] See: *Race Disparity Audit*, https://www.gov.uk/government/publications/race-disparity-audit, October 2017.

Home ownership is another good example. The proportion of white British senior managers owning their homes at 82% compares to only 55% among senior managers from other ethnic groups. But here's the problem with this stat: it doesn't normalise the positive impact of inheritance and therefore doesn't give a truer picture of race-related injustice. That is, broadly speaking, if the white population has been living on the British Isles for hundreds of years, it's only normal to expect that at a macro level they fare better on a measure of home ownership. Moreover, a disproportionate concentration of black and ethnic minorities living in major cities where property prices tend to be higher compared to more rural areas means that affordability is naturally lower for black and ethnic minorities, especially with the lack of real-terms growth in wages in recent years.

Similarly, on unemployment, black and ethnic minorities have roughly twice the level of unemployment as white people across all regional and demographic segments. We know from other studies how prejudices lead to real race-inequality injustices. Most egregious is perhaps the mounting evidence of unfair discrimination that an applicant with a "foreign-sounding" name faces simply by virtue of their name. There's also mounting discomfort among some Muslim women applicants who forgo their *hijab* (head scarf) just so that they can be considered on the basis of their skills and aptitude, and not have to worry about being judged based on the kind of clothing they wear.

However, at the same time, many have said that solutions remain elusive and of course no single policy can do it all. That said, as I've argued here, there are many policy interventions which the government can quite easily institute. Some of which may not need incremental spending. I would even argue that they have the potential to kick-start wider positive impacts to social cohesion, productivity and cultural innovation for a UK that thrives as a rich, inclusive, cosmopolitan society.

For example, the government could introduce legislation compelling employers (private and public) of a certain size to reflect diverse society in their workforces and to make it a legal obligation to publish equality audits each year. The government could also institute into law recruitment based on name- and address-blind applications, as recommended in the

Citizens UK report.[213] This links in well with a more hidden problem at the heart of race-inequality injustices: the prevalence of unconscious bias. There is no doubt that the government needs to fund research to identify and overcome the impact of unconscious bias in public life within organisational culture, recruitment, training and development and access to public services etc.

To improve home ownership, the government could increase the threshold for stamp duty, but crucially link it to affordability indices, and only for first time buyers in target areas, which could be funded perhaps by a small increase in the rate of stamp duty for high-end properties. The government could also target housing vouchers to those on low incomes. However, any intervention in housing almost certainly would require an increase in the supply of new homes if we're to avoid simply boosting demand that couldn't be supplied and therefore increasing prices, which would unwittingly risk widening socio-economic disparities. And there's a whole raft of other proposals in the government's own briefing paper[214] which are worth considering.

Of course, there's so much more to say on this and for government to do - only a few examples have been produced here for illustrations purpose. If we're looking at this from a holistic point of view, Damian Green MP is absolutely right in saying that addressing racial injustices "will require a concerted effort by government, partners and communities working together." However, from a leadership point of view, it's clear that we need far more intelligent and bold involvement from the government to break down structural barriers and institutional racism, to provide opportunities, and to institute nuanced policies that help level the playing field, rather than forcing people from black and ethnic minorities, as the Equality Trust called it, "to sprint just to stay still."[215]

Otherwise, the Race Disparity Audit risks being yet another report

---

[213] *The Missing Muslims - Unlocking British Muslim Potential for the Benefit of All*, *Citizens UK*, 2017, http://www.citizensuk.org/missing_muslims.

[214] *Extending home ownership: Government initiatives*, Briefing Paper Number 03668, http://researchbriefings.files.parliament.uk/documents/SN03668/SN03668.pdf, 28 December 2017.

[215] The Equality Trust, *Government and Business Must Do More On Social Mobility*, https://www.equalitytrust.org.uk/government-and-business-must-do-more-social-mobility, 21 June 2017.

that has all the jingoism of hope (for example: "build a country that works for everyone") but emphatically fails to deliver any beneficial change. And with that, the opportunity to create a country that has the ambition of being the epitome of the world carrying the hopes and aspirations of millions of our own current and future generations could lay in ruin. That's in no one's interest.

## 3.7 Co-opting Muslim charities into the politics of cultural self-assertion

As human beings we crave recognition of our efforts. Whether it's a pat on the back or something more, it's always nice to be recognised by peers, teachers or senior managers at work. So it seemed this was no different in the recent *A Very Merry Muslim Christmas*[216] report by the All Party Parliamentary Group (APPG) on British Muslims highlighting the work of Muslim charities in the UK. This was British Muslims showcased for the charitable value they contribute to British society. The context, however, wasn't so clear cut, which got me thinking. Why would politicians and members of civic groups suddenly want to become bastions of the collective effort of Muslim charity organisations from soup kitchens feeding the homeless to institutional *zakat* distributors, and to do so in Christmas?

Now, before we go further, I want to clear up a couple of things. Firstly, as far as numbers go the Muslim charity sector overall is very impressive, punching well above their weight. For example, according to the Charity Commission, British Muslims as a whole donated money at a rate of £38 per second during Ramadhan 2016, which is a staggering £371 per individual.[217] In *A Survey of Charitable Giving in the British Muslim Community* in December 2014 by the independent organisation, Cause 4, 48.9% of respondents said that they gave at least £20 per month on average to charitable causes, which equates to over £240 per year, and 22.4% of respondents said that they make an average monthly donation of at least £50, which equates to over £600 per year. Yet, in the NPC's *Money for Good* report, the average donation for donors generally in the UK was £303 over the past 12 months. All of this clearly shows that there is a significant segment of British Muslims who don't just show intent for but actually donate twice as much as the average Brit.[218] For a diverse community that

---

[216] All Party Parliamentary Group on British Muslims, *A Very Merry Muslim Christmas*, December 2017.
[217] *Charity Commission hails 'sheer scale' of fundraising by British Muslims during Ramadan*, The Independent, 22 July 2016.
[218] Ali Khimji, *A Survey of Charitable Giving in the British Muslim Community*, Cause 4, December 2014.

consistently comes among the lowest socio-economic classes, this is a very significant display of generosity.

Secondly, there is an ongoing debate among British Muslims, including its most erudite scholars, about how best to engage with the cultural elements of Christmas, which is in many respects a religio-cultural festival and not intrinsic to Islam. But Muslims as a minority group, and arguably, living increasingly in a Makkan context[219] must face and deal with this question. It's a reconciliation that remains unfinished with varied arguments and positions. Certainly, it isn't helped by the fact that the politics of identity are much thornier, fragmented and more complex today than in the 1980s and 90s when many Muslim children grew up happily singing hymns like "Kumbaya my Lord" or "In His Hands" in school assemblies. This article isn't about this debate or the identity boundaries that might define whether, or in what contexts, we can say "Merry Christmas."[220]

My argument is a little deeper and goes to the very heart of principles that we apply in "how" we engage with the public in the politics of cultural recognition and inner dignity of our "Muslimness." The APPG on British Muslims is about celebrating the contribution of British Muslims to Britain, and Christmas being a period of happiness and fun might seem like the right kind of "Norman Tebbit immigration test" to engage with. The downside is that by so overtly linking Muslims to Christmas in the run-up to Christmas you run the risk of being accused of cultural encroachment, the so-called "creeping-*Shari'ah*" type, which is difficult to placate in today's social media environment. Though, I am a little wary

---

[219] Refers to the socio-religious and political context in the first 13 years of Prophethood in the city of Makkah, where there were few followers, with Muslims without much influence or support from the wider society, and where the focus was on teaching the foundations of Islam and cultivating the strength of belief.

[220] Much like our use of language generally, according to Islam the permissibility of saying "Merry Christmas" would depend entirely on one's context and intentions. As a cultural goodwill message which is what most Muslims base it on, it's completely fine and one that would fall under the broader principle of building good relations and civility that Islam encourages. However, it would be impermissible if one intends to tacitly acknowledge or support the Christian doctrine of Jesus as son of God - this is the opinion of Shaykh Mohammad Akram Nadwi, Shaykh Mohammed Nizami and others.

that those Muslim charity workers, who refrain from engaging Christmas due to its roots in the Trinitarian doctrine, might have unwittingly become the sacrificial turkey as it were despite their love and hard work as Britons.

After all, unlike those who have argued that "a very merry Muslim Christmas" is a social media slogan for both politically-correct "good" Muslims and, worst still, that Muslims need humanising,[221] the reality is that in the realm of public self-assertion there is always a need to make the case for something, rather than simply expecting the world to automatically recognise or accede to a certain moral value. A very painful example of this is the lack of pro-EU PR campaigns in the decade leading up to Brexit. Positive things don't just happen out of thin air or inaction, which is why we elect people to govern and rely on civic bodies to help shape policy in order to correct failure in our society.

Nor, as some have argued, does the report necessarily have to include "all" charities or mention irrelevant details like the charity workers who were stripped of their citizenship while doing charity work because they were deemed security risks. The reality is that this report was never meant to be exhaustive. In fact, the report focuses on charity work done in Britain. And on that note, we know very well that the overwhelming majority of charity donations by British Muslims leaves the UK. Thus, the idea that Muslims have somehow overcome negotiating multiple attachments to local, national and transnational belongings is not yet true. This happens even for *zakat* payments most of which leaves the UK, despite the Prophetic imperative to prioritise local distribution.

These points aside, my main contention is that it is questionable whether the *A Very Merry Muslim Christmas* report itself passed the "trustworthy test." Self-exaggeration is an un-Godly tactic in the politics of self-assertion. As cultural anthropologists like Stuart Hall (1932-2014) note, "it is only through relation to the Other, the relation to what it is not, to precisely what it lacks, to what has been called its constitutive outside that the 'positive' meaning of any terms - and this its 'identity' - can be constructed."[222]

---

[221] Shaista Aziz, *A very merry Muslim Christmas: the slogan for 'good' Muslims*, The Guardian, 21 December 2017.

[222] Hall, S. *Who needs identity?* in S. Hall and P. du Gay (eds.) Questions of Cultural Identity, Sage, 1996.

In other words, in relation to our discussion here, the Muslim charity sector is miniscule in context to the wider non-Muslim charity sector which is worth approx. £39 billion yearly, with 760,000 paid employees. Put in this context, the claim that Muslim charities are a "fourth emergency service" in Britain during Christmas seems somewhat self-exaggerated. Unchallenged claims of greatness can often be perceived to deny the real achievements and cultural pride of others, which lead not only to a breakdown of trust but also to culturally-ingrained grievances that incite equally embellished counter-claims. This is exactly the kind of politics we need to move away from, to have at our fingertips emotionally intelligent responses, in order to at least have a chance of winning the hearts and minds of those who may have trouble seeing successful Muslims.

The APPG on British Muslims could have avoided this if they contextualised the report to the wider charity work of non-Muslims; even mentioning that there are some 167,000 registered charities in England and Wales, most of whom also go quietly about charity giving and volunteering during Christmas. They could have also been much more explicit about the annualised numbers quoted to remove the impression from the title of the report that it all happens in Christmas, something which Sadiq Khan recognised in his tweet where he explicitly called out "...and throughout the year."

## 3.8 What "Britain First" should know to put Britain first?

Whenever the far-right BNP splinter group Britain First march, it reignites the focus on their misguided views.[223] The name "Britain First" was coined by its closed-minded founders to suggest that so-called "newcomers" to Britain, particularly Muslims, aren't willing to integrate and have no interest in putting Britain first. As if in one single sweep everything about British Muslims, including their love for their home in the UK, and their aspirations and hard work to help build a thriving society, can be quite simply reduced to nothing. Used in this way, the term itself is consciously dishonest.

Zealot suspicion of "otherness" is of course nothing new whether in the UK or elsewhere for that matter. In the diaries of Samuel Pepys (1633-1703) we find, for instance, that the Great Fire of London was blamed on French immigrants. Similarly, the history of persecution of Catholics is another terrible memory. In all cases, for a small group of bigots, anger and a lack of recourse to address simmering socio-political grievances or self-righteousness, was expressed in ill-treatment or intolerant attitudes towards immigrants - known otherwise as xenophobia.

Similarly, Britain First is a phenomenon of narrowed worldview where the hate-filled surround themselves in social media swarms of clickbait of completely inaccurate and dishonest information about people whom they know little about. Unsuspectingly, people are lured to its online pages with politicised "honey trap" images, memes and infographics.[224] And once there, people often passively consume its hyperbolic and scaremongering infotainment. Whilst much of this reflects a rather unedifying aspect of social media culture, it also reveals ignorance and an unwillingness to make meaningful contact with Muslims to learn about the Islamic

---

[223] This article was in response to the Britain First's march in Luton on 27 June 2015. The points raised apply to other far-right nationalist leaders and groups like the English Defence League (EDL), Pediega, British Nationalist Party (BNP), Klu Klux Klan (KKK) etc.

[224] Thomas G. Clark, *12 things you should know about Britain First*, http://anotherangryvoice.blogspot.co.uk/2014/06/12-things-britain-first.html?m=1, 7 June 2014, retrieved 3 June 2015.

faith, inasmuch as Muslims haven't done enough to convey their religion contextualised to the UK.

But the fears of Britain First can only be described as irrational. British Muslims make up only 5% of the UK population, which is around one Muslim for every 20 or so people. There are about 2000 mosques in Britain amidst over 40,000 churches.[225] These are hardly reasons for banners saying "No more mosques" or scaremongering the public.

Britain First's crude understanding of "otherness" is not any better either. Indigenisation of "otherness" has always been an ongoing process. For example, whatever one thinks of them, cultural expressions that only a few years ago would have been considered alien (ethnic foods, music and dance routines are good examples) have become absorbed into British popular culture today. Equally, it is of course impossible for people to simply delete the memory of their forefathers and places of ancestral origin. Naturally, one should expect the characteristics of second and third generation immigrant communities to still reflect, to varying degrees of course, "their country of origin, their pre-migration status, period of migration, settlement histories and legal, language, educational and employment issues that they face."[226]

Besides, cultural self-assertion has always been an inviolable part of human societies. The encounter of new ideas, peoples and ways in the process of cultural evolution creates, as to be expected, transitive periods where cultures meet and coalesce. In fact, if it wasn't for "mutually- assured diversity"[227] human societies couldn't have evolved over time from the level of "semi-permanent peasant village" some 5000 years ago to the global communities today.

In response to cultural self-assertion, the British have quite rightly grown to appreciate and adopt such diversity. Not merely because it makes economic sense, that people are more productive if they feel at home, but by the quintessentially British attitude that, "immigration has happened, that we have new neighbours, and that it is our absolute duty to get on with

---

[225] *English Church Census 2005*, http://www.eauk.org/church/research-and-statistics/ english-church-census.cfm, 20 March 2008.

[226] *Understanding Muslim Ethnic Communities*, Change Institute, 2009, p. 5.

[227] Zia Uddin Sardar, *Beyond Difference: Cultural Relations in the Twenty First Century*, British Council, 2004.

them as best we can."[228] Pragmatism, tolerance and conviviality have long been core to Britishness, much more so than Britain First or the far-right generally care to recognise.

It works the other way too. It would have been unheard of among British Muslims in the villages and towns of their ancestors to celebrate birthdays, wedding anniversaries, Mother's Day, Bonfire Night, and a whole host of other British cultural expressions that, whether one agrees with them or not, have comfortably found a place in the ongoing hybridised experience of British Muslims. Islam allows local styles to evolve whilst maintaining the broad bounds of Islam - it's always been like that in every part of the world. The British influence on Islamic culture is still in the making; it is "For British Muslims to explore and publicise."[229]

The religion that Britain First so despise itself commands Muslims to "come to a common word" (3:64) with others by uniting in mutual harmony on what is agreed between them - and there is so much to agree and share in order to "know one another" (49:13). In spite of their hatred of Muslims, Muslims are still commanded to care for those who abuse out of ignorance, to look after their poor and orphans, to give neighbourly assistance and to protect them against wrongdoing.[230]

British Muslims can only therefore extend the hand of friendship to Britain First and call upon them to abandon hate for mutual affection and respect. Surely, to put the interests of all British people first is to put Britain first?

---

228 Peter Hitchins, *It's not a Muslim issue. In our modern nation you're an extremist, too,* Mail Online, 15 June 2014.
229 Tim Winter, *British Muslim Identity*, Muslim Academic Trust, 2003, p. 24.
230 Abu Aaliyah, *The Basic Rules of Religious Activism*, The Humble "I", 25 September 2012.

## 3.9 Overcoming apathy in the politics of condemning terrorism

In the aftermath of the horrific, mind-numbing attack in Westminster on 22 March 2017 some have taken to expressing views about why Muslims shouldn't condemn acts of terrorism. In one case, up to 75 reasons have been cited, even sarcastically suggesting that condemning terrorism has for some people become something of a sixth pillar of Islam.[231] Others have claimed that the right-wing media and Islamophobes have created a climate of social pressure trapping Muslims into exaggerating their condemnation rhetoric only to unwittingly reinforce the association between terrorism and Muslims and Islam in the public's minds. There is yet, it is argued, a moral equivalence with Christian groups, the media and politicians, who appear unmoved to condemn the near daily occurrence of acts of mass killings by terrorists in places like Syria, Afghanistan, Yemen and Iraq etc. Others cite how some face backlash from Muslim congregations when the perception is that they "never talk about issues related to the global *ummah*" yet are quick to condemn acts of terrorism nearer to home.

However, reading all of this it pains to see the lack of basic human fraternity and emotional intelligence (empathy, expressing sadness etc.) among those making such claims. For whom, the relevance of social perception in the ebb and flow of being sensitive to, and winning, the hearts and minds of people in wider society seems completely blocked out.

There is also the context of "who" is doing the condemning. Organisations which seek to represent Muslims are duty-bound to publicly and emphatically condemn terrorist atrocities, to be seen as decent, empathetic and in solidarity with the wider society. Thankfully, Muslim organisations have generally got better at doing this over the years, which has helped signal Muslim "in-group" identity tuned into the wider society's conversations and feelings at such momentous times. Acts of politically-motivated malice are designed to draw wedge between people. And hence, in the immediate aftermath it becomes incumbent to step up in symbolic shows of genuine concern, love and solidarity. The human heart

---

[231] Ismail Ibrahim, *75 Reasons Why Muslims Must Stop With Their Terrorism Condemnation Ritual*, Muslimmatters.org, 10 August 2016.

is programmed by God to desire harmony and to recognise when good is done to us (91:8) and in momentous times this is more so than ever.

Our human nature and how societies work means that we're more likely to be moved by events happening closer to home. This is just the reality of how consequences unfold. Thus, when the mainstream media or politicians aren't seen to be giving enough attention to daily occurrences of terrorism in other parts of the world, it isn't in itself an indication of utter disregard. The simple fact is that it might be more important to us as Muslims to take an interest but to expect everyone else seems somewhat unrealistic.

Admittedly, in an increasingly interconnected world we're exposed to things that happen far away from the day-to-day realities of our lives. Mass media tends to create false consciousness, opening our eyes to problems "out there" without giving us the local contexts, necessary capacity or competence to do something productive about it. For many it's a distraction that heightens their sense of looming crises and instability to be always around the corner. Not to mention, those arguing against condemning apply a "chaos theory"-like approach that seems to unwittingly make everything wrong in the world the responsibility of individual Muslims to not only be aware of but also to fix. Yet, looking at the plight of Muslim communities around the world, you would think a little humility won't go amiss. It is, after all, God who reminds us that the "soul isn't burdened beyond what it can bear" (2:286) and, as individuals, we won't be judged on something that we're not responsible for (41:46).

There is of course a time, place and manner to have mature debates about things. Not that the drench of anger-filled populist sentiments of many today can be expected to deal with anything appropriately, least of all be an example of virtue. Firebrand rhetoric whether from the mosque *minbar* or on social media is something that certainly appears strong, yet it is utterly inert to its core. Lacking in deeper thought, self-awareness, competence and the organising power to bring about lasting change, it is in fact a subtle hypocrisy (*nifaq*) in religious culture which has arguably been normalised.

In some sections, condemnation apathy has set in based on the argument that condemnation culture since 9/11 hasn't won Muslims any friends, citing the hardening of Counter Terrorism laws as proof. However, to correlate the two as causally linked you would have to assume that Counter Terrorism laws, as problematic in their application in places as they might be, exist only because of the Muslim community's failure to condemn terrorism and not because society actually needs protection from terrorism. We know this is not the case since the threat of terrorism is real.

Condemning terrorism is also not about apologising for something done in the name of Islam, as some interpret it. Rather, it's about building solidarity against destructive forces and ensuring that the distinction between what Islam is versus its perversion by individuals and groups is continually reinforced in public. This becomes even more important given that the British public arguably hasn't had a sustained and fruitful interaction with contextualised Islam which is partly a reflection of Muslims not doing enough to sort out their own house and to convey and demonstrate the value of their faith. And of course, showing solidarity against terrorism can be expressed in so many ways, in vigils, peace walks, stand-up events, seminars, talks, songs, poems, official statements, articles, tweets, interfaith work, documentaries, plays, giving charity etc.

The fact that Christian groups, the media and politicians may not condemn the near daily occurrence of acts of mass killings by terrorists in places like Syria and Iraq is not to in any way to condone such atrocities, but perhaps reflects other psychological effects which are worth being aware of. The daily occurrence of atrocities in regions of conflict is to be expected since, sadly, that's what happens in conflict. As a result, people find themselves feeling desensitised in what psychologist's term "psychic numbing." Moreover, thinking too much about traumatic events such as refugee crisis, school shootings or terrorist bombs exploding in crowded markets can easily lead people back in the UK to become overly anxious or depressed. In response, they may consciously or subconsciously take protective steps to shut out or pacify the significance of such news, succumbing to what is known as "compassion fatigue."

It's also natural that we take less interest in events happening on the other side of the world if the UK overall, or as communities within the UK, we have limited interactions over there. Many Muslims get caught up here because they see a "globalised Muslim community" (*ummah*) as a single body and anything traumatic happening anywhere within it becomes equally significant. Yet, they struggle to realise that we can't expect non-Muslims to think along the same lines. The same effect happens from a diaspora perspective too. For example, events such as a bomb explosion or flooding in Bangladesh would naturally be more relevant and interesting to first and second generation British Bangladeshis than, say, British Pakistanis. These are yet more reasons why it's imperative to get the art of condemning terrorism right, recognising that there are important psychological variables at play.

Admittedly, the so-called "condemnation ritual" can at times seem quite monotonous, apologetic or even opportunistic.[232] No doubt, our take on it will depend on our appetite for different styles of engagement, and in particular seeing prominent Muslims ritualise public engagement. However, not condemning terrorism at all would only give strength to terrorists and the far-right will claim to be vindicated. Many Muslims will also be more deeply entrenched into a vicious cycle of post-colonial imaginings, feeling yet more marginalised and perpetuating victim mentality. Thankfully, we have diverse Muslim organisations and individuals who can pick up the baton.

---

[232] A good example of opportunism was following the killing of Scandinavian tourists in Morocco in December 2018, some scholars and activists went onto social media to causally link violent extremism to a default animosity to *Sufism* and *Ash'arism,* rather than making the point that they have a more general hatred and intolerance of difference that goes beyond theology and into political ideology. Similarly, minority groups with grudges against majority Muslims are also known to engage opportunistically.

# 3.10 Reflections on Mak Chishty - why journalists must ask tough questions

The press and other news organisations are well-known for their biases, investigative oversights, omissions, and of course, in popular press, a compulsion to gossip about the private antics of public figures. Whilst not all journalism wittingly starts-off with this in mind, knowing that these things happen sometimes with disastrous consequences can be a constant anxiety. This tension was summarised by Justice Leveson in his public inquiry into British newspaper ethics in 2011. "The press," he said, "provides an essential check on all aspects of public life. That is why any failure within the media affects all of us."[233]

Modern society thus trusts and relies on journalists and the media at large, whose mark of integrity cannot therefore rest on anything but an unflinching standard to be truthful, to assist in the public's well-being, and to alert the public about things that they might have otherwise uncritically gone along with. These points are well-recognised by journalists. John Simpson, for example, rightly commented on what he called the role of "unsafe but vital" good journalism. "Putting tough questions to those in power, or finding out what is really going on, instead of what vested interests say is going on ... A country requires the vibrant, competitive, accurate flow of news if it is to thrive."[234] Inconvenient truths, it seems, can be as unpalatable at times for governments and others in public office that champion freedom as they are for those that don't.

Thus, the challenge for the press is to have the highest levels of criticality and a fair-minded approach to journalism. Get that even slightly wrong and you get the kind of bigoted, almost fascist-like comments talking of "exterminating Muslims" that were so shamelessly left on social media and on websites following the interview with the then head of community engagement for the Metropolitan police, Commander Makhdum (Mak)

---

[233] *The Leveson Inquiry: Culture, Practice and Ethics of the Press,* 22 January 2014.
[234] John Simpson, *Egypt Al-Jazeera case: Good journalism not safe, but vital,* BBC News website, 7 April 2014.

Chishty.[235] God knows what kind of demonic impressions about ordinary Muslims it's left on people who have perhaps never meaningfully interacted with Muslims. The kind of "damaging stereotypes" which leads to what human rights experts are increasingly warning is an "intensification of hate speech against vulnerable groups and racist violence … against immigrants, Muslims and Roma people in particular."[236]

It's become far too common that when it comes to writing about Muslims too many journalists aren't fair and balanced enough. 150 years ago at the height of Orientalism and human zoos, journalists might have been forgiven for not doing a decent job. Of course, back then writing anything remotely favourable about the non-Western world, dubbed "the Orient," would have been seen as inherently "biased" and possible only when lacking scruple. But things are of course very different today; we have much better access to information for instance. However, despite this, and notwithstanding the fact that we still have a long way to go to better understand people's lived experiences, cultures and the effect of unconscious bias etc., it remains perplexing as to why disproportionately focusing on Muslims should be so fashionable.

The pretext, as all journalists perhaps instinctively realise, is that the views of those in public office who look to raise the profile of extreme ideology or "Muslim extremism" will always be more newsworthy than the quiet and detailed work carried out by communities in the background to engender respect and harmony. That's all fine, and arguably it's only natural that this should be the case. However, the process is only right and proper if journalists put "tough questions" to those in public office, particularly if their views are patently weak.

In the interview with Chishty, it seems his idealism and unbalanced views about "early indicators of extremism" in context to the interaction between parents and children went completely unchallenged. All of the factors that he listed (such as: refusing to celebrate Christmas, not shopping at M&S, sudden refusal of alcohol, wearing a particular type of clothing

---

[235] This article was written in response to an interview by Mak Chisty (retired since June 2017) with the Guardian newspaper, published 24 May 2015, *Jihadi threat requires move into 'private space' of UK Muslims, says police chief.*

[236] European Commission against Racism and Intolerance, *Annual Report on ECRI's Activities,* 2013.

etc.) in truth have nothing directly to do with extremism, radicalisation, criminal behaviour or incitement to hatred. You don't need to open up a sociology textbook or attend parenting classes to realise just how patently weak Chishty's views were.

Journalists must ask themselves, then, why questionable views by those in public offices can go so unchallenged when it comes to what Muslims or others under scrutiny get up to in their private spaces?

# 3.11 The doctrine of a "Muslim block vote"

In the run up to the surprise 2017 General Election (8 June 2017), there was a fair share of the usual cries of "voting is *haram*." As nefarious as these calls are, they continue rearing their ugly head whenever there's a General Election be it on social media or in verbal confrontations outside mosques. Amongst this, there are calls which have arguably been simmering for a while for a "Muslim block vote." This is the doctrine that if Muslims represent a single united block vote, for the Labour Party as it currently happens to be, they stand a better chance of being a more potent electoral group and thus make their political voice count more effectively. On the face of it, it sounds quite appealing. However, when you dig into it, it isn't as straightforward as advocates claim.

A review of demographics based on the 2011 census shows that there are 2.71 million Muslims in the UK, with most living in England - that's about 5% of the UK. Of them, 66% (1.8 million) are above 15 years old. Breaking this out into the relative share of votes across constituencies, it turns out that the Muslim share of the electorate is largest in constituencies that are already Labour Party safe seats. This isn't surprising. It merely reflects the post-war settlement history of working-class immigrant communities in industrial towns and cities across the country. As for marginal seats, again, the assumption that Muslims generally aren't already voting Labour is less probable than not.

A "First Past the Post" (FPTP) voting system, as ours is, favours continuity over returning different governments each and every time. As one analysis showed, roughly 61% of all seats (400 out of 650) are safe in what is known as "safe parliament." That is, the majority of constituencies rarely change. In fact, some haven't changed since the Victorian times (e.g. North Shropshire has been Tory since 1835 and Doncaster North has been Labour since 1918) whilst many others haven't changed since the 1960s.

In light of these factors, the question isn't about absolute Muslim voter numbers but about how many Muslim voters are incrementally undecided in marginal seats (when other factors are normalised). We shouldn't just gloss over this point; they're undecided for very good reasons. Many voters prefer not to have an automatic loyalty to any particular political party and have special interest in specific policy areas to do with health, taxation, education, Brexit, immigration etc. which might be overriding in their decision.

You would also have to assume that all Muslim voters have registered which is very unlikely since the overall voter registration is about 80%,[237] and then come the day will actually turn out to vote since only 66% overall did so in 2015. People often struggle to vote not because they don't want to, but because they've missed the chance to register, or they're away from home, or the daily grind conspires against them on polling day etc. And I'm sure some are in a dilemma about whether to back their current MP if he or she doesn't represent their views on such an important matter as Brexit.

Now, let's put the above into the mix of other voter movements. One of the large shifts that we're likely to see, at least if we believe the analysts, are UKIP votes going to the Conservatives. This alone could in many constituencies completely offset other voter movements. The other big cluster are the undecided swing voters from the wider electorate. We just don't know whether or not they're still looking for a government to finish off delivering Brexit, to see through the sentiment against immigration and EU power, or if Jeremy Corbyn has done enough to sway at least some of them.

Aside from this, there is another potentially damaging twist to a Muslim block vote. It could stigmatise those who for perfectly good reasons choose to vote for another party. You can almost foretell the accusation of being "sell outs." Yet, no one should feel compelled or guilty for voting as they wished.

Moreover, hedging political loyalties in such an explicit way is arguably a naïve tactic for a community like ours seeking mutually-assured cultural self-assertion. In this scenario, we need to make friends with as wide a political spectrum as possible. This entails not being so narrow-minded as tying up the fate of an entire social group with the fortunes of a political party. Moreover, singling out a "religious identity vote" would suggest that all Muslims have the same political affiliation and, equally egregiously, for whom only religion is operative. Yet, it's a fact that Muslims have diverse

---

[237] See: https://www.electoral-reform.org.uk/campaigns/upgrading-our-democracy/voter-registration/, retrieved 1 October 2018.

interests, political leanings and worries about jobs, security, taxation, healthcare etc.

And so, post-GE2017, whether one votes for the Conservatives or Labour or another party, it's in our collective interest for an emphatic rethink in the way Muslim organisations and politically active individuals engage wider political parties by reaching out to them, working with them productively for mutual benefit and holding back from needless cynicism and suspicion.

## 3.12 Brexit: a ship without rudders

In the aftermath of the EU Referendum, most of us woke up to a Brexit shock. It was an exercise of direct democracy, with just over half of the electorate deciding to untie four decades of institution building and partnership in the EU. This initial shock, which turned out to be greater than the Credit Crunch, sent the value of the Pound and financial markets tumbling. It wasn't until the Governor of the Bank of England intervened with a message of stability and liquidity of the financial markets that the Pound and the FTSE 100 stabilised and recovered slightly.

This referendum has brought into sharp focus many long-standing disparities within British society. The older generation's apparent fear of losing control and "old Brit" identity stands in sharp contrast to the younger generations' yearning and hope for a "global urban class" with the right to settle in EU countries even if they have no job there to go to. However, as some moderate Brexiteers have argued, many ordinary people, particularly among the older demographics voted for Brexit because they perceived the founding EU principles of the freedom of movement and labour to be a business-driven one to import cheap goods and labour and is perceived to put local workers out of a job. Newcomers who've never paid into the NHS or education are also able to take advantage of both, blocking up the welfare system for everyone else, impacting on the localities where the locals may have lived all of their lives. While such objections have encouraged xenophobia, they're not unreasonable complaints in themselves.[238] However, studies carried out show that

---

[238] Gavid Goodhart argues this in his book *The Road to Somewhere: The Populist Revolt and the Future of Politics*, Hurst, 2017.

all things considered, Eastern European migration since the 2004 A8 European Union enlargement has been on balance good for the UK.[239]

Unlike those who identify themselves as Anglican or Church of England, who backed the UK leaving the EU by 60% compared to 40% who supported staying in, Muslims were clearly in the remain camp, with 69% choosing this option and 31% in favour of leaving the EU.[240] Muslim demographics, arguably, favoured the pro-EU vote with a disproportionately younger age profile (40% below 19 years as at 2011) who naturally have a more pro-EU sentiment compared to the rest of the population (24%). Moreover, Muslims are geographically more concentrated in large cities like London, Manchester, Glasgow etc. which voted remain. There were anomalies to this too. For example, Bradford, with about 25% Muslims, voted 54.2% Leave, and Birmingham, with a 22% Muslim population, voted 50.4% Leave.

Then there is the contrast of academia-dominated cities like Cambridge, Oxford, London, Bristol and Manchester embracing cosmopolitanism versus the more provincial, perhaps inward-looking white working-class

---

[239] With the A8 European Union enlargement in 2004, the UK was one of the few countries to have allowed immigration without any transitional arrangements/limitations from the start. By 2013 it meant that around 600,000 Polish people came to live in the UK, which is roughly equivalent to the population of British Bangladeshis who took almost 50 years to reach the same number. During this time, the positive benefits of Eastern European immigration wasn't generally communicated in public. These benefits included: increased aggregate demand in the economy; increased tax base; contribution to the economy outweighed consumption of public services; provided downward pressure on the UK's age demographic problem; supplied critical labour in industries with labour shortage such as construction and nursing; revitalised derelict areas of towns and cities like Peterborough; and improved geopolitical ties with A8 countries. The evidence suggests that A8 migration didn't cause statistically significant displacement of UK natives from the labour market in periods when the economy was strong, but some labour market displacement did happen when the economy was in recession, see: Dhiren Patel *et al.*, *Impacts of migration on UK native employment: An analytical review of the evidence*, 2014, Home Office; Full Fact, *How immigrants affect jobs and wages*, 2017, https://fullfact.org/immigration/immigration-and-jobs-labour-market-effects-immigration/, retrieved 12 December 2018.

[240] Ben Clements, *How religious groups voted in the 2016 referendum on Britain's EU membership*, http://www.brin.ac.uk/2017/how-religious-groups-voted-at-the-2016-referendum-on-britains-eu-membership/, April 2017, retrieved 16 October 2018.

areas, where immigrants from Europe, and further afield, might be perceived as unfairly getting ahead with school places, benefits, housing and jobs etc. There is also the contrast of pro-Europeanism in Scotland and Northern Ireland versus, what is now evident, a rampant Euroscepticism in England driven by xenophobic leaders like Nigel Farage.

Efforts to shrug off the symbolism of "little England" that Brexit inevitably brings were quickly under way. Within a day of the Brexit vote, universities like Imperial College, London reiterated their European and internationalist identity. Even Boris Johnson, who somewhat sheepishly got onto the podium to give his not so victory-like speech, offered the most astonishing of self-contradiction. "Young people," he said, "who may feel that this decision in some way involves pulling out a draw bridge or any kind of isolationism because I think the very opposite is true. We cannot turn our backs on Europe. We are part of Europe. Our children and our grandchildren will continue to have a wonderful future as Europeans travelling to the continent, understanding our languages and cultures that make up our common European civilisation, continue interacting together in a way that is open and friendly and outward looking." The speech was hardly the stuff of euphoria of a referendum win. Rather, it had all the hallmarks of a surprise win, something which Boris's sister hinted at, and also of great anxiety about the uncertainties that now lie ahead.

As uncertainties go, it actually doesn't get any bigger, spanning economic, constitutional, social and legal; all of which will continue to unfold as time goes on. Credit rating agencies quite swiftly downgraded the UK. At some point this could make the cost of national borrowing higher. Something which may well add to the sense of missing out if, as expected, it leads to less investment and welfare cuts, it will hit working-class voters most. Ironically, these are the very people who fear losing the "old Brit" identity due to the EU's founding principles. And then there is the matter of the UK's ongoing debt pile and current account deficit. Somehow, with banks having passed their post-Credit Crunch stress tests, the huge debt-to-GDP ratio has remained at its historic highs, above 80%, as the annual deficit hasn't come down fast enough despite austerity measures, and now seems politically less significant.

Politically, we've seen David Cameron resign from what became an immediately untenable position, and Theresa May beating her rivals to become the new Prime Minister. In the aftermath, May misjudged the mood of the electorate and Corbyn as an opponent, and in unexpectedly calling for an early General Election, she's self-inflicted a weakening of her own mandate. Out of nowhere, it's giving the Northern Irish party, the DUP, a power broker position to prop up May's Government. May has paid the ultimate price, forced to resign knowing that she's failed to deliver Brexit. We've also seen many ministerial resignations, including the chief Brexiteers Boris Johnson and David Davies; all complaining about the direction Brexit negotiations have gone. Meanwhile, to deliver some notion of "Brexit means Brexit" May has had to square off the need for continuity and minimal disruption to the economy, while contending with tricky conventions of border control and finding a customs regime that gives the UK the freedom to do its own trade deals outside of the EU. Negotiations have been fraught with almost hour-by-hour media commentary, and both the EU and the UK Government using delays, leaks and offhand comments as part of their negotiating tactics to gain leverage or to manage stakeholders and pressure points in their own camps.

As for the Labour Party, Jeremy Corbyn has had to deal with charges of anti-semitism, directed at him as well the party. Labour now looks set to preside over an extended period of power struggles between the more "centrist" faction borne out of the Blair-Brown days, many of whom have London constituents who voted remain, and the more radical left leadership borne out of classical socialism that generally eschews EU founding principles designed to create the largest possible free market. Indeed, Corbyn is widely seen to have had a lacklustre campaign in the EU Referendum which wasn't surprising given his dislike of the UK's EU membership in 1975. If the Labour Party is to have a chance of winning an outright majority in the next General Election Corbyn will need to unite many of the Parliamentary Labour Party members behind him. The decent man of politics appears ideologically too leftist and devoid of the muscular leadership that parliamentary politics, and indeed the office of Prime Minister arguably requires.

The EU faces uncertainties too. However, at this stage talk of the beginning of the end of the EU seem somewhat exaggerated. There is little sympathy from across the continent either, with leading EU foreign ministers having piled pressure on the UK to swiftly invoke Article 50 in order to officially kick-start exit proceedings. It's very likely that the new legal frameworks will turn out to be a cut and paste job of EU law, at least initially. And, whatever trade deals are done with the EU, whether in an EEA, Canada-style, WTA framework, or something else, it will necessarily require some level of freedom for people to move around and costs for the UK. Modelling the plausible trade scenarios after Brexit, it's clear that the UK will be economically worse off outside of the EU at least in the short to medium term, though exactly how much worse off isn't clear.[241] The challenge for the UK Government is thus to strike deals with the EU and others to limit the impact. However, the EU will not want to be seen to be giving economic advantage to the UK outside of the EU for fear of emboldening populist nationalist sentiment across Europe, and weakening the EU institution further. Equally, a no deal outcome is politically and economically damaging to both the UK and the EU.

For many, the uncertainty of the referendum lies in legitimised xenophobia and giving an open ticket to racists in the likes of the EDL, BNP, Britain First, UKIP and National Action. That such an important decision was made by many on the back of mostly a xenophobic leave campaign, lies about £350m a week to the NHS and "taking back control" is significant for its populist nationalism, a trend unlikely to disappear anytime soon. This will be worrying as much for the millions of European expats and ethnic minorities in the UK as the 1.3 million British expats who live and work in the EU.

All of this is unprecedented stuff. No one really knows where it will all end and how the UK will fare with the rest of the world outside of the EU. But one thing is for sure, divorce is never sweet and we're in for turbulent waters in the lead up to Brexit and in what follows after. That's of course assuming that a second referendum dubbed "Peoples Vote" or a General Election doesn't undo the course set. The ship has well and truly sailed without rudders.

---

[241] See: The RAND Foundation, *Examining Economic Outcomes After Brexit*, https://www.rand.org/randeurope/research/projects/brexit-economic-implications.html, retrieved 18 December 2018.

# — 4 —

# Concluding remarks

## 4.1 Unlocking the theocentric value of being British Muslims

In the 1950s, the Muslim population of the UK stood at around 100,000[242] (0.2% of the UK population of 50 million), with less than a handful of mosques.[243] In 2018, the number of Muslims stood at around three million (5% of the UK population of 67 million), with about 2000 mosques (compared to over 40,000 churches). So much of course has happened during this time which has driven the increase. Most notably, immigration from territories once ruled by Britain, under the British Nationality Act, in support of post-war rebuilding and labour shortages. Early immigrants were workers in the NHS, steel and textile mills, food industries, manufacturing and tailoring, and contributed in important ways to the cultural, economic and social life of the UK. At current growth rates, by 2050 the proportion of the UK's Muslim population is projected to increase to about 10% (6.5

---

[242] Houssain Kettani, *Muslim Population in Europe: 1950-2020*, International Journal of Environmental Science and Development, Vol. 1, No. 2, June 2010

[243] *Registered Mosques, 1915-1998*, http://www.brin.ac.uk/figures/registered-mosques-1915-1998/, retrieved 18 October 2018.

million).[244] Similar projections have been made for Europe as a whole.[245] In the UK, most of this growth is expected to be from natural birth, especially given the disproportionate skew towards a younger Muslim demographic with 40% under the age of 19 as at 2011 compared to 24% for the UK overall.[246]

There is thus a great need I would argue for British Muslim communities to create a strategic vision of social development. But it's got to be based on a shared vision that strengthens and broadens their epistemological horizons, capacity and outlook. Future generations depend on this not only to feel comfortable with being God-centric, but also to bring original and refreshing faith-based perspectives, and to be effective in discharging their civic roles and responsibilities for the greater good of society. Being effective means avoiding issues of cognitive dissonance, religious illiteracy,

---

[244] See: *Europe's Growing Muslim Population*, Pew Research, 29 November 2017. The Pew Research paper modelled three scenarios which gave different projections for the % share of Muslims among the total population in countries in Europe. In the "zero migration scenario" it is 9.7% or 6.5 million; in the "medium migration scenario" it is 16.7% or 13 million; in the "high migration scenario" it is 17.2% or 13.5 million. I am much more inclined to believe a figure closer to the "zero migration scenario" since: (1) the forecast uses an overestimated starting population of 4.1 million Muslims in the UK for 2016, which would have inflated the long-term numbers. The figure is more likely to be around 3 to 3.2 million; (2) as the researchers also explained, Muslim identity in some cases is estimated indirectly based upon the national origins of migrants which isn't necessarily accurate for all cases; (3) asylum seekers who aren't granted refugee status is a source uncertainty; and (4) in the UK, immigration of Muslim spouses from Muslim countries as well as new asylum seekers are both on a long-term decreasing trend. These figures don't factor in the likely changes to migration post-Brexit, and also assume that future generations of Muslims will all remain Muslim.

[245] European nationalists will of course protest the growth of the Muslim population, as often seen in press headlines, but they would do well to know that: (1) there were proportionately more Muslims in Europe during the medieval times than today, in places like Spain, Sicily, Malta, Hungary, Balkans etc.; (2) today, European countries like Bosnia, North Cyprus, Albania and Turkey are majority Muslims countries; and (3) with the onset of modernisation in recent years there's been a decrease in Muslim fertility rates in Morocco and Turkey, which suggests that one cannot assume that Muslim birth rates will indefinitely continue at current levels.

[246] 2011 census data on religion by age.

lacking in the right skills, marginalizing women, seeing non-Muslims as others, inward-looking attitudes, endemic racism, colourism and so on.

As discussed in this book, the word "Muslim" describes a plethora of people whose faith is Islam but come from different ethnic and cultural backgrounds, primarily of Pakistani, Indian, Bangladeshi and Somali ancestry (and all their intricate sub-ethnicities). As of 2018, roughly 50% of the UK's Muslim population was born in the UK. The experience and stories of the first generation has largely gone undocumented, and most of it remains perhaps only in the memories of the second generation. With this shift comes on one hand the loss of "old-ways" of experiencing the world and navigating one's place within it, and on the other hand it comes with the excitement and opportunity to make "new culture." The questions now facing British Muslims are: "From where can British Muslims get their inspiration?"; "How are we to manage the dislocation?"; "What should be the nature of this new culture?" and "How are we to construct it?" In the essays in this book I have attempted to contribute to these questions.

For the earliest migrants in the 1950s and 60s who came as economic migrants, religion wasn't an overt priority, nor did they explicitly self-identify as "British Muslims" but, instead, as "British Pakistanis," "British Bangladeshis," "British Indians" etc.[247] This was due to limitations they had for publicly expressing their religious identity, which was shaped by a number of factors.

(1) The first generation who settled in the UK was primarily men aged between their late teens and mid 30s who had relatively low levels of literacy.[248] They possessed basic knowledge of Islam limited to ritual worship, religious celebrations and building mosques etc., which reflected the understandings and cultural conventions of South Asian Muslims at the time. As the first generation aged,

---

[247] See survey results which show that in 2009 British Bangladeshis considered themselves as such: *The Bangladeshi Muslim Community in England: Understanding Muslim Ethnic Communities*, Change Institute, 2009, *https*://swadhinata.org.uk/wp-content/uploads/2017/08/Bangladeshi_Muslim.pdf, retrieved 20 December 2019.

[248] Literacy level for men in India in 1951 was around 26% (and 18% for both men and women), where literacy is defined as "being able to both read and write with understanding in any language," see: Sandeep Kapur *et al.*, *Literacy in India*, August 2009.

they became more settled, grew in religious consciousness and achieved a great deal such as building mosque communities and contributing to the social and economic life of the UK. What they didn't develop, however, was the stock of contextualised Islamic knowledge and a wider theocentric cultural capital for formulating a shared vision of engaging the public and social development.[249] Similarly, the second and third generations are yet to meaningfully contribute to this area.

(2) Ethnic and country of origin categories took prominence. Firstly, this happened explicitly due to the structures within society, such as in the way the Home Office documented immigration in terms of ethnicity and country of origin categories, which was later adopted by public and private organisations for recording workplace diversity. Secondly, this happened implicitly with first and second generation British Muslims maintaining their ethno-nationalistic identities, ignoring the need to forge greater

---

[249] This is not to say that there weren't any religious scholars in the UK. In fact, there were enough senior scholars to establish a number of *Darul 'Uloom* seminaries and schools which taught the *'alimiyyah* course where the teachers were foreign born. Similarly, as mosques were founded across the country they recruited imams from South Asia. However, these scholars didn't grow up in the UK, nor did they interact much with the wider society. While some scholars were aware of theological arguments to root into societies in which they lived, the supportive environment failed to come about, primarily as a result of: (1) push back from political "Islamist" groups who argued ideologically against Western integration and damaging public perception of "being Muslim"/"doing Islam"; (2) scholars and imams, as traditionalists, shifting their pastoral and intellectual focus, to a larger extent, to stem the tide of *Salafism* which was seen as an attempt to deconstruct principles (*usul*) of theology; and (3) lack of effective organisation and leadership within Muslim communities to get away from being reactionary and factional, and to build and execute on a vision and strategy for the long-term. In fact, very stern warnings about the dangers of not contextualising Islam were vocalised by the Indian scholar Abul Hasan 'Ali al-Nadwi in a speech at the opening of the Dewsbury Markaz (the main UK centre for the politically quiet Tablighi Jamat) in 1982 in which he spoke about the consequences of not applying the lessons of Prophetic *sirah* (life history), the dangers of living isolated and insulated lives and the idea of earning a place in the UK etc. See transcript of his speech: *For Effective Da'wah in the West*, http://www.ilmgate.org/for-effective-dawah-in-the-west/, retrieved 15 October 2018.

intra-Muslim integration among themselves especially on matters pertaining to public religion.[250] The glaringly obvious example are mosques which became fossilised symbols of Asian and sectarian affiliation, such as "Bangladeshi *Barelvi/Deobandi* mosque," "Pakistani *Barelvi/Deobandi* mosque," "Gujrati mosque," "Somali mosque," "*Salafi* mosque" etc.[251] What was initially perceived to be an "identity crisis" among the second generation captured in the question "Are you Pakistani/Bangladeshi or British first?" as time went by shifted radically to the self-identity of "British Muslim." This shift occurred despite at the underlying level British Muslims are still far more rooted in their ethno-cultural identities than a shared religious outlook. Nor are they one large community, but made up of various ethnic communities with their own particular interests.

This identity shift seems to have occurred initially through the vocabulary of the "war on terror" and by virtue of being superficially judged by those on the outside to be alike due to their ostensibly shared "brownness." In turn, British Muslims for convenience also appropriated the term to simplify the intersectionality of their multiple identities. "British Muslim" became, then, cognate of being subservient to God

---

[250] Some notable examples of failure to achieve consensus in the interest of public religion include: moonsighting for declaring the start of Ramadhan and Eid; establishing UK-wide governance and standards for children's Islamic education; establishing standards for women's access to mosques and female scholarship; formulating a strategy for dealing with extremist political radicals and those who incite hatred; campaigning against racism by Asian Muslims against black Muslims; ensuring *zakat* is distributed locally to meet the needs of the impoverished Muslims of the UK first etc.; encouraging marriage between Muslims from different ethnic backgrounds.

[251] Luton is a good example of how mosques in the 1970s and 1980s were established upon ethno-national identities which has since remained and set the unfortunate trajectory for British Muslims. Following the independence of East Pakistan from West Pakistan in 1971, which led to the formation of Bangladesh, Luton's Bangladeshi Muslims were supposedly expelled from Luton Central Mosque (initially at 2 Westbourne Road, Luton) which was managed and dominated by West Pakistanis, but till then had been the single shared place of worship for, the then, East and West Pakistani Muslims.

which demanded recognition by others. It is in this paradigm that the term "British Muslim" is used in the politics of identity today, which from a *Qur'anic* perspective you could argue remains circumstantial and self-exaggerating.

(3) A lack of or gaps in statutory laws to protect race relations and equal opportunities meant that racism was for the most part left institutionally unopposed, making the focus of society on race, ethnicity and civil and worker rights etc. as opposed to God and faith.

(4) Values or concepts like "diversity," "inclusion," "multiculturalism," "cosmopolitanism," "pluralism" etc. for progressing modern Britain hadn't achieved the kind of wide acceptance that was necessary, even as vague, notional concepts, nor become important considerations in public policy.

(5) Strong emotional connections with the countries of origin sustained an overarching assumption among the first generation that their time in the UK was merely transitional and that one day they would return back. Questions about integration and cultural self-assertion were less relevant. However, with time, self-evidently this became a "myth of return": a romanticised notion of "going back," not a living reality. Whilst first generation men got married in what they saw was their "back home" and brought their families over, the next generation by consequence became increasingly dislocated both emotionally and by virtue of their lived experiences and up-bringing in the UK. This trend continued into the second and subsequent generations. By the third generation there was a significant drop in such marriages, and increasingly frowned upon.[252] Whilst there are still pockets of "first generation in every generation," a phenomenon in which each new generation grows up with a foreign-born parent who retains much of the cultural outlooks of their country of birth, it is increasingly less prevalent,

---

[252] This is based on trends over time in spouse visa and citizenship applications as a proportion of the total populations of those from ethnically Pakistani and Bangladeshi heritage. Data sourced from the Home Office.

partly due to the tightening of immigration rules[253] and also partly due to the increasing cultural and emotional disconnection and changes to social mores that time naturally brings about.[254]

Ever since the day the first generation migrated to the UK a process of indigenisation into Britishness has been at play. "The first glance," Anthony Giddens is right to note, "accords recognition of the other as an agent and as potential acquaintance."[255] However, the making of Britishness always faced considerable barriers. There are those who Amartya Sen labelled "old Brit,"[256] who embrace a fixed vision of "being British." Their somewhat narrow, ill-informed and culturally predatory views maintain the perception of Britain's "unbridged" ancient Anglo-Saxon-Roman roots primarily represented in white skin colour, and in casting "newcomers" as not "fitting in" at face value, nor willing to explore other identities and belongings. The recognition of "newcomers'" inner identity and contribution to daily life or Britishness and intrinsically belonging to the British Isles is thus seen as a legitimate area for debate and to otherize. In turn, for British Muslims, the challenge was always to see how Islam impelled earlier Muslims to settle into the localised contexts and intuitions of people as it expanded out of Makkah into Africa, Asia and Europe. For whom, today, there is a striking lack of self-confidence to make British Islam and to advance their theocentric cultural imperatives amidst people who aren't necessarily familiar or receptive.

In respect of the latter, addressing topical religious challenges has

[253] For example, since July 2012 the UK's Immigration Rules have required non-EEA nationals to satisfy a financial, "minimum income" requirement in order to secure a visa to join a British/settled spouse or partner in the UK. Available maintenance funds equivalent to a minimum gross annual income of £18,600 is required. See: https://researchbriefings.parliament.uk/ResearchBriefing/Summary/SN06724, retrieved 18 October 2018.

[254] See: Charsley, K., Bolognani, M., Spencer, S., Ersanilli, E., Jayaweera, H. (2016) *Marriage Migration and Integration Report*, Bristol, UK: University of Bristol, https://www.bristol.ac.uk/media-library/sites/ethnicity/documents/Marriage%20 Migration%20and%20Integration_final%20report.pdf, retrieved 16 October 2018.

[255] Anthony Giddens, *The Consequences of Modernity*, Polity Press, 2009, p. 81.

[256] See: Amartya Sen, *Identity and Violence: The Illusion of Destiny*, W. W. Norton & Company, 2007.

always been the domain of Muslim scholars operating as thinkers, jurists, philosophers and theologians. It was through their intellectual enquiry that perceptive thought was formulated, debated and developed. The immense amount of social, political, scientific and cultural change witnessed in modernity and the growing citizenship of British Muslims necessitates the realisation of an Islamic discourse that speaks to British life, its epistemological paradigms and operative variables in a manner that relates to peoples' intuitions and experiences of living in the UK. Intellectual activity remains integral to the progression of Muslims, not least to the enterprise of rethinking paradigms and methods that inform cogent and compelling narratives on religious identity, context and space. This requires reinvigorating rigorous and high-quality religious literacy that lead to mature reflection and thought. In the absence of this, the best possible formulations and responses to the new realities Muslims face in the UK, and more broadly in the West, will struggle to emerge.

Indeed, it would perhaps be the first time ever that a sizeable group of Muslims who settled into new territories and failed to advance its civility through an engagement of what God wants of them. Many historical examples are testament to this responsibility. For example, Muslims transformed the likes of the Tartars into a civilised people in the 13th century. Similarly, in Moorish Spain and North Africa, Muslims protected Jews from persecution in Europe. On the challenges of cultural preservation, Muslims have a long history of enabling other cultures to flourish. The preservation of ancient Greek thought and disseminating Greek works into other language like Sanskrit in India are good examples. And it was the introduction of new ways of thinking (deductive logic, empiricism etc.) and learning (science, mathematics, medicine, legal systems, international governance, geography etc.) from medieval Muslim scholars through Spain and the Mediterranean region which arguably sparked-off the Renaissance in Europe. References to the likes of Ibn Tufayl's (1105-1185) *Hayy Ibn Yaqdhan*[257] by European scholars as important as Hume (1711-1776), Locke (1632-1704), Voltaire (1694-1778) and Rousseau (1712-1778) etc.

---

[257] *The Tale of Living Son of Vigilant* is a fictional story written in the 12th century about how human beings develop perception, learn tolerance and show respect for different perspectives.

over many centuries shows the vast extent of the influence.[258] That's just one example of many. Much of this is of course how civilisations interact, share and cross-influence each other, with the good and value-creative influences standing the test of time.

The more significant reason is at the very heart of the *Qur'an* itself. If Muslims are to be God-centred, holding God as the central interest and ultimate concern, it would be binding on them to take interest in the obligations set by God to be an emphatic force for good: to be a stalwart for truth (*haqq*); service (*khidma*); uprightness (*'amal al-salihat*); security (*salam*); and compassion (*rahmah*) to people and nature. Indeed, knowledge of revelation, and the very act of testifying belief in God (*shahadah*), should bring a deep sense of responsibility to contemplate and discern what God wants of us, and the fine line between good and bad, ethics and immorality, and praiseworthy and blameworthy actions in every aspect of life.

The question each generation of Muslims face, both collectively and as individuals, is: "What is their defining expression of being Godly that could help society flourish?" It's clear that this question for most British Muslims hasn't yet provoked a deep mining of the *Qur'an* and *Sunnah* to explore expressions of what God wants of them contextualised to 21st century UK, even among the most active individuals and institutions, and organisations that claim to represent them. Often, attempts struggle to go beyond one or more of: reinforcing ritualism; sectarian outlooks; academic minutia; missionary-like expressions; identity politics; and ethno-culture. This isn't necessarily out of choice, but rather reflexive of the historical consequences which today's British Muslims find themselves grappling with.

(1) The situation of British Muslims today hasn't come about in a vacuum, but the product of diverse immigration histories and ethnic backgrounds, and subsequent social policies and socio-economic standards. While much of these impacts are external, there are things which Muslims can do to bring about transformations in their condition. But it requires people to come together in mutual

---

[258] Samar Attar, *The Vital roots of European Enlightenment: Ibn Tufayl's Influence of Modern Western Thought*, Lexington Books, 2010.

respect to organise properly, to choose the right priorities and to create strategies that are then pursued in communities in an agreed upon way. Such an approach has struggled to materialise, and certainly the realisation that revelation can meaningfully steer Muslims towards it remains unexplored.

(2) Unlike pre-modern times, Muslims living as minorities in the West today arguably enjoy greater levels of civility (justice, welfare, liberty, security etc.) than those living in majority-Muslim countries. This has, in turn, made it perhaps more challenging for Muslims to express their own original, theocentric ideas and values. It's hard enough contending with the general indifference to religion in British society, which is of course a liberty people enjoy on their own terms and contexts. To complicate things, additional trends are also at play which shape the socio-political headwinds in which British Muslims find themselves, such as: secularisation; the ubiquity of entertainment and materialism; identity politics (white nationalism, muscular liberalism etc.); and preconceived and media-led public misconceptions of Islam and Muslims.

(3) Religious literacy remains poor among Muslims. Inevitably this means that Muslims not only struggle formulating credible responses to the big theo-political discussions of today, but even grasping the connection between being kind, forgiving, easy to work with, reasonable-minded, having a positive, gracious outlook etc. as signs of one's commitment to God (*iman*) isn't necessarily a straightforward realisation for many either. This lack of religious literacy permeates the ordinary Muslim's lack of insight into the multiple layers of being or identity that we traverse; that what we mean by "being Muslim" should ultimately be about "being Muslim to God" without which a graceful, refreshing and intellectually robust approach to the politics of identity that rages on today may not be possible.

In light of this, the exploration of contentions in this anthology should be taken as an introductory guide to some of the most pertinent areas of focus in the making of a confident, theocentric expression of British

Muslim. I also hope that the arguments I have put forward strengthen the roots of faith (*iman*, *yaqeen*) in the minds and hearts of Muslims of the UK. Finally, I hope that non-Muslims can gain insight into the intricacies of the multifarious crossroads that are at play in the ongoing making of British Muslims.

# 4.2 A charter for British Muslims

I end the book with some final words of good counsel. Below I outline a seven-point charter, or first-principles, for contextualising Islam in the UK and developing a British Muslim experience that isn't beholden to ethnic commitment to religion or identity politics. These aren't necessarily novel and can be found explicitly stated, or derived based on *Qur'anic* and Prophetic reasoning or even by common sense. Having them at our fingertips and placed in the context of considerations around being British Muslims will help the making of a theocentric British Muslim culture, unlocking the potential for not only contributing to but inspiring the conscience of society more generally.

Bringing change is never easy, and we can expect denial and resistance to persist for some time. However, we should realise that "God doesn't change the condition of people until they change what's within themselves" (13:11). The deep wisdom in this is that God has placed cause and effect relationships between variables at the centre of the human condition and in human activities that make the world work. The believer is in this sense tasked to rationally probe what is internal and external to them, and to create an environment that sustains all that is good and beneficial. Simply by doing this, natural consequences would dictate that new doors will open and transformations will be possible. This is perhaps why God tells us that doing good is itself its own reward (55:60) and the focus for the believer is to muster the courage to do good.

## 1. Gaining contextualised and deeper knowledge of how to be Godly.

From as far back as the Prophet Abraham, Islam as subservience to God has always had a unique set of benefits to offer any society that craves holistic paradigms, wisdom, meaning and ethics. And just as it does for those non-Muslims who might be receptive to its message today, revelation needs to be approached even by Muslims with a clear mind, and a desire to bring benefit and profound insights to today's experiences. But this is only possible if sufficient numbers of Muslims become serious about going beyond superficial learning to gain deeper contextualised knowledge from which they can draw guidance in a manner that relates to peoples' intuitions and experiences of living in Britain.

However, care is needed to avoid learning from individuals whose intelligence remains untested, or whose authority to teach is limited, or who harbours political, ideological, ethnic or sectarian tendencies. Indeed, appearances and speech can be highly deceptive. The cloak of piety and insincerity lies in self-righteousness. As Muslims we should take knowledge that benefits us from wherever we can. But knowledge must lead to rational, constructive action and a graceful manner if it's to have a chance of benefiting and enlightening wider society in a more profound way.

## 2. Valuing the power of the intellect and deep thinking.

We should strive to restore the intellectual foundations of Islam by reacquainting ourselves with the legacy of Islamic scholarship and reasoning. We need to formulate our own narratives by thinking for ourselves and embracing opportunities that demonstrate the value and profoundness of the paradigms within revelatory texts. God gave us the intellect (*'aql*) and the ability to reason for the purpose of understanding reality so that we can draw from guidance and build upon the stock of knowledge imparted to us from past scholars. We should acquaint ourselves with knowledge of the rational, reasoned and logical nature of *Qur'anic* and Prophetic examples. We should learn history to grasp how polities have changed over time, and how Islamic scholars applied techniques in reasoning with the challenges they faced. We shouldn't become hermits who fear that by having something original to say, or taking an interest in Western intellectual traditions, we risk diluting the distinctiveness of Islam.

## 3. Establishing reputable institutes of learning, platforms and standards.

An immense amount of intellectual energy is needed to find cogent answers of contemporary relevance by an intellectually deeper reading of the *Qur'an* and Prophetic life contextualised to our lived experiences. This requires the energised like-minded to come together to: (1) establish reputable institutions of learning that produces enlightening and clarificatory content, and individuals who can competently engage in this activity; (2) establish platforms that confidently trains and encourages individuals in the art of enlightening the human conscience; and (3) establish well-defined standards across different realms of British Muslim enterprise. We must avoid things (like the lack of professionalism and wasteful duplication of resources etc.) that diminish our effectiveness to truthfully uncover the vastness of the Islamic tradition, to help heal the divisiveness of the world and to pursue workable, ethical and responsible outcomes in all walks of life, whether in communities, commerce, governance, environment, social policy and so on. Whilst institutions, platforms and standards need to be creative, down-to-earth, open and convivial, they need our support to help them become sustainable and independent in their own contexts. However, while we should maintain forbearance (*hilm*) when they err, we should also realise that there are advantages to failing fast.

## 4. Seeking to be a type of "total Muslim" with a "God-centred ethic."

We should strive towards being a type of Muslim who begins with God in mind. This entails being truthful and righteous, and presenting ourselves in an enlightening and aesthetically pleasing way, paying emotionally intelligent attention to people's preconceptions, cultures and identities. God commands fairness (*'adl*) and excellence (*ihsan*) for everything (16:90), so everything about a Muslim, our intentions, thoughts, goals and actions, need to at least set out to reflect this. Conducting ourselves respectfully, smiling, leaving a good impression, thanking people, having probity in our transactions, answering with honesty and working hard in the different realms of life will go a long way to develop social capital with others, the kind that a commitment to God demands. Having belief is seldom sufficient for transforming or enlightening society, we should therefore be action-orientated to seek benefit (*fa'idah*) and affirm our commitment to God in that way. To be action-orientated requires applying intelligence, gaining experience and skills, and becoming competent. In striving we should never assume that we've succeeded in pleasing God, even if others congratulate us for having achieved a certain positive outcome.

## 5. Taking care in social interactions.

The Prophet said: "The most hated person with God is the most quarrelsome person."[259] Muslims should keep away from seeing ourselves as superior or better endowed in any realm of life simply by virtue of being Muslim. Instead, we should strive to be humble and grateful beings. In the context of social interactions, this means that we see others including non-Muslims as souls on their own journeys back to God. It also means listening to and being easy with others, being constructively critical of ourselves, keeping things real, striving for fairness and integrity, particularly in positions of authority, whether as parents, friends, elders, professionals, managers, public figures, scholars or activists. Being emotionally intelligent means tailoring our interactions appropriately. This means, for example, recognising that people have a hard time talking about their biases, that identity and behaviours are emotional subjects and that there hasn't been sustained meaningful interaction with contextualised Islam by both ethnically-committed Muslims and non-Muslims alike.

The Prophet's mode of action was to build trust, to be inclusive, motivating, putting others before his own interests, thinking better of others, showing tact and insight and so on. Since God sent the Prophet "as a mercy" and made him firm on these qualities, they should be the core features of following him. While the *Sunnah* is to find excuses for the shortcomings of others on a personal level, and coming forward to make things easy for others, we're equally at liberty to evaluate people's conduct for uprightness and competence, so long as we recognise that only God guides and has the right to judge people's ultimate fate. Equally, we can't coerce others to take heed of our counsel (*nasihah*), cultivation (*tarbiyyah*), or encouragement and warning (*targhib wa al-tarhib*).

## 6. Being careful with language.

---

[259] *Hadith* narrated by A'isha in *Sahih al-Bukhari*.

We must learn to manage the way modern life can decay our natural inclination towards God by offering us confusing new terms and all kinds of distractions. Undoing this irreverence requires us to evaluate our experiences and thoughts to their deeper meanings and implications. The more we do this, the less we may become, for example, preoccupied with consuming entertainment, and the more informed, rich and profound our realisation of revelatory meanings may become. Through a more thoughtful and precise use of language, we can better appreciate the aesthetics of virtue and metaphysical connection with the unseen realm (*ghaib*). Part of this is about being careful in everyday language we use to convey ourselves and our attitudes, and to signal trustworthiness and compassion in our own contexts and day-to-day lives. The Prophet's advice was that either we have something good to say that facilitates the good, builds trust and constructively moves things forward or we refrain from speaking. We shouldn't neglect the power of simple words and the additive effects of seemingly small actions. We need to intelligently express the falsity of being Godly as a historical idea appropriate for a previous time only, knowing that this is by no means easy to grasp for those uninterested, taken unawares or consumed by other preoccupations. Equally, the language we use needs to be inviting and friendly, being firm in the right way when needed, and to avoid shouting from the sidelines, or making sweeping generalisations due to our lack of control or insight.

## 7. Adding value in every action.

We should come to terms with the idea that shortcomings in people and institutions will always exist and dwelling on them out of stubbornness or to prove a point will trip us into unhealthy scepticism of people and the world around us. In these situations, we should at first exert forbearance (*hilm*) and recognise that the seemingly insignificant or misplaced interactions and phenomena are in themselves both powerful critiques and warnings of our own conditions (*hal*), and also manifestations in themselves of God's attributes (*Al-Qadar, Ar-Rahman* etc.). Equally, we should be easy to work with by being forthcoming and constructively critical. Adding value is to elevate people or to reason with them "in the best possible way," not to intellectually bludgeon others down or to cow them in their weaknesses and obscuring factors. We must highlight the value of Islamic perspectives, yet recognise that there are many very reasonable overlaps with secular, atheist and other religious and ethical philosophies which we can mutually and productively interact with to enhance well-being all-round.

This entails removing hardships, standing for the downtrodden, being positive and optimistic, restraining our egos, protecting nature, and easing the path for others to achieve their potential. However, we should understand the limits of our own influence and responsibilities. In extending the reach of our influence, we can't add value everywhere or approach everything with a "fix it" attitude, and must therefore be selective in what we do. Nor can we afford to lose sight of maximising value within our own families and localities in which we live. Part of this is about learning to become good all-round effective individuals and communities by "seizing the day" because every day is a day closer to our reckoning (*Akhirah*), our time being up. The Prophet said, describing them as easy things that require little effort: "Take advantage of five matters before five other matters: your youth before your old age; and your health before your illness; and your riches before your poverty; and your free time before your work; and your life before your death."[260]

God knows best.

---

[260] *Hadith* narrated by Ibn 'Abbas in Imam al-Bayhaqi's *Shu'b al-Iman* ("*Branches of Faith*").

# About the Author

Mamnun Khan completed his undergraduate degree in Biochemistry from Imperial College London, and subsequently gained a PhD in Molecular Immunology from Cambridge University. In recent years, Mamnun has advised a number of UK organisations on projects and strategy, as well as founding grassroots initiatives. His passion is to bring critical insight and thought leadership in advocating contextualised Islam and making the British Muslim experience God-centred. For ongoing exploration and research papers visit www.beingbritishmuslims.com.

Printed in Great Britain
by Amazon